UTAH GUN LAW II:
PANCHO'S WISDOM

The FULL TEXT of EVERY
UTAH
GUN LAW
under
ONE COVER!

with
Interesting, Entertaining, and Easy
to Read
"PLAIN TALK"
Summaries

by Attorney James D. "Mitch" Vilos

Written and published in the United States of America
by James D. Vilos.
ISBN 0-9669721-1-2

James D. "Mitch" Vilos, P.C.
PO Box 1148
Centerville, UT 84014
1(800) 530-0222
Mobile and Voice Mail: (801)560-7117
E-Mail: mitchv@firearmslaw.com
Internet Home Page: www.firearmslaw.com

ABOUT THE COVER: Wanted Poster of Revolutionary Pistolero Pancho
on his spirited mount "Tom" (courtesy of the infamous "Cold Water
Gang") deep in the red-rock badlands of the West's Great Basin.

Dedication

To my lovely wife Bonnie who has tolerated with good humor my consuming fascination with firearms law and guns ever since I turned forty, chalking it up, I'm sure, to mid-life crises. She astutely recognizes shooting as a relaxing diversion for a stressed-out trial lawyer. You might say she has bought into my excuse of playing cowboy for medicinal purposes. She even refrains from initiating commitment proceedings when I dawn the garb (sombrero, leather bandoliers, holsters, guns and bullets) of the notorious pistolero "Pancho Vilos" and shoot it out with the gringos of the Deseret Historical Shootist Society and Wasatch Desperadoes. What a woman, every gun owner's dream!

To my two sons Jason and Evan. My oldest son, Jason recently completed a mission for the L.D.S. Church in Richmond, Virginia, a fact of which I am very proud. He also happens to be Utah's foremost expert in the art of primitive bow and arrow making and a walking book on Indian culture. How about that, a cowboy and an Indian in the same "fam." Moving completely to the other end of the political spectrum, my youngest son, Evan, is an accomplished "head-banger" guitarist who began composing rock music at the tender age of 17. Although he has completed recording his first "80's rock" CD, he decided to delay superstardom to serve a mission in British Columbia. My sons' pursuit of their passions, almost at the exclusion of everything else, has given me the assurance that it is "O.K." to divert occasionally from the pursuit of earning a living, to "chill out," as the teenagers put it, and do "gun stuff."

To my three exquisitely beautiful daughters, all accomplished dancers, who have leavened my life with music and culture. But back off boys, they know how to shoot! I affectionately refer to them as Pancho's Angels.

Like most Western children outside the "Metro," my kids feel safer and more secure because their dad has guns and knows how to shoot (I wonder if they would fit in at Stanford?).

To my cousins Mike and Randy Rasley who instilled in me the love of shooting and hunting and the courage to speak up for what is right despite the unpopularity of my comments among the politically-correct elite.

To my secretary, Melia White, without whose help this edition could never have been completed, my friends and law student volunteers for countless re-reads, my design artist Clarence Bowman and my printer, Mike Everton. Finally, I dedicate this edition of my book to those who have brought to my attention the "unanswered questions" in the first printing.

Disclaimer

Every attempt has been made to insure the accuracy of this book but state and federal statutes and regulations are often vague and subject to different interpretations. They are often amended, replaced and repealed with little notice to the public. Therefore, the author accepts no liability, express or implied, for damages of any kind resulting from reliance on any aspect of this book, including but not limited to, consequential damages. This book should be used as a guide only and not considered as legal advice. Because the gun laws may change from year to year, you may want to ask us to place you on our mailing list (see form in Appendix D) to keep you informed of changes.

FURTHERMORE, because laws are subject to different interpretations, there is no guarantee that police, wildlife officers, prosecuting attorneys and ultimately the courts will agree with the author's interpretation. Even if the author's interpretation is right, you may still have to pay an attorney to defend you, if charges are brought.

FINALLY, the author has no authority to express opinions on behalf of any of the several organizations mentioned in this book. The controversial opinions expressed herein are those of the author. Any material the reader finds to be outrageous or offensive should be attributed solely to the infamous Revolutionary Pistolero, Pancho.

PREFACE

Pancho's Wisdom
If liberals don't wail and gnash their teeth
'bout what yer sayin', you ain't tellin' it like
it is!

Here it is, the sequel! Utah Gun Law II: Pancho's Wisdom. **This edition is current through the 2001 Legislative Session.** Its coverage of Utah's gun laws is even more comprehensive than the first edition, Utah Gun Law: Good, Bad and Ugly. For example this edition covers areas of federal law e.g. possession of firearms on federal facilities, post offices, and national parks, that the first edition did not include.

And so 's up with the "Pancho's Wisdom" theme? You'll notice it has replaced the "Good, Bad and Ugly" format of the First Edition. Nowadays many Utahns seem hesitant to admit in public that they are gun owners, hunters or concealed weapon permit holders. Is it any wonder with the media portraying guns as evil and gun owners as "haters, ignorant hicks, right-wing extremists and terrorists?" In addition to completely updating shooters and hunters about Utah's gun laws, this edition assures Westerners that IT'S OKAY to be a gun owner and hunter. WHO SAYS? PANCHO SAYS! Pancho's Wisdom constitutes AFFIRMATIVE ACTION[1] and EQUAL TIME for the most persecuted and misunderstood segment of modern American society - the gun owner. Pancho Vilos (related to the author only by ego) is a "revolutionary pistolero."[2] He boldly proclaims what most gun owners are thinkin', but are too bashful to utter in public. Watch anti-self-defense liberals tweak as Pancho slams 'em with bursts of wisdom such as:

---

1. Double action, lever action, single action, bolt action, pump action, cowboy action and rootin-tootin quick re-action!

2. Whatever the heck that means . . . . sounds dramatic though. Ya' hafta admit, though, beats being called a "widget" (law student joke).

Pancho's Wisdom
Gun confiscation is tyranny; so gun
registration is attempted tyranny.

A helpful new addition to this second edition is Appendix H "Quick Draw Gun Law." It is conveniently positioned at the end of the book to give fast shooters quick access to laws governing "guns in cars," "guns in schools," "guns at work," "federal facilities, national parks etc." The references in that Appendix point the reader to more in-depth coverage within the preceding chapters.

Utah's gun laws are scattered throughout thousands of pages, in dozens of law books that contain countless laws relating to everything from "adoption" to "water rights." Consequently, Utah legislators, county commissioners, city council members, judges, lawyers and police officers (let alone shooters and hunters), have a tough time keeping up with firearms law. To make gun laws easier to find, we boiled off all the "fat" from these law books (stripped away the laws having nothing to do with guns), leaving only the gun laws, and then we stuck them all under this one cover.

This book is the only publication in existence that contains virtually ALL Utah State gun laws and regulations in ONE volume. Notice we said "State" gun laws, not "local" ones. Because most city, town and county ordinances are not readily available to the public, it would be impossible for us to compile and comment upon all of them. To be safe, just assume that all cities and towns prohibit shooting within their boundaries, except at public shooting ranges. You'll be surprised to learn that the counties have not been given authority by the Utah Legislature to pass gun laws (except relating to spotlighting and night hunting). There are several federal gun laws that impact Utahns. We discuss these in detail in Chapter XIII. In short, this book contains all of the information you need to conduct yourself safely and legally with a firearm anywhere in the state of Utah.

This new edition more aggressively "shoots holes" through the impotent arguments in favor of gun control (infringement). It contains numerous updates in the law. The summary at the end of the chapter on Concealed Weapon Permits (Chapter VIII) is the most comprehensive and authoritative work yet explaining exactly where concealed weapon permit holders can and cannot take their concealed weapons. In the First Edition we suggested establishing a Utah Gun Owner's Legal Defense Fund. GOOD NEWS! A non-profit organization has been established with the mission that no individual Utah gun owner should have to shoulder the entire financial burden of paying legal fees to defend his or her right to bear arms. Read about the Utah Gun Owners Legal Defense Fund (U-Gold) in Chapter XVI. Learn also about the Concealed Weapon Permit Holders Association, Inc. (CWPA), a new organization representing the interests of permit holders and offering a host of membership benefits. Its most innovative benefit is a PRE-PAID legal plan. As soon as a member's application for membership is accepted, she immediately has an attorney on retainer to represent her if she is charged with a felony as a result of a defensive shooting. Chapter XVI also contains contact information about several other Utah pro-self-defense organizations.

Pancho's Wisdom

After seeing what the Clinton Administration was capable of, the question ISN'T, "Why does anyone need an 'assault rifle'?" The REAL QUESTION IS, "Why don't all law-abiding citizens own machine guns with hundred-round drums and night-vision scopes?"

TABLE OF CONTENTS

Pancho's Wisdom
The Right to Bear Arms is a Right to Life

APPENDIX A:
    Parental Consent Form for Minor to Possess Handgun

APPENDIX B:
    Order form for additional copies of
    Utah Gun Law II: Pancho's Wisdom

APPENDIX C:
    Order form for the
    Utah Spotlighting and Night Hunting Manual

Pancho's Wisdom
Speak softly, but carry a BIG SIG!

CHAPTER I: INTRODUCTION

Pancho's Wisdom
You can tell a lot about a man by the calibers he keeps.

The RIGHT to BEAR ARMS is an extremely important right to all free people for at least three reasons: (1) It is a vital "check" on government tyranny, (2) It is an important deterrent to foreign invasion, (3) It allows free citizens to defend themselves from violent criminal attack.

1. A"CHECK" ON GOVERNMENT TYRANNY - The Founding Fathers of our country knew that it is the character of every government to grow and become more powerful; to evolve from a state of freedom to a state of tyranny. They and their forefathers had witnessed this phenomenon for centuries in Europe culminating with Great Britain's tyranny over the American Colonies.

At the time the Bill of Rights was adopted, several notable citizens commented on the importance of the Right to Bear Arms in protecting the newly formed republic from tyranny:

"Whereas civil-rulers, not having their duty to the people duly before them, may attempt to tyrannize, and as military forces, which must be occasionally raised to defend our country, might pervert their power to the injury of their fellow citizens, the people are confirmed by the article in their right to keep and bear their private arms."

-- Tench Coxe, in Remarks on the First Part of the Amendments to the Federal Constitution.

"To preserve liberty it is essential that the whole body of the people always possess arms and be taught alike, especially when young, how to use them."

-- Richard Henry Lee, Letters from the Federal Farmer to the Republic (1787-1788).

"The best we can hope for concerning the people at large is that they be properly armed."

-- Alexander Hamilton, The Federalist Papers at 184-188.

"No freeman shall ever be debarred the use of arms."

-- Thomas Jefferson, Draft Virginia Constitution, 1776.

"Before a standing army can rule, the people must be disarmed; as they are in almost every kingdom in Europe. The supreme power in

America cannot enforce unjust laws by the sword; because the whole body of the people are armed, and constitute a force superior to any band of regular troops that can be, on any pretense, raised in the United States. A military force, at the command of Congress, can execute no laws, but such as the people perceive to be just and   constitutional; for they will possess the power, and jealousy will instantly inspire the inclination, to resist the execution of a law which appears to them unjust and oppressive."

--Noah Webster, An Examination of the Leading Principles of the Federal Constitution (Philadelphia 1787).

"Who are the militia? Are they not ourselves? Is it feared, then, that we shall turn our arms each man against his own bosom. Congress have no power to disarm the militia. Their swords, and every other terrible implement of the soldier, are the birthright of an American...[T]he unlimited power of the sword is not in the hands of either the federal or state governments, but, where I trust in God it will ever remain, in the hands of the people."

--Tenche Coxe, The Pennsylvania Gazette, Feb. 20, 1788.

In their Declaration of Independence from Great Britain, the Founding Father's proclaimed when "any Form of Government" begins to destroy its citizens' inalienable rights to "Life, Liberty and Pursuit of Happiness." "It is the Right of the People" to "throw off" [abolish] "Such Government." How do completely disarmed citizens (or even those relegated to archaic, ineffective, ssslllllooooowwwww-loading-and-shooting guns) tell a ruthless tyrant, brandishing flesh-consuming weapons that Old Testament prophets saw in their nightmares, "we are abolishing your Hilaryschumerfeinsteinness because you are trampling on our inalienable rights?" So the Founding Fathers incorporated a number of checks and balances in our Constitution to reduce the possibility that the federal government could become so powerful that it could destroy the liberty and freedom of it's citizens. One of the most important "checks" on this power was the right to bear arms. The theory was that all of the armed citizens, the "militia," would be better armed that a "standing army" (one assembled by the federal government in times of war). This would prevent tyrants from using the standing army to force a free citizenry to submit to their tyranny.

I could reveal my paranoia here and talk about Bill Clinton and Janet Reno and the possibility of a bunch of little Bill Clinton clones running around not knowing yet who their daddy is, but I won't. Let me just say, just in case you haven't heard, that the federal government has banned the manufacture of "assault weapons" and "high-capacity magazines" (Chapter XIII) and the state of California is now confiscating certain semi-automatic rifles. To make matters worse, prominent members of the United Nations want participating countries (including ours) to completely disarm all of their civilians. Does this upset anyone besides me, myself and Pancho?

So you don't think I pulled these ideas out of Pancho's sombrero, I urge you to buy and read a remarkable book about the political thought that culminated with the drafting of the Second Amendment of the United States Constitution. The book is entitled *That Every Man Be Armed: the Evolution of a Constitutional Right* by Stephan Halbrook, Ph.D. It contains a difficult-to-refute analysis of the development of the Second Amendment that persuasively establishes the points I am making in the limited space of this introduction. Dr. Halbrook is a well-respected constitutional scholar. He is the attorney who argued the *Printz* case discussed in Chapter XIII holding part of the "Brady Handgun Violence Prevention Act" unconstitutional. His book was cited with authority in that case in a concurring opinion by Justice Thomas of the United States Supreme Court. Every Utah gun owner should have Dr. Halbrook's book, my book and John Lott's book, *More Guns, less Crime* in their "arsenal." (Yeah, keep 'em in yer gun safe!)

2. A DETERRENT TO FOREIGN INVASION - I spent two years as a missionary in the tiny country of Switzerland which has enjoyed its independence for over two thousand years. Switzerland issues every militia member (every able-bodied man) a machine gun and trains him how to use it. It did this well before the Nazis took control in Germany. Hitler never attacked Switzerland. Golly, I wonder why? Instead he attacked countries all around Switzerland, the citizens of which were not nearly as well armed as the Swiss. Currently Switzerland still issues its citizens FULLY AUTOMATIC weapons and trains them how to use them, while the U.S. prohibits its citizens from possessing SEMI-AUTOMATIC rifles with HIGH CAPACITY MAGAZINES.

It's an awful thought, but suppose someday a powerful enemy "nukes" the U.S. in a few strategic locations and this convinces a whimpy, Democratic president to surrender (for a small sum of money and a European prostitute named Olga). With the number of guns we presently own, do you suppose a foreign army could occupy our country maintaining any degree of safety for its troops? Not hardly. Varmint hunting would take on a new meaning. Why attack us if you have to spend so much time dodging bullets you can't enjoy the spoils of war?

Comprende how an armed citizenry acts as a deterrent to ambitious foreign despots drooling over our resources?

3. CRIME PREVENTION - An exhaustive analysis of crime statistics compiled by the FBI over an 15 year period involving 3,054 counties in the U.S. proves statistically that gun control does not work. The book containing this research is entitled *More Guns, Less Crime*. The second edition of the book is now available in paper back. Every gun owner should arm himself with this book's findings because it persuasively refutes claims by the uninformed that gun control reduces crime. Briefly, the book convincingly establishes that states and counties that encourage gun ownership and liberally issue concealed weapon permits have significantly less violent crime than states that enact oppressive gun control laws. For example, Vermont, the state with the least restrictive gun laws, in the latest comparison between states, had the nation's lowest rape rate and second lowest murder rate. Additional statistics of interest in Lott's two editions include: States that ban the concealed carry have murder rates 127% higher than those with the most liberal concealed-carry laws. (2d ed. p. 47) For each additional year that concealed carry laws were in effect, murders fell by an additional 1.5%, and rape, robber, and aggravated assault fell by 3% per year. (2d ed. p. 170) After states enacted "must issue" concealed-carry laws, the number of multiple-victim public shootings declined by 84%, deaths declined 90% and injures declined 82%. (2d ed. p. 196) "The very few attacks that still occur in states after enactment of right-to-carry laws tend to occur in particular places where concealed handguns are forbidden, such as schools." (2d ed. p.196) In the first two years after Australia's sweeping gun bans, armed robberies had risen by 73 %, unarmed robberies by 28 %, assaults by 17% and kidnaping by 38%. (2d ed. p. 241) More children died from bicycle accidents than die from all types of firearm accidents. (1st ed. p. 9) Almost twice as many children drown each year in bathtubs as die from all types of firearms accidents. (2nd ed. p. 9) Anyway, you can't expect me to do all your readin' for you, so buy the book and read it yourself.

But Lott's statistics don't tell us red-necked cowpokes what we didn't know all along. . . . bad guys are allergic to lead. Think about it. If you were a "home invader," would you rather break into a residence in Washington D.C. where almost nobody has a gun, or Virgin, Utah that has an ordinance REQUIRING every adult to own a gun? I rest my case.

Many of Utah's gun laws are based upon the false premise that gun control works. It doesn't. If Utah were to adopt less restrictive gun laws, our citizens would be much safer. For example, Vermont, the state with the least restrictive gun laws has the nations lowest rape rate and second lowest murder rate. Until Utah adopts less restrictive weapon laws, Utahns need to know and obey the laws presently in force. It is for this purpose that I have written this book; to help keep my fellow Utah gun owners out of trouble. Pancho's mission, however, is to use his "armor piercing" revolutionary wit to reveal the ridiculous nature of many of the state and most of the federal gun laws. I take full credit for my controversial opinions. Please do not attribute them to any of the organizations mentioned herein; I do not have authority to speak in their behalf. However, all statements believed to be outrageous and offensive should be attributed solely to Pancho. Enjoy mis amigos! We'll see you at the range!

Pancho's Wisdom
I'd rather endure public humiliation and die broke, than give up my battle for the right of the innocent to protect themselves and their families!

CHAPTER II: HOW THIS BOOK IS ORGANIZED

Pancho's Wisdom
A poncho is a South-of-the-Border concealed ARSENAL permit!

A. OVERVIEW OF ALL THE CHAPTERS

There ain't nothin' more boring than reading code section after code section in a law book. (Actually, there is - knocking over bowling pins with a bowling ball rather than bullets!) So we decided to break up the monotony by throwing in some fun stuff like Pancho's Wisdom. We added so much salsa to this edition that we worried it might get a little confusing, so we put this chapter up front as kind of a road map. Even the most experienced shooters and hunters will be astonished at how little they know about Utah gun law when they take the test in Chapter III called the Gun Owners' Gauntlet. You too may have many misconceptions. So run the Gauntlet if you dare. The answers are in Chapter IV.

No gun owner wants to unintentionally commit a felony and lose his or her right to bear arms. Anyone with a conscience knows it's a crime to murder, rape, or assault another person. In contrast, the acts prohibited by many gun control laws are only crimes BECAUSE THE GOVERNMENT SAYS SO! If you haven't read the law, you might not know that some of the things you do with guns are felonies. In Chapter V, we warn of more than twenty ways gun owners can commit a felony without realizing it.

The "meat" of this book are the parts of the Utah Constitution, Utah Code Annotated and Utah Administrative Code ("Utah Regulations") comprising what we call "Utah Gun Law." Our analysis begins with Utah's Constitution in Chapter VI and then covers everything from weapons laws to the law of self defense. These chapters appear as follows:

CHAPTER VI:	Utah's Constitution
CHAPTER VII:	Utah Weapons Laws
CHAPTER VIII:	Concealed Weapon Permits
CHAPTER IX:	Hunting Laws and Regulations

B. THE BREAKDOWN OF EACH CHAPTER

Each chapter begins with an explosion of wisdom compliments of your pontificating pistolero. Then every law reported in the chapter is carefully dissected and explained using the following subtitles:
-Code Section or Regulation Number and Title
-"Plain Talk" Summaries
-The Actual Text of the Law
-Our Commentary
-Proposed Changes in the Law

1. **Pancho's Wisdom** - Today's great revolutionaries know that wielding a pen with wisdom is a powerful weapon. Pancho blasts weak-minded-anti-self-defense liberals with clever logic containing more foot pounds of energy than a .50 Cal. BMG. Pancho's hot and spicy bumper-stickers-in-a-book express the sentiments of every true Westerner. Like picante, Pancho's quips burn gun haters from the lips to the hips. His persuasive, yet entertaining blossoms of "blam!" are interspersed throughout the book to activate your axons. Look fer 'em in boxes sportin' this design:

Pancho's Wisdom
Tell your doctor you refuse to take Prozac
until he's tried you on a steady regimen of

> **blowing up plastic water bottles with high-powered-expanding bullets!**

2. Numbered Code Section or Regulation and Title

Utah gun laws appear as either code sections (Utah Code Annotated, abbreviated U.C.A.), or regulations (abbreviated by a capital "R" followed by a number). After the number, both code sections and regulations have a descriptive title. For example, the title of the state spotlighting code section looks like this, **"U.C.A. 23-13-17. Spotlighting of coyote, red fox, striped skunk, and raccoon--County ordinances--permits."** This means Utah Code Annotated, Title 23, Chapter 13, Section 17 contains the state spotlighting statute. When we say, "Utah gun law," we mean only the state law. We are not talking about county or city ordinances. Although many counties have enacted spotlighting ordinances under the authority of and patterned after the state statute, this book does not contain county ordinances.[3] To make the book easier to use as a reference guide, we organized every chapter like this:

a. Code sections (designated by "U.C.A." e.g. U.C.A. 76-3-1) generally appear before regulations (designated by "R" e.g. R724-3-1).

b. Both code sections and regulations appear numerically within any given chapter usually beginning with the smallest numbers first.

c. For some unexplained reason, regulations relating to the same subject matter as code sections often repeat verbatim the text of the code section. When this occurs we will include the code section, but omit the corresponding regulation.

d. Sometimes when a code section is so closely related to a regulation, we break the pattern referred to above and simply lump the two together. This allows the reader to read the entire law covering the subject matter without having to skip around in the book.

e. When a code section is long and many of the subsections do not contain "gun law," we cut these subsections out to spare you the bother of digging through depleted soil. You know we cut something out when you see the three little dots [. . .] together.

---

[3] If you want to spotlight legally, get a copy of *The Utah Spotlighting and Night Hunting Manual.* It analyzes in detail the state spotlighting law as well as the ordinances of those counties permitting spotlighting. We have attached an order form at the end of this book.

f. Occasionally, we insert a federal law at the end of a discussion of state law when the two are closely related. The penalties for violating the state law may not be as severe as federal law and we wanted to alert you. For example, under state law it's a misdemeanor to carry a concealed weapon into an airport. The same act under the antiterrorist provisions of federal law calls for severe felony-like penalties. See our Commentary under the discussion of U.C.A. 76-10-529.

3. "Plain Talk" Summaries

Unfortunately, most laws are written in "legalese," a language spoken and written only by lawyers. Legalese is similar to English, but boring, complicated, convoluted, lengthy, circumlocutious, redundant, and confusing to boot. In this book we translate legalese into "Plain Talk." This translation follows the title but precedes the actual text of the code section or regulation in a double-bordered box that looks like this:

```
┌──────────────────────────────────────────┐
│                                          │
│             "Plain Talk"                 │
│                                          │
└──────────────────────────────────────────┘
```

The title appears in large, bold print, and the Plain Talk translation appears in a larger print to help you distinguish our translations and commentary from the actual text of the code section or regulation. We have not translated every subsection of every gun law into Plain Talk. Some subsections need no explanation and others are simply too dull and irrelevant to our discussion to include in the Plain Talk summaries.

4. Actual Text of Code Section or Regulation -The actual text of the code sections and regulations is smaller, plain, non-bold print like this paragraph preceded by a bold heading indicating "**ACTUAL TEXT**." We have not drawn single or double-bordered boxes around the actual text of the law. This is for lawyers who CAN'T HANDLE the "Plain Talk."

5. Commentary - Sections entitled "Commentary" give us a chance to compliment, poke fun at or explain sundry code sections and regulations. These comments are enclosed in a single-lined box like this:

```
┌──────────────────────────────────────────┐
│                                          │
│             Commentary                   │
│                                          │
└──────────────────────────────────────────┘
```

6. Proposed Amendments - Bad and ugly gun laws should be amended or repealed. When legislators introduce amendments to

existing state law they use a specific format. Undesirable language is stricken out by using the ~~strike out~~ key. New statutory language is inserted as underlined text. We use the same format in this book for changes we propose. Send a copy of this book to your legislator so he or she can submit the changes during the next legislative session.

7. **Appendices** -The appendices contain a parental consent form and order forms for books and updates. Parents can use the form in Appendix A to give their minor children permission to possess a firearm for certain purposes such as target practice, farming and ranching activities. It complies with both Utah and federal gun law (see discussion on federal gun law requiring minors to have written permission from their parents to possess a handgun, Chapter XIII). Appendix B contains an order form for this book, *Utah Gun Law II: Pancho's Wisdom.* You may want to purchase copies for your friends and legislators. Appendix C is an order form for the *Utah Spotlighting and Night Hunting Manual* that reveals how and where hunters can use spotlights at night to hunt certain predators and varmints. If you would like to be informed of future changes in Utah gun law, Appendix D is a request form that you can mail to us. You will be placed on a list reminding us to contact you when there are changes in the law. You may then purchase supplements, if any, or a new, revised edition of the book. Appendix E contains a list of addresses and phone numbers of every state's Office of Attorney General. With this information travelers can call ahead to find out about the gun laws in states and cities they will be visiting. This information alone, is worth the price of this book.

Appendix F will keep you from frying your brain trying to sort out all of the state and federal laws governing when and how juveniles can possess guns and ammo. Appendix G is a copy of a contour map showing the forest service property in Davis County subject to a federal "No Shooting" order. Appendix H contains the convenient reference guide Quick Draw Gun Law. Finally, don't forget to check out the footnotes.[4] They'll keep you amused.

---

[4] No Keith, you can't read these with a scope, it takes a magnifying glass!

CHAPTER III: GUN OWNERS' GAUNTLET: HOW WELL DO YOU UNDERSTAND UTAH GUN LAW?

Pancho's Wisdom
Don't forget, Cain didn't use a gun.

How badly do you NEED this book? Take the following test and find out. Don't feel too bad if you fail; heck, most lawyers, judges and police officers don't know the answers either, at least not without looking them up.

1. QUESTION: Under the Utah Constitution, the right to bear arms is a COLLECTIVE right (for example, a state having the right to organize a militia) and NOT an INDIVIDUAL right possessed by every law-abiding adult citizen. T____ F____

2. QUESTION: A person who does not have a concealed weapon permit may legally carry a loaded gun in a holster on a public street ("open carry") as long as it is not concealed. T____ F____

3. QUESTION: On the other hand, a person with a concealed weapon permit MUST CONCEAL his weapon and may not carry it openly ("open carry"). T____ F____

4. QUESTION: Under Utah law, a gun "containing ammunition" is not necessarily "loaded." T____ F___

5. QUESTION: A double action revolver is considered loaded even if there is not a bullet aligned with the barrel, if the next cylinder to rotate to line up with the barrel contains a cartridge. T____ F____

6. QUESTION: A person, without a concealed weapon permit, who hides a gun in his car (1) that is unloaded, (2) that contains ammunition, (3) completely zipped up in a cloth "zipper bag" (4) within his immediate reach, is guilty of carrying a concealed weapon, a felony. T____ F____

7. QUESTION: A college or university may adopt a policy prohibiting adult students and university employees who are licensed concealed weapon holders from carrying concealed weapons on campus. T____ F____

8. QUESTION: A city or county can pass an ordinance making it illegal to possess a firearm except during hunting season. T____ F____

9. QUESTION: A Utah concealed weapon permit allows you to conceal a pocket knife with a three-inch blade. T____ F____

10. QUESTION: The Brady Handgun Violence Prevention (sic[k]) Act, may require local Utah law enforcement agencies to use state and local funds to enforce the Brady Act. T____ F____

11. QUESTION: To possess a handgun or handgun ammunition, a minor must have the written permission of a parent or guardian in his possession at all times, although the parent or guardian accompanies the minor. T____ F____

12. QUESTION: Any person who keeps a loaded handgun in his home, temporary home, place of business, or camp must have a permit. T____ F____

13. QUESTION: Upland game birds (like pheasants and quail) may be hunted with a pistol. T____ F____

14. QUESTION: It is no longer legal to spotlight or night hunt anywhere in the state. T___ F___

15. QUESTION: A person who has a guardianship or conservatorship placed over him or his financial estate may lose his right to bear arms. T___ F___

16. QUESTION: A person who has taken another person's prescription drug may not legally possess a handgun. T___ F___

17. QUESTION: A person without a concealed weapon permit, who is otherwise hunting legally, may conceal a handgun if its barrel length exceeds 4 inches. T___ F___

18. QUESTION: To be convicted of "carrying" a concealed weapon, a person must have a weapon hidden somewhere on his body or under his clothing. T___ F___

19. QUESTION: The civil rights of law-abiding citizens to protect themselves from criminal attack with firearms are less important than the civil rights of women to kill their own unborn children, of homosexuals to keep their jobs, and of atheists to keep God-fearing school children from praying at school. T___ F___

20. QUESTION: It's legal to shoot from a vehicle as long as the vehicle is at least 200 feet from a highway, you don't shoot across the highway, and you are at least 600 feet from a building. T___ F___

21. QUESTION: If you accidently shoot someone during the deer hunt, your homeowner's insurance company will pay an attorney to defend you in a negligence lawsuit brought by the injured hunter. T___ F___

22. QUESTION: If your cousin Randy from Reno, who has a clean criminal record and a Nevada concealed weapon permit, attempts to conceal his .50 caliber Desert Eagle on the streets of Salt Lake City, he commits a felony under Utah law. T___ F___

23. QUESTION: Under no circumstances may a Utah gun dealer sell rifles or shotguns to residents of other states. T___F___

24. QUESTION: A Utah citizen 21 years of age or older with a clean criminal record MUST be issued a concealed weapon permit, whether she has a good reason for having one or not. T___F___

25. QUESTION: A concealed weapon permit is valid throughout the state without restriction. T___F___

26. QUESTION: A person who has been acquitted of murder charges on the grounds of self defense, cannot be sued by the heirs of the person he killed. T___F___

27. QUESTION: Cities and towns have been given authority by the Legislature to pass ordinances regulating the discharge of firearms, but the counties can only pass ordinances regulating spotlighting and night hunting. T___F___

28. QUESTION: Repentance brings forth the blessings of the 2nd Amendment. T___F___

29. QUESTION: You pass through a school zone on the way home from the deer hunt. Your deer rifle is unloaded and zipped in a gun case behind your seat. You do not have a concealed weapon permit. You are guilty of a crime punishable up to 5 years in prison and if convicted, you could lose the right to possess a firearm or ammunition for the rest of your life. T___F___

30. QUESTION: Although federal law prohibits a gun dealer from selling a gun to an individual under the age of 21, a Utah resident who is not a gun dealer can sell a handgun to another Utah resident who is 18 years of age or older but less than 21 years of age. T___F___

31. QUESTION: You can hunt deer on a farmer's hay field as long as it is not posted "No Trespassing!" T___F___

Pancho's Wisdom

GUN CONTROL and RAPE are not about guns or sex, they're about CONTROL; but we've GOT GUNS and we refuse to be CONTROLLED or RAPED!

Pancho Meditating for Wisdom

CHAPTER IV: ANSWERS TO GUN OWNERS' GAUNTLET

> ## Pancho's Wisdom
> ## Gun FREE zones COST innocent lives.

1. ANSWER: FALSE. Utah's Constitution, Article I, Section 6 guarantees the right to keep and bear arms to each INDIVIDUAL Utahn. Chapter VI.

2. ANSWER: FALSE. Only law officers and concealed weapon holders (CWPs) can "open carry" with a LOADED gun. See discussion of U.C.A. 76-10-505 in Chapter VII. Theoretically, anyone can "open carry" with an UNLOADED gun, but he must be careful no one claims that wearing a gun is intended as a threat.

3. ANSWER: FALSE. As shown in the answer to Question 2, above, CWPs can "open carry." Therefore, it does not matter if their guns can be seen. Pancho lets his concealed weapon show from time to time to make a political statement!

4. ANSWER: TRUE. See U.C.A. 76-10-502. When weapon deemed loaded. Chapter VII.

5. ANSWER: TRUE. See U.C.A. 76-10-502. When weapon deemed loaded. Chapter VII.

6. ANSWER: FALSE. CAUTION: This answer is a close call and slight variations of the facts could make the difference between an acquittal and a conviction. The answer to this question is false for two reasons. First, a person may keep an unloaded gun in his car, even if it contains ammunition,[5] if it is unloaded and in plain view or "securely encased."[6] A gun in a "zipper bag" is securely encased if the bag is closed.

The second reason the answer to the question is "false" is that carrying a concealed dangerous weapon is not a felony. It used to be

---

[5] See U.C.A. 76-10-502. When Weapon Deemed Loaded, Chapter VII.

[6] U.C.A. 76-10-501(17) "Securely encased" means not readily accessible for immediate use, such as held in a gun rack, or <u>in a closed case or container, whether or not locked,</u> **OR** in a trunk or other storage area of a motor vehicle, <u>not including a glove box or console box</u> (emphasis added).

(see Commentary to U.C.A. 76-10-504), but now it's a   class B misdemeanor to conceal a firearm not containing ammunition and a class A misdemeanor if it contains ammunition.[7] **The key to carrying a gun in a car _without_ a concealed weapon permit is to carry it (1) UNLOADED and (2) NOT CONCEALED. It may be kept hidden, however, (to prevent theft) if it is (1) unloaded AND (2)securely encased (see definitions in Chapter VII, U.C.A. 76-6-501).**

7. ANSWER: FALSE. Concealed weapon permits are valid throughout the state without restriction except in "secured areas." College campuses are not secured areas. See U.C.A. 53-5-704 These issues are discussed in detail in Chapter VIII.

8. ANSWER: FALSE. See U.C.A. 76-10-500(2), Chapter VII.

9. ANSWER: TRUE. See U.C.A. 76-10-523 excepting concealed weapon holders from the applications of sections 504(1)(a)(b) in Chapter VII.

10. ANSWER: FALSE. See discussion in Chapter XIII of 18 U.S.C. Sec. 922(s)&(t), the Brady Handgun Violence Prevention Act and the summary of the _Printz_ case, in which the United States Supreme Court held portions of the Brady Act UNCONSTITUTIONAL!

11. ANSWER: TRUE (as ridiculous as it sounds). See discussion in Chapter XIII of 18 U.S.C. § 922(x).

12. ANSWER: FALSE - U.C.A. 76-10-500(1) guarantees that Utahns do not have to have a permit to keep a gun in these places. See also U.C.A. 76-10-510, 511, 505. Under U.C.A. 76-10-511, a person may have a loaded firearm at his home, including any temporary residence or camp. However, if he is going to keep a firearm loaded in a vehicle or on a public street, a concealed weapon permit is required (U.C.A. 76-10-505). We discuss these code sections in detail in Chapter VII.

13. ANSWER: TRUE - But you must use "bird shot" instead of a single lead bullet. See R657-6-9(2)(a) Firearms . . .[Upland Game], Chapter IX.

14. ANSWER: FALSE - See U.C.A. 23-13-17, the State Spotlighting Statute, Chapter IX. Commercial Break: For a VERY detailed analysis of the State Spotlighting Statute and Regulations and the corresponding county ordinances, read my book, _THE UTAH_

---

[7] Hey, I warned you this stuff can get complicated!

SPOTLIGHTING AND NIGHT HUNTING MANUAL. An order form is located in Appendix C.

15. ANSWER: TRUE - A person who is protected by a conservatorship or guardianship must be either mentally or physically incapacitated under the Utah Probate Code. If the person is mentally incapacitated this could be construed to be the same thing as mentally defective within the meaning of U.C.A. 76-10-503(1)(b)(vii) and federal law 18 U.S.C. Sec. 922 (g)(4).[8] See Chapters VII and XIII.[9]

16. ANSWER: TRUE - U.C.A. 76-10-503(1)(b)(3), Chapter VII. (Isn't this a bit of an overkill in some situations? What if a cop takes one of his wife's anti-inflammatories because he has a backache. Did the Legislature intend to disarm him?)

17. ANSWER: TRUE - U.C.A. 76-10-504(4), Chapter VII.

18. ANSWER: FALSE - See *State v. Williams*, 636 P.2d 1092 (Utah 1981) discussed in Chapter VII. The defendant was convicted of "carrying a concealed weapon" for concealing a pistol in a bag on the passenger's seat of his car. The court held that a concealed weapon need not be concealed under a person's clothing, if it is easily ACCESSIBLE to him or her.

19. ANSWER: FALSE - Surprise! A few enlightened judges have ruled that gun owners have civil rights too! See discussion of the civil rights of gun owners in Chapter XIV.

20. ANSWER: FALSE - You can't shoot from a vehicle, PERIOD, unless you are disabled and on a big-game hunt. If you get caught violating this section, you lose your drivers license, even if you are 70 miles from nowhere. Hill Air Force Base top guns can blow up scrapped school buses with air-to-ground missiles in the same general location where you will get arrested for shooting a .22 short into a red-

---

[8] Our computerized legal research did not reveal that the term "mentally defective" was defined anywhere in the United States Code or Code of Federal Regulations. Therefore the term could be interpreted broadly by a court to encompass mentally incapacitated persons as defined under the Utah Code, who are protected by a conservatorship or guardianship.

[9] A law that declares a mentally incompetent person a felon for possessing a firearm, is a legal anomaly. If the person does not have the mental capacity to formulate criminal intent, he cannot be guilty of a crime!

ant hill from your vehicle. See U.C.A. 76-10-508 and U.C.A. 53-3-220, Chapter VII.

21. ANSWER: TRUE - Most homeowner insurance policies cover such an accident and the insurance contract may allow you to choose the lawyer you want to represent you. See discussion in Chapter X.

22. ANSWER: FALSE - First, it is not a felony to carry a concealed weapon (U.C.A.76-10-504) unless you are already a felon or restricted person (U.C.A. 76-10-503) or unless you conceal a weapon on a bus or airplane. (See discussion in Chapters VII and XIII.) Furthermore, as of 2001 Utah recognizes the permits of all other states and counties. (See Chapters VII and VIII.)

23. ANSWER: FALSE - Utah law (U.C.A. 76-10-524) coupled with federal law (18 U.S.C. 922(b)(3)) permit gun dealers to sell rifles and shotguns to residents of other states, if the sale is legal in Utah and home state of the buyer (see Chapter VII).

24. ANSWER: TRUE - See discussion in Chapter VIII and U.C.A. 53-5-704.

25. ANSWER: TRUE - See U.C.A. 53-5-704. Caution: even concealed weapon holders cannot carry weapons into "secured areas" at courthouses, prisons, jails, airports and federal buildings. These issues are discussed in detail primarily in Chapters VII and VIII.

26. ANSWER: FALSE - A civil lawsuit has nothing to do with the outcome of a criminal prosecution. You can be found innocent of murder, but still be held liable in money damages for killing or injuring another. If you don't believe us, ask O.J. Simpson! See discussion in Chapters X and XI below.

27. ANSWER: TRUE - See the discussion in U.C.A. 10-8-47 and Chapter IX.

28. ANSWER: TRUE - If they have gone without an offense or conviction for a long time, even felons can sometimes have their criminal records wiped clean. The process is known as "EXPUNGEMENT." Through expungement, a convicted criminal can have his civil rights restored. See U.C.A. 77-18-10 *et.seq.*, Chapter XII. However, those convicted of a capital felony, first degree felony, second degree forcible felony or a sexual act against a minor, can forget about expungement.

29. ANSWER: TRUE - You cannot possess a firearm in a school zone, 18 U.S.C. § 922(q), Chapter XIII, even if it's unloaded, unless it's <u>locked</u> in a gun rack or case. Because the gun, in this example, is in a zipper case (the way many deer hunters carry their guns in Utah) and not in a locked container, you would be guilty of a crime punishable of up to 5 years in prison, 18 U.S.C. 924(4). If convicted of a crime punishable for more than one year in prison, you cannot legally possess a gun or ammunition, 18 U.S.C. § 922(g). If federal agents set up road blocks in school zones during the 10 day Utah deer hunt, they could use this law to send ten thousand Utah deer hunters to prison and strip them of their right to bear arms![10] Fortunately, concealed weapon permit holders are exempt from this outrageously overly-broad federal statute (see discussion of the Gun Free School Zone Act in Chapter XIII).

30. ANSWER: TRUE - As long as the non-dealer isn't acting as a "middle man" to help gun dealers sell handguns and handgun ammo to individuals under 21 years of age. The non-dealer cannot have the intent to transfer the handgun to an individual who is less than 21 years of age at the time he, the non-dealer, purchases the gun from the dealer (see Chapter XIII).

31. ANSWER: FALSE - Under the new law passed during the 2000 legislative session, a cultivated field is PRESUMED to be posted "No Trespassing." (See U.C.A. 23-20-14, Chapter IX.)

---

[10] Sarah Brady and the rest of the anti-self-defense crowd tell us they want gun control legislation because they simply want to reduce violent crime. Why then do they pass laws such as this that set snares for law-abiding citizens?

CHAPTER V: HOW TO BECOME A FELON IN THIRTY SECONDS OR LESS USING A FIREARM

> ## Pancho's Wisdom
> ## Neither clothes nor guns make the man; but guns make him HAPPY!

Felons do not have the right to bear arms under either federal or state law. Unfortunately, there are several ways shooters and hunters can unwittingly commit a felony and lose their right to bear arms forever. This chapter reveals some of those ways.

1. Sell a gun to a minor outside the presence of his parent, e.g., two 17-year-olds trade a gun for a car (See U.C.A. 76-10-509.9, Chapter VII).

2. Conceal a handgun while riding the bus without a concealed weapon permit (U.C.A. 76-10-1504, Chapter VII).

3. Kiss your boyfriend under the mistletoe hanging in the doorway of the local bus station (one foot in the bus station and one foot out) while having an unloaded pistol in your purse (yes, you read it right, UNLOADED), U.C.A. 76-10-1507, Chapter VII.

4. Pretend you're John Dillinger and stick your grandpa's old sawed-off shotgun down your pants (even if you have a concealed weapon permit).

5. Let your 17-year-old neighbor handle your UNLOADED, fully automatic M-16 machine gun for ten seconds to admire it (See 76-10-509.4(2) and (4), Chapter VII). (This assumes you have complied with the federal laws that permit you to own and possess a fully automatic weapon.)

6. Intentionally give false information to a gun dealer when purchasing a handgun (U.C.A. 76-10-527, Chapter VII).

7. As a gun dealer, sell a handgun to a person whom you know cannot legally own or possess one (U.C.A. 76-10-527, Chapter VII).

8. Buy a handgun from a dealer with the intent to transfer it to someone you know can't legally own or possess one, for example, a felon or a person under 21 years of age (U.C.A. 76-10-527, Chapter VII).

9. Take someone else's prescription medication and possess a handgun (U.C.A. 76-10-503(3)(a)(iii), Chapter VII).

10. Concealed weapon permit holder or not, attempt to take your gun into a "secured area" of a jail, prison, mental institution or

courthouse. Most offenses under these sections are third degree felonies if committed "knowingly or   intentionally"(U.C.A. 76-10-523.5, 76-8-311.1, 76-8-311.3, and 78-7-6, Chapter VII). It's a big-time federal felony to attempt to take a firearm into the passenger compartment of a commercial airliner. (49 U.S.C. 46505, Chapter VII)

11. As a parent, get convicted twice of allowing your problem child, who has been convicted of a violent crime such as manslaughter, rape, robbery, burglary, or house breaking, to possess a firearm (U.C.A. 76-10-509.6, Chapter VII).

12. Possess a firearm if you are under indictment for a felony (U.C.A. 76-10-503(1)(b)(i), Chapter VII).

13. As a minor, pick up the Road Warrior's UNLOADED sawed-off shotgun, having a barrel length of less than 18 inches (U.C.A. 76-10-509.4, Chapter VII).

14. Take a box of bullets to your little brother, who is incarcerated in a mental health facility for drug abuse, to encourage him to get well soon, so you can go shooting together [Duh!] (U.C.A. 76-8-311.3, Chapter VII).

15. It's a FELONY to intentionally or RECKLESSLY and UNLAWFULLY injure or kill any of the following species of wildlife:

- bison,
- big horn sheep,
- rocky mountain goats,
- moose,
- bear,
- a member of any endangered species (see discussion in Chapter IX),
- elk, (one fellow I know was charged with a felony for shooting an elk a few hundred yards outside his poorly-defined area),
- threatened species (see discussion in Chapter IX),
- trophy deer with an antler spread of 24 inches,
- a pronghorn antelope buck with horns exceeding 14 inches (U.C.A. 23-13-1, U.C.A. 23-20-4, Chapter IX).

16. Illegally and intentionally or recklessly kill or injure two or more non-trophy deer or antelope. U.C.A. 23-20-4.5 gives animals an arbitrary monetary value. If the value exceeds $500, killing the animal without a valid hunting license is a felony. However, for the animals that have been given an arbitrary value of less than $500, if you kill

enough animals in that species to equal or exceed $500, you have also committed a felony. Non-trophy deer and antelope have been given an arbitrary value of $400. Poaching two of either of these species, is a felony. The same is true for intentionally or recklessly killing or injuring the following combinations of animals without a license or permit:

      a. a non-trophy antelope and a non-trophy deer,

      b. a bobcat and two turkeys,

      c. five turkeys and a loon (no, we're not talking about O.J.'s legal "dream team!"), and

      d. one swan a diving, two sandhill cranes a craning, three Utah milk snake a milking, one Utah mountain king snake a reigning (without even killing a partridge in a pear tree).[11] See U.C.A. 23-20-4(4)(f), Chapter IX.

    17. You shoot and kill what, at a distance, looks like a "monster" of a moose with gigantic antlers. When you get closer you realize it was just an average moose with embarrassingly small antlers. Because a bull moose hunt is a once-in-a-lifetime hunt, you abandon the moose without tagging it in hopes of finding the bull with enormous antlers you saw while scouting. It's a felony to intentionally abandon the flesh of a bull moose (U.C.A. 23-20-4(1)(c)(ii)).

    18. You are deer hunting in Hackberry Canyon in Kane County, with your trusty .270 Remington BDL strapped over your shoulder. All of a sudden, crawling on the damp rocks on a cliff above the trail, you see the elusive Kanab Ambersnail (Oxyloma Haydeni Kanabensis). You think to yourself how amusing it would be to splatter this slimy mollusk all over the hieroglyphs of this forty-foot-high red rock wall. Now what are you going to do, kiddies?

    You carefully place the cross hairs of your Leopold Gold Ring scope at 10.5 power on the snail's oviduct to avoid the risk of wounding your prey! The adrenaline is rushing and your heart is pounding. In fact, you have "snail fever," so you eject two cartridges without firing. Finally, you get a hold of yourself and squeeze the trigger like your Boy Scout merit badge instructor taught you. You hear the gun's report and feel the dull jolt against your shoulder. The snail disappears from the scope's image. You see a light spray of what appears to be soy sauce descending in the midst of the sun's rays penetrating the narrow gorge. Without warning, three Special Forces Officers from the Division of Wildlife Resources, suddenly rappel from the top of the cliff. They are

---

[11] Tell me this book wouldn't make a great Christmas gift!

clad in a full array of bullet-proof vests, black hoods and combat boots. They immediately subdue and handcuff you.   As they bring you shamefully before the Federal United States District Court, Central Division, you hang your head as the Judge asks you, "Are you guilty of a felony?" ANSWER: Yes. The Kanab Ambersnail is listed as an endangered species that inhabits Kane County.   It's a felony to kill a member of an endangered species, U.C.A. 23-20-4.   Kane County residents in the mood for escargot, BEWARE! No wonder there are no French restaurants in Kanab!

19. Shoot carp in the shallow waters of Muddy Creek with your .458 Winchester Magnum, knowing that endangered Razorback suckers are swimming nearby. See U.C.A. 23-20-4, and discussion of endangered species, Chapter IX. See also U.C.A. 76-2-103 that defines "intentional," "knowingly, or with knowledge," and "recklessly or maliciously."[12] You don't necessarily have to INTEND to kill, if you "consciously disregard a substantial and unjustifiable risk" that your actions will result in the death of an endangered species. If there are endangered fish mixed in with carp, which are not endangered, and you shoot, although you can't see what you are shooting at, you could be found guilty of a felony.

20. Simply possess a pipe bomb, U.C.A. 76-10-306(1), (although this doesn't involve using a firearm, we threw it in as a bonus, because some gun enthusiasts like to hear things go "Bang!")

21. Obviously stealing a firearm is a felony (second degree, U.C.A. 76-6-412.) Did you realize that "borrowing" one from a friend without his permission without the intent to deprive him of it permanently is a third degree felony? (U.C.A.76-6-404.5. Wrongful Appropriation)

22. I recently represented two young men who accidently shot a trophy bull elk in a spike-only area. It was their first big-game hunt without their parents and they hadn't surveyed the area boundaries in order to fully understand the ambiguities found in the hunting proclamation. They were both charged with felonies! Fortunately we were able to convince the prosecutor that they had made an innocent mistake and had not intentionally killed the giant bull outside their area boundaries. Most Utah hunters do not realize that they can be charged with a felony for intentionally or recklessly killing certain big game

---

[12] U.C.A. 76-2-103 appears in Chapter IX as a footnote under the discussion of U.C.A. 23-20-4, Wanton destruction of wildlife.

animals even though they have a license to hunt that particular species. See U.C.A. 23-20-4, Chapter IX.

CHAPTER VI: UTAH'S CONSTITUTION

Pancho's Wisdom
Citizens bear arms; subjects don't!

Constitution of Utah, Article I. Declaration of Rights. Section 6. Right to bear arms.

"Plain Talk"
The statesmen who drafted this section understood that the right to bear arms is essential to the protection of life, liberty and the pursuit of happiness. Therefore, the Utah Constitution contains a Declaration of Rights similar to the Bill of Rights in the United States Constitution. Article I, Section 6 of Utah's Constitution preserves the rights of law-abiding Utahns to bear arms to defend themselves, their homes, their families, and their freedom. This right also extends to "other lawful purposes" (undoubtedly referring to hunting and recreational shooting).

ACTUAL TEXT
The individual right of the people to keep and bear arms for security and defense of self, family, others, property, or the state, as well as for other lawful purposes shall not be infringed; but nothing herein shall prevent the Legislature from defining the lawful use of arms.

C. of U. Article 1. Section 6.

Commentary
The drafters of this Article wanted to make sure that the right to bear arms was interpreted to be an individual right and not just a collective right.[13] The wording also makes it clear that the

---

[13] The Second Amendment of the United States Constitution says, "A well regulated militia, being necessary to the security of a free state, the right of the people to keep and bear arms, shall not be infringed." Unfortunately, many judges, not understanding the historical meaning of the term "militia," have interpreted the right to bear arms as a collective right associated with military service. However, at the time the 2nd Amendment was drafted, "militia" meant "the people" rather

Legislature does not have the authority to infringe upon this right in defining the lawful use of firearms.

Pancho's Wisdom
Who are Michael Jordan, Mark McGwire, John Elway or Tiger Woods? My sports heros are Annie Oakley, Bob Munden, China Camp and Rob Leatham.

---

than a standing army. "...I ask, who are the militia? They consist now of the whole people, except a few public officers." George Mason, Virginia's U.S. Constitution Ratification Convention, 1788. See also S. Halbrook, *That Every Man Be Armed, The Evolution of a Constitutional Right* (1984). Therefore, the right belongs to all the people, not just a few members of state militia groups. The drafters of the Utah Constitution wanted no misunderstanding. Therefore, they used the phrase, "individual right to keep and bear arms."

CHAPTER VII: THE WEAPON LAWS

Pancho's Wisdom
There ain't NOBODY as worthless as
SOMEBODY with an unloaded gun!

U.C.A. 76-10-500. Uniform Law

"Plain Talk"

It's not often these days that a gun law "giveth" rather than "taketh away." Section 500 emphasizes that the right to keep and bear arms is an important constitutional right. Local governments may not pass laws prohibiting law-abiding citizens or legal aliens[14] from owning, possessing, purchasing, transporting or keeping firearms in their homes, on their properties, at their businesses or in their vehicles (although there are severe restrictions on carrying a loaded gun in a vehicle - see discussion below). We have a right to protect our "castles" with a loaded gun. This applies to temporary dwellings like apartments, hotel rooms, campers and tents. State and local governments cannot require permits to possess firearms in these places. Counties and cities cannot pass firearm ordinances, unless state law specifically authorizes them to do so. The only authority the State has given counties to regulate shooting relates to the spotlighting of varmints at night, like coyotes and skunks. (See U.C. A. 23-13-17). If you are spotlighting jack rabbits, don't forget to trade your real gun in for a BB gun when you cross the Tooele County line.[15]

ACTUAL TEXT
(1) The individual right to keep and bear arms being a constitutionally protected right, the Legislature finds the need to provide uniform laws throughout the state. Except as specifically provided by state law, a citizen of the United States or a lawfully admitted alien shall not be:

---

14 "Non-immigrant status" aliens may generally not possess firearms under federal law. See discussion about this in Chapter XIII.

15 The Utah Spotlighting and Night Hunting Manual also written by Attorney "Mitch" Vilos discusses the state law and county ordinances relating to spotlighting of varmints and predators.

(a) prohibited from owning, possessing, purchasing, selling, transferring, transporting, or keeping any firearm at his place of residence, property, business, or in any vehicle lawfully in his possession or lawfully under his control; or

(b) required to have a permit or license to purchase, own, possess, transport, or keep a firearm.

(2) This part is uniformly applicable throughout this state and in all its political subdivisions and municipalities. All authority to regulate firearms shall be reserved to the state except where the Legislature specifically delegates responsibility to local authorities or state entities. Unless specifically authorized by the Legislature by statute, a local authority or state entity may not enact or enforce any ordinance, regulation, or rule pertaining to firearms.

U.C.A. 76-10-500

Commentary

How many state college and university administrators are violating this state law by denying adult students the right to keep a firearm in their apartments and dormitories?[16]

Pancho's Wisdom
College coeds with concealed weapons are dangerous and should be banned from campus dormitories. Ted Bundy[17]

U.C.A. 76-10-501. Definitions.

"Plain Talk"

The definitions in section 501 create the foundation for restrictions relating to persons with criminal backgrounds and the concealment of weapons. The definition of "dangerous weapon" includes anything that is capable of causing death or serious bodily injury. This could mean a

---

[16] The federal law which prohibits a person from taking a gun into a school zone does not prohibit guns on the college campus. Federal law defines "schools" as institutions providing elementary and secondary education, which does not include colleges and universities (18 U.S.C. 921(a)(26)).

[17] If he didn't say it, he thought it!

crocheting needle, a sharp stick,[18] a nail, brass knuckles, a piece of glass, a small pocket knife, a pointed can opener, a screw driver, a hat pin, or a pair of scissors.[19] If you are carrying such items and do not hurt anyone, because most of these objects have lawful uses, you probably would not be arrested or convicted of carrying a concealed dangerous weapon. Ever wonder why thugs use screw drivers rather than knives to mug people on buses and subways? That's right, so it will be hard to prosecute them for simply carrying the object. If however, someone is robbed or stabbed with such an object, the police and the courts can look at how the object was used and what kind of wound resulted. If your grandma inflicts a "long, deep and ugly" cut with her crochet needle, she could be convicted of assault with a deadly weapon.

"Fully automatic weapon" means a machine gun or sub-(pistol caliber) machine gun (ala Rambo).

The definition of "securely encased" is interesting. The Legislature did not want people convicted of carrying a concealed weapon if they had an unloaded weapon on a gun rack or in a gun case, methods by which many Utahns carry their firearms.

The definition of concealed dangerous weapon is troublesome. Notice that in addition to the words "hide" and "secret" the definition uses the word "covered." Does this mean fully covered or partially? It is unclear and the use of the word covered may suggest to a court that the defendant does not have to intend to conceal to be guilty. This could mean that if you were driving down the street with your gun unloaded on the floor boards of the back seat and you slam on your brakes causing your groceries to fall on the gun, you might be found guilty of carrying a concealed weapon. The courts should hold this statute void for vagueness (see discussion under "Commentary" after discussion of U.C.A. 76-10-505.5 below) and the Legislature should remove the word "covered" from the definition to make it clear that a prosecutor has to prove "specific intent to conceal" to get a conviction under this code section.

Amendments to this section in 1999 clarified a couple of provisions and also added definitions of the following terms: "enter," "house of residence," "residence," "state entity." Section (1)(a)(i) added "selling" and "transferring" to the list of activities including owning, possessing and

---

[18] If vampire hunting's your game.

[19] How many women do you know who DON'T carry concealed dangerous weapons of this nature in their purses?

purchasing firearms that citizens and legal aliens[20] cannot be prohibited from doing. The amendments in this subsection relating to the "lawful possession or control of a vehicle" restrict persons from having a firearm in a stolen car or truck.

Subsection (b) beefed up the state uniformity statute. It expressly added "state entities" to the list of political subdivisions that cannot enact or enforce an ordinance, regulation, or rule pertaining to firearms unless specifically authorized by the Legislature. This should put an end to claims by the University of Utah and other "state entities" (including the executive branch) that have created internal regulations or policies attempting to restrict concealed weapon permit holders. The definitions of "house of worship" and "residence" are pretty straight forward.

The major change in the year 2000 was the substitution of the term "violent felony" for the term "crime of violence" which expanded the types of crimes which prohibit a person from possessing a firearm (covered extensively in Chapters VII and XIII) or having a concealed weapon permit (see Chapter VIII).

2001 legislative changes exempted certain "antiques and curios" from the definition of "firearm." Many collectors do not collect guns to shoot them, but rather to as an investment or antique. Most of these guns are so old they cannot be fired safely. This law recognizes such use and exempts them from the definition of "firearm." Thus, that the restrictions existing on the possession and transfer of firearms do not apply to these collector items.

ACTUAL TEXT

As used in this part:

(1) (a) "Antique firearm" means any firearm:

(i) (A) with a matchlock, flintlock, percussion cap, or similar type of ignition system; and

(B) that was manufactured in or before 1898; or

(ii) that is a replica of any firearm described in this Subsection (1)(a), if the replica:

(A) is not designed or redesigned for using rimfire or conventional centerfire fixed ammunition; or

(B) uses rimfire or centerfire fixed ammunition which is:

(I) no longer manufactured in the United States; and

(II) is not readily available in ordinary channels of commercial trade; or

---

[20]   Apparently our Legislators were unaware that this year Congress passed a law prohibiting a whole class of legal aliens, "nonimmigrant-status aliens," from possessing a firearm. See discussion in Chapter XIII.

(iii) (A) that is a muzzle loading rifle, shotgun, or pistol; and

(B) is designed to use black powder, or a black powder substitute, and cannot use fixed ammunition.

(b) "Antique firearm" does not include:

(i) any weapon that incorporates a firearm frame or receiver;

(ii) any firearm that is converted into a muzzle loading weapon; or

(iii) any muzzle loading weapon that can be readily converted to fire fixed ammunition by replacing the:

(A) barrel;

(B) bolt;

(C) breechblock; or

(D) any combination of Subsection (1)(b)(iii)(A), (B), or (C).

(2) (a) "Concealed dangerous weapon" means a dangerous weapon that is covered, hidden, or secreted in a manner that the public would not be aware of its presence and is readily accessible for immediate use.

(b) A dangerous weapon shall not be considered a concealed dangerous weapon if it is a firearm which is unloaded and is securely encased.

(3) "Criminal history background check" means a criminal background check conducted by a licensed firearms dealer on every purchaser of a handgun through the division or the local law enforcement agency where the firearms dealer conducts business.

(4) "Curio or relic firearm" means any firearm that:

(a) is of special interest to a collector because of a quality that is not associated with firearms intended for:

(i) sporting use;

(ii) use as an offensive weapon; or

(iii) use as a defensive weapon;

(b) (i) was manufactured at least 50 years prior to the current date; and (ii) is not a replica of a firearm described in Subsection (4)(b)(i);

(c) is certified by the curator of a municipal, state, or federal museum that exhibits firearms to be a curio or relic of museum interest;

(d) derives a substantial part of its monetary value:

(i) from the fact that the firearm is:

(A) novel;

(B) rare; or

(C) bizarre; or

(ii) because of the firearm's association with an historical:

(A) figure;

(B) period; or

(C) event; and

(e) has been designated as a curio or relic firearm by the director of the United States Treasury Department Bureau of Alcohol, Tobacco, and Firearms under 27 C.F.R. § 178.11.

(5) (a) "Dangerous weapon" means any item that in the manner of its use or intended use is capable of causing death or serious bodily

injury. The following factors shall be used in determining whether a knife, or any other item, object, or thing not commonly known as a dangerous weapon is a dangerous weapon:

(i) the character of the instrument, object, or thing;

(ii) the character of the wound produced, if any;

(iii) the manner in which the instrument, object, or thing was used; and

(iv) the other lawful purposes for which the instrument, object, or thing may be used.

(b) "Dangerous weapon" does not include any explosive, chemical, or incendiary device as defined by Section 76-10-306.

(6) "Dealer" means every person who is licensed under crimes and criminal procedure, 18 U.S.C. § 923 and engaged in the business of selling, leasing, or otherwise transferring a handgun, whether the person is a retail or wholesale dealer, pawnbroker, or otherwise.

(7) "Division" means the Criminal Investigations and Technical Services Division of the Department of Public Safety, created in Section 53-10-103.

(8) "Enter" means intrusion of the entire body.

(9) (a) "Firearm" means a pistol, revolver, shotgun, sawed-off shotgun, rifle or sawed-off rifle, or any device that could be used as a dangerous weapon from which is expelled a projectile by action of an explosive.

(b) As used in Sections 76-10-526 and 76-10-527, "firearm" does not include an antique firearm.

(10) "Firearms transaction record form" means a form created by the division to be completed by a person purchasing, selling, or transferring a handgun from a dealer in the state.

(11) "Fully automatic weapon" means any firearm which fires, is designed to fire, or can be readily restored to fire, automatically more than one shot without manual reloading by a single function of the trigger.

(12) (a) "Handgun" means a pistol, revolver, or other firearm of any description, loaded or unloaded, from which any shot, bullet, or other missile can be discharged, the length of which, not including any revolving, detachable, or magazine breech, does not exceed 12 inches.

(b) As used in Sections 76-10-520, 76-10-521, and 76-10-522, "handgun" and "pistol or revolver" do not include an antique firearm.

(13) "House of worship" means a church, temple, synagogue, mosque, or other building set apart primarily for the purpose of worship in which religious services are held and the main body of which is kept for that use and not put to any other use inconsistent with its primary purpose.

(14) "Prohibited area" means any place where it is unlawful to discharge a firearm.

(15) "Readily accessible for immediate use" means that a firearm or

other dangerous weapon is carried on the person or within such close proximity and in such a manner that it can be retrieved and used as readily as if carried on the person.

(16) "Residence" means an improvement to real property used or occupied as a primary or secondary residence.

(17) "Sawed-off shotgun" or "sawed-off rifle" means a shotgun having a barrel or barrels of fewer than 18 inches in length, or in the case of a rifle, having a barrel or barrels of fewer than 16 inches in length, or any dangerous weapon made from a rifle or shotgun by alteration, modification, or otherwise, if the weapon as modified has an overall length of fewer than 26 inches.

(18) "Securely encased" means not readily accessible for immediate use, such as held in a gun rack, or in a closed case or container, whether or not locked, or in a trunk or other storage area of a motor vehicle, not including a glove box or console box.

(19) "State entity" means each department, commission, board, council, agency, institution, officer, corporation, fund, division, office, committee, authority, laboratory, library, unit, bureau, panel, or other administrative unit of the state.

(20) "Violent felony" means the same as defined in Section 76-3-203.5.

[U.C.A.76-3-203.5(c))(i)defines **"Violent Felony"** as follows: "Violent felony" means any of the following offenses, or any attempt, solicitation, or conspiracy to commit any of these offenses punishable as a felony:

(A) aggravated arson, arson, knowingly causing a catastrophe, and criminal mischief under Title 76, Chapter 6, Part 1, Property Destruction;

(B) aggravated assault under Title 76, Chapter 5, Part 1, Assault and Related Offenses;

(C) criminal homicide offenses under Title 76, Chapter 5, Part 2, Criminal Homicide;

(D) aggravated kidnaping and kidnaping under Title 76, Chapter 5, Part 3, Kidnaping;

(E) rape, Section 76-5-402;

(F) rape of a child, Section 76-5-402.1;

(G) object rape, Section 76-5-402.2;

(H) object rape of a child, Section 76-5-402.3;

(I) forcible sodomy, Section 76-5-403;

(J) sodomy on a child, Section 76-5-403.1;

(K) forcible sexual abuse, Section 76-5-404;

(L) aggravated sexual abuse of a child and sexual abuse of a child, Section 76-5-404.1;

(M) aggravated sexual assault, Section 76-5-405;

(N) sexual exploitation of a minor, Section 76-5a-3;

(O) aggravated burglary and burglary of a dwelling under Title 76, Chapter 6, Part 2, Burglary and Criminal Trespass;

(P) aggravated robbery and robbery under Title 76, Chapter 6, Part 3, Robbery;

(Q) theft by extortion under Subsection 76-6-406(2)(a) or (b);

(R) tampering with a witness under Subsection 76-8-508(2)(c);

(S) tampering with a juror under Subsection 76-8-508.5(2)(c);

(T) extortion to dismiss a criminal proceeding under Section 76-8-509 if by any threat or by use of force theft by extortion has been committed pursuant to Subsections 76-6-406(2)(a), (b), and (i);

(U) damage or destruction of school or institution of higher education property by explosives or flammable materials under Section 76-8-715;

(V) possession, use, or removal of explosive, chemical, or incendiary devices under Subsections 76-10-306(3) through (6);

(W) unlawful delivery of explosive, chemical, or incendiary devices under Section 76-10-307;

(X) purchase or possession of a dangerous weapon or handgun by a restricted person under Section 76-10-503;

(Y) unlawful discharge of a firearm under Section 76-10-508;

(Z) aggravated exploitation of prostitution under Subsection 76-10-1306(1)(a);

(AA) bus hijacking under Section 76-10-1504; and

(BB) discharging firearms and hurling missiles under Section 76-10-1505; or

(ii) any felony offense against a criminal statute of any other state, the United States, or any district, possession, or territory of the United States which would constitute a violent felony as defined in this Subsection (1) if committed in this state.]

U.C.A. 76-10-502. When weapon deemed loaded.

> ### "Plain Talk"
> Obviously, a firearm with a bullet in the chamber is loaded. Pistols and revolvers are loaded if the operation of any mechanism once would cause the gun to fire. A double-action revolver with no bullet aligned with the barrel is still considered "loaded" under this definition, if pulling the trigger would cause the cylinder to rotate and fire the gun. A semi-automatic pistol, however, is NOT loaded even if it has a magazine or clip in it, if there is no bullet in the barrel.

ACTUAL TEXT

(1) For the purpose of this chapter, any pistol, revolver, shotgun, rifle, or other weapon described in this part shall be deemed to be loaded

when there is an unexpended cartridge, shell, or projectile in the firing position.

(2) Pistols and revolvers shall also be deemed to be loaded when an unexpended cartridge, shell, or projectile is in a position whereby the manual operation of any mechanism once would cause the unexpended cartridge, shell, or projectile to be fired.

(3) A muzzle loading firearm shall be deemed to be loaded when it is capped or primed and has a powder charge and ball or shot in the barrel or cylinders.

U.C.A. 76-10-503. Restrictions on possession, purchase, transfer, and ownership of dangerous weapons by certain persons.

"Plain Talk"

This section was completely revamped in 2000. It creates two categories of restricted persons, Category I (really bad dudes - violent felons either as adults or juveniles) and Category II (bad dudes - "normal felons" either as adults or juveniles, druggies, mentally deficient persons, illegal aliens etc.). None of these people can possess a firearm, but Category I restricted persons are subject to a higher classification of felony than Category II restricted persons. Those who plead not guilty by reason of insanity and who are mentally incompetent to stand trial cannot possess a firearm. Most of these people are already restricted under the Gun Control Act of 1968; why not let the feds prosecute them for possessing a firearm (refer to explanation of federally restricted persons in Chapter XIII)?

ACTUAL TEXT

(1) For purposes of this section:

(a) A Category I restricted person is a person who:

(i) has been convicted of any violent felony as defined in Section 76-3-203.5;

(ii) is on probation or parole for any felony;

(iii) is on parole from a secure facility as defined in Section 62A-7-101; or

(iv) within the last ten years has been adjudicated delinquent for an offense which if committed by an adult would have been a violent felony as defined in Section 76-3-203.5 .

(b) A Category II restricted person is a person who:

(i) has been convicted of or is under indictment for any felony;

(ii) within the last seven years has been adjudicated delinquent for an offense which if committed by an adult would have been a felony;

(iii) is an unlawful user of a controlled substance as defined in Section 58-37-2 ;

(iv) is in possession of a dangerous weapon and is knowingly and intentionally in unlawful possession of a Schedule I controlled substance as defined in Section 58-37-2 ;

(v) has been found not guilty by reason of insanity for a felony offense;

(vi) has been found mentally incompetent to stand trial for a felony offense;

(vii) has been adjudicated as mentally defective as provided in the Brady Handgun Violence Prevention Act, Pub. L. No. 103-159, 107 Stat. 1536 (1993), or has been committed to a mental institution;

(viii) is an alien who is illegally or unlawfully in the United States;

(ix) has been dishonorably discharged from the armed forces; or

(x) has renounced his citizenship after having been a citizen of the United States

(2) A Category I restricted person who purchases, transfers, possesses, uses, or has under his custody or control:

 (a) any firearm is guilty of a second degree felony; or

 (b) any dangerous weapon other than a firearm is guilty of a third degree felony.

(3) A Category II restricted person who purchases, transfers, possesses, uses, or has under his custody or control:

 (a) any firearm is guilty of a third degree felony; or

 (b) any dangerous weapon other than a firearm is guilty of a class A misdemeanor.

(4) A person may be subject to the restrictions of both categories at the same time.

(5) If a higher penalty than is prescribed in this section is provided in another section for one who purchases, transfers, possesses, uses, or has under this custody or control any dangerous weapon, the penalties of that section control.

U.C.A. 76-10-504. Carrying concealed dangerous weapon -- Penalties.

"Plain Talk"

Unless you have a concealed weapon permit, it's illegal to carry a concealed weapon. It is a class B misdemeanor if you conceal a knife or other dangerous weapon that is not a firearm unless you're at home, on your property or at your place of business. This penalty also applies to firearms that are not loaded. If the firearms "contain ammunition," the violation is a Class A misdemeanor. Remember, a gun can be "unloaded" but still contain ammunition (U.C.A. 76-10-502). For example, a semi-automatic pistol contains ammunition, but is unloaded if the magazine is in the gun, but there is no bullet in the chamber. Concealed weapon holders are exempt from paragraph (1)(a) and (b) of Section 504, but are not exempt from the remaining provisions of the Section. Even a concealed weapon permit holder cannot legally conceal a sawed-off shotgun or sawed-off rifle. He can legally pretend he is Wyatt Earp, who carried a loaded Buntline Special on his hip, but not John Dillinger, who reportedly concealed a sawed-off shotgun in his baggy trousers. ~~Strikeout~~ and <u>underlining</u> indicate changes for 2000.

ACTUAL TEXT

(1) Except as provided in Section 76-10-503 and in Subsections (2) and (3):

(a) a person who carries a concealed dangerous weapon, as defined in Section 76-10-501, which is not a firearm on his person or one that is readily accessible for immediate use which is not securely encased, as defined in this part, in a place other than his residence, property, or business under his control is guilty of a class B misdemeanor; and

(b) a person without a valid concealed firearm permit who carries a concealed dangerous weapon which is a firearm and that contains no ammunition is guilty of a class B misdemeanor, but if the firearm contains ammunition the person is guilty of a class A misdemeanor.

(2) A person who carries concealed a sawed-off shotgun or a sawed-off rifle is guilty of a second degree felony.

(3) If the concealed firearm is used in the commission of a [~~crime of violence~~] <u>violent felony</u> as defined in Section [~~76-10-501~~] <u>76-3-203.5</u> , and the person is a party to the offense, the person is guilty of a second degree felony.

(4) Nothing in Subsection (1) shall prohibit a person engaged in the lawful taking of protected or unprotected wildlife as defined in Title 23, [~~Fish and Game~~] <u>Wildlife Resources Code</u>, from carrying a concealed weapon or a concealed firearm with a barrel length of four inches or greater as long as the taking of wildlife does not occur:

(a) within the limits of a municipality in violation of that municipality's ordinances; or

(b) upon the highways of the state as defined in Section 41-6-1.

U.C.A. 76-10-504

Commentary

In the case *State v. Williams*, 636 P.2d 1092 (Utah 1981), the defendant was convicted of "carrying a concealed weapon" for concealing a pistol in a satchel on the passenger's seat of his car. The court held it was not necessary for the weapon to actually be concealed under a person's clothing if it was within arm's reach and easily accessible. This case illustrates why it's so hard to predict whether you are in violation of certain laws. The word "carrying" suggests that a person is "totin'" the weapon on his person. Here the defendant was convicted of a felony for carrying the weapon in his car within his immediate reach. Luckily, the law under which this defendant was convicted has since been amended to be more lenient. Now, possession of a concealed loaded firearm is a class A misdemeanor (Section 504(1)(b)) instead of a felony, unless the firearm is a sawed-off shotgun or sawed-off rifle, in which case the offense is a second-degree felony (Section 504(2)).

U.C.A. 76-10-505. Carrying loaded firearm in vehicle, on street, or in prohibited area.

"Plain Talk"

This code section and the preceding section (504) govern how persons WITHOUT concealed weapon permits must carry guns in cars — (1) NOT CONCEALED and (2) UNLOADED. A gun that is securely encased (see definition in section 500 above) is not concealed. Securely encased does NOT permit a person to place a gun in the console or glove box.

THE STRANGER WITH THE BIG IRON ON HIS HIP -- Cowboys can strap their LOADED smoke wagons on their hips and strut down public streets as long as they don't conceal, right? WRONG! It's illegal to carry a loaded gun on a street, in a vehicle or in a "posted prohibited area" (which means any place [like a city?] Where signs say it is illegal to shoot). This does not apply to concealed weapon permit holders, cops, judges, or nonresidents with concealed weapon permits from other states (See U.C.A. 76-10-523).

ACTUAL TEXT
(1) Unless otherwise authorized by law, a person may not carry a loaded firearm:
> (a) in or on a vehicle;
> (b) on any public street; or
> (c) in a posted prohibited area.

(2) A violation of this section is a class B misdemeanor.

U.C.A. 76-10-505.5. Possession of a dangerous weapon, firearm, or sawed-off shotgun on or about school premises -- Penalties

"Plain Talk"

It is illegal under both state and federal law (see Chapter XIII) to take a gun or other type of dangerous weapon onto school (elementary and secondary) property. This applies to students, teachers, administrators and parents. The exceptions are concealed weapon permit holders, U.C.A. 53-5-704, temporary concealed weapon permit holders, U.C.A. 53-5-705, people keeping a loaded weapon at their temporary residences, residences or camps, U.C.A. 76-10-511, federal and state police officers, mail carriers making deliveries, concealed weapon permit holders from other states, non-residents with unloaded weapons that are securely encased, and judges, U.C.A. 76-10-523. We discuss this topic again in Chapter XIII to show how it relates to the federal statute known as the Gun Free School Zone Act. When successful applicants for a Utah concealed weapon permit receive their permit in the mail, they get a letter from the Bureau of Criminal Investigation (BCI) specifically telling them they can take their concealed weapons onto school property.

ACTUAL TEXT

(1) A person may not possess any dangerous weapon, firearm, or sawed-off shotgun, as those terms are defined in Section 76-10-501, at a place that the person knows, or has reasonable cause to believe, is on or about school premises.

(2) (a) Possession of a dangerous weapon on or about school premises is a class B misdemeanor.

(b) Possession of a firearm or sawed-off shotgun on or about school premises is a class A misdemeanor.

(3) This section applies to any person, except persons authorized to possess a firearm as provided under Sections 53-5-704, 53-5-705, 53A-3-502, 76-10-511, 76-10-523, Subsection 76-10-504(2), and as otherwise authorized by law.

(4) This section does not prohibit prosecution of a more serious weapons offense that may occur on or about school premises.

U.C.A. 76-10-505.5

Commentary

There are few misguided prosecutors and school board members that take the position that a related, but obscure "school statute" U.C.A. 53A-3-502 prohibits concealed weapon permit holders from taking weapons onto school property. That code section states:

(1) A person who possesses a weapon, explosive,

flammable material, or other material dangerous to persons or property in a public or private elementary or secondary school, on the grounds of the school, or in those parts of a building, park, or stadium which are being used for an activity sponsored by or through the school is guilty of a class B misdemeanor, unless a higher penalty is prescribed in Title 76, Criminal Code, in which case the penalty provisions of that title control.

(2) Subsection (1) does not apply under the following circumstances:

(a) possession is approved by the responsible school administrator; or

(b) the item or material is present or to be used in connection with a lawful, approved activity and is in the possession or under the control of the person responsible for its possession or use (emphasis added).

U.C.A.53A-3-502(1) does not apply if the weapon is used "in connection with a lawful, approved activity." Because concealed weapon permits are "valid throughout the state without restriction" (See Chapter XIII), a permit holder carrying a concealed weapon is engaging in a "lawful, approved activity." Notice that U.C.A.53A-3-502 doesn't have any specific language, such as in U.C.A. 76-10-523 exempting police officers, federal marshals, or judges performing their official duties unless such duties come within the language about "a lawful, approved activity." Certainly the Legislature did not intend to disarm police officers performing their duties on school grounds. The Legislature could clarify this situation for police officers and concealed weapon permit holders by adding a paragraph (c) that states:

(c) does not apply to the classes of individuals referred to in sections (1) and (2) of U.C.A. 76-10-523, including concealed weapon permit holders.

When a statute is confusing or vague, **people cannot be expected to understand what it means.** The courts can invalidate laws like this under a doctrine known as "void for vagueness." **The concern is that the vague terms will permit law enforcement personnel and the courts to enforce ordinances without giving citizens fair notice of what is illegal.** *Coates v. City of Cincinnati*, **402 U.S. 611, 614 (1971)**[21] If a concealed weapon permit holder was arrested for violating U.C.A. 53A-3-502 for carrying a weapon on the school grounds, his lawyer should walk into court

---

[21] Lawyers have a habit of citing cases that illustrate the principle of law just stated. The United States Supreme Court discussed the concept "void for vagueness" in the *Coates* case.

screaming, "void for vagueness!" In my opinion, he should win. One is truly led to believe by the language of U.C.A. 76-10-505.5(3), that concealed weapon permits are valid on school property.

U.C.A. 76-10-506. Threatening with or using dangerous weapon in fight or quarrel.

"Plain Talk"
You can't legally threaten deadly force unless someone is first threatening you with deadly force (see detailed discussion of the law of self defense in Chapter XI). If you threaten without justification, it's a class A misdemeanor. The wording, "in the presence of two or more persons" is unclear. It appears there must be two or more witnesses to convict someone of this offense.

ACTUAL TEXT
Every person, except those persons described in Section 76-10-503 **[felons etc.]**, who, not in necessary self defense in the presence of two or more persons, draws or exhibits any dangerous weapon in an angry and threatening manner or unlawfully uses the same in any fight or quarrel is guilty of a class A misdemeanor.

U.C.A. 76-10-506
Commentary
I have represented several clients charged with violating this code section. Unfortunately, these cases often stem from verbal arguments or road rage incidents. Consequently, I train my concealed carry students to set "macho" aside when they are packing heat. The object of concealed carry is to survive, not win arguments or prove that you "had the right of way." Shun verbal disputes before they escalate into conflicts that force you to use a gun to defend yourself. Avoiding gestures with your middle finger, will save wear and tear on your trigger finger (and on your pocket book by not having to hire a lawyer to defend you for threatening with a weapon).

U.C.A. 76-10-507. Possession of deadly weapon with intent to assault.

"Plain Talk"
Possessing a dangerous weapon with the intent to assault is a class A misdemeanor. This statute makes 90% of the rest of the gun laws unnecessary.

ACTUAL TEXT
Every person having upon his person any dangerous weapon with intent to unlawfully assault another is guilty of a class A misdemeanor.

U.C.A. 76-10-508. Discharge of firearm from a vehicle, near highway, or in direction of any person, building, or vehicle.

"Plain Talk"

You cannot shoot your gun out of your car window or the back of your truck unless you are disabled (see R657-12-4 entitled "Obtaining Authorization to Hunt from a Vehicle", Chapter IX). This section applies to all dangerous weapons including slingshots, blowguns, BB guns, and crossbows. "Vehicle" includes ATVs, motorcycles, dune buggies and Jeeps. U.C.A. 41-6-1 (21) defines, "Motor vehicle" as "every vehicle which is self-propelled and every vehicle which is propelled by electric power obtained from overhead trolley wires, but not operated upon rails, except vehicles moved solely by human power [bicycles[22]] and motorized wheel chairs."

You cannot shoot from or across a highway. The term "highway" has a very broad definition under the Utah code. "Highway" means "the entire width between property lines of every way or place of any nature when any part of it is open to the use of the public as a matter of right for vehicular travel" (U.C.A. 41-6-1 (15)). So even if you're off the road, if you are on the "right of way," you can't shoot. It probably doesn't mean dirt roads on private property unless there is a public right of way. If the public has a right of way over a private dirt road, the road is considered a highway under this definition.

It is a crime to shoot at road signs, communications equipment, railroad equipment, in Utah State Park buildings (duh!), state park camping and picnic sites, overlooks, golf courses, boat ramps, and developed beaches. Don't shoot your gun (or your blowgun for that matter) within 600 feet of any building or structure where a domestic animal is kept, without the permission of the owner or person in charge of the property. Police officers and people acting in self defense are exceptions to the prohibitions contained in this code section.

---

[22] Looks like it's legal to shoot at jack rabbits with a pistol from a mountain bike (while sippin' on a Mountain Dew), unless you're on a road or shooting across a road. Uh, while we're on the subject of jack rabbits and pistols, why do people shoot them with shotguns? It's like really no compo (O.K., maybe it's cool to let your 6 year old use a .410, just to get the hang of it, but not to kill bushels of 'em unless they're threatening crops). Try shootin' 'em with a handgun if you want a REAL challenge. It's kinda like "catch and release" without the "catch!" That way there'll be plenty of bunnies when you go back next time.

ACTUAL TEXT

(1)(a) A person may not discharge any kind of dangerous weapon or firearm:

    (i) from an automobile or other vehicle;

    (ii) from, upon, or across any highway;

    (iii) at any road signs placed upon any highways of the state;

    (iv) at any communications equipment or property of public utilities including facilities, lines, poles, or devices of transmission or distribution;

    (v) at railroad equipment or facilities including any sign or signal;

    (vi) within Utah State Park buildings, designated camp or picnic sites, overlooks, golf courses, boat ramps, and developed beaches; or

    (vii) without written permission to discharge the dangerous weapon from the owner or person in charge of the property within 600 feet of:

    (b) a house, dwelling, or any other building; or

    (c) any structure in which a domestic animal is kept or fed, including a barn, poultry yard, corral, feeding pen, or stockyard.

    (d) It shall be a defense to any charge for violating this section that the person being accused had actual permission of the owner or person in charge of the property at the time in question.

(2) A violation of any provision of this section is a class B misdemeanor unless the actor discharges a firearm under any of the following circumstances not amounting to criminal homicide or attempted criminal homicide, in which case it is a third degree felony:

    (a) the actor discharges a firearm in the direction of any person or persons, knowing or having reason to believe that any person may be endangered;

    (b) the actor, with intent to intimidate or harass another or with intent to damage a habitable structure as defined in Subsection 76-6-101(2), discharges a firearm in the direction of any building; or

    (c) the actor, with intent to intimidate or harass another, discharges a firearm in the direction of any vehicle.

(3) This section does not apply to a person:

    (a) who discharges any kind of firearm when that person is in lawful defense of self or others; or

    (b) who is performing official duties as provided in Sections 23-20-1.5 and 76-10-523 and as otherwise provided by law.

U.C.A. 76-10-508

Commentary

    Sections (1)(a)(i) and (ii) of U.C.A. 76-10-508, which prohibit the discharge of <u>any kind</u> of dangerous weapon or firearm . . .from an <u>automobile or other vehicle</u> or from, upon or across <u>any highway,</u> are too broad. As shown above, the definitions of "vehicle" and "highway" are very expansive. These sections prohibit shooting a slingshot or air rifle on the most remote dirt roads in the most isolated sections of the state. The Legislature should amend these laws to permit shooters and hunters to discharge various weapons from a vehicle, in remote areas, if it can be done with reasonable safety.

Although shooting from a vehicle can be dangerous, many sports, such as rock climbing, horseback riding (e.g., the tragedy surrounding Christopher Reeve's paralysis), kayaking, river running, swimming, and golf, involve some risk. (I once handled a case where a six-year-old at a city golf clinic drove a chipping wedge through the forehead of another six-year-old!) As most hunters can attest, a Utah general season deer hunt can be spooky. More hunters have probably been killed or injured deer hunting than have ever been shot or killed simply shooting from a vehicle. If safety alone were the issue, why would the state allow disabled persons to hunt big game from a vehicle? (See R657-12-4 Obtaining Authorization to Hunt from a Vehicle, Ch. IX) No offense to the disabled, but it seems more dangerous to allow a person with a disability to shoot from a vehicle under the excitement of bagging a trophy buck or bull elk, than to allow a healthy individual to shoot jack rabbits out of his truck window thirty five miles northwest of Delta (Dude, we're talking desolate!).

This state statute should be amended to allow hunters to shoot from a vehicle under certain conditions. For example, the activity could be limited to unimproved dirt roads that are not state or county roads. The driver of the vehicle could be prohibited from shooting. Other restrictions could be enacted which could make the sport much safer, including limiting the number of shooters, the types of weapons, and the number of shots per weapon. With a little effort the sport could be made reasonably safe. Also, persons protecting their livestock on their own property should be permitted to shoot from a vehicle. By the time a sheep herder climbs out of his truck, marauding coyotes are likely to be loooooonnnnng gone.

A reasonable person might consider "highway" to mean a road that is paved and traveled by a substantial number of vehicles. However, the definition in U.C.A. 41-6-1 (15) is broader and may include dirt roads.[23] The state should define "highway" more narrowly. Most heavily traveled roads contain a federal, state or county road number such as "Interstate 15," "State Road 89," and "County Road 14." The state could enact a law prohibiting the discharge of a firearm from or across any federal, state or county highway or road. Another approach could be to prohibit shooting

[23] "'Highway' means the entire width between property lines of every way or place of any nature when any part of it is open to the use of the public as a matter of right for vehicular travel", (Utah Code Ann. 41-6-1 (15)).

on interstates, highways, principal roads and improved roads, but allow shooting on unimproved roads, except within 600 feet of another vehicle owned by persons not voluntarily participating in the shooting activity.

Another criticism of sections (i) and (ii) is that they treat all weapons the same. Most cowboys, Indians, medieval knights, and other warriors know that all weapons are not created equal. It's dangerous to zing a .223 caliber 55 grain boat tail at light speed out of your truck window on Interstate 15, three miles south of Cedar City. But it's not unsafe to shoot a .45 Long Colt out of the back of your Jeep, twenty five miles southwest of Trout Creek on a dirt road that hasn't seen another vehicle besides yours, in forty five days. Section 508 does not distinguish between the two situations. The .223 boat tail has a muzzle velocity of over 3200 feet per second, but the .45 Colt, depending on the powder charge, pushes a 250 grain bullet at only 750 to 900 feet per second. The boat tail might skip on a rock and cause injury up to a mile away. My experience has been that a .45 Colt 250 grain lead round nose travels a hundred yards at most after it hits the ground. The statute be rewritten as follows:

U.C.A. 76-10-508:

(1) (a) A person may not discharge any kind of dangerous weapon or firearm:

(i) from an automobile or other vehicle:

a) during daylight hours (½ hour before sunrise until ½ after sunset), while said automobile is on an interstate, paved highway, principle road, or an improved road, or within 600 feet of other persons or vehicles occupied by persons not participating in the same shooting activity as the person discharging the firearm or dangerous weapon; and the shooting activity must be in compliance with all other state laws and city ordinances;

b) at night time (½ hour after sunset until ½ hour before sunrise), except as provided in U.C.A. 23-13-17 [the state spotlighting statute] and in accordance with the county ordinances pertaining to spotlighting; or within 600 feet of other persons or vehicles occupied by persons not participating in the same shooting activity as the person discharging the firearm or dangerous weapon; and the shooting activity must be in compliance with all other state laws and city ordinances; and in addition thereto,

i) participants in the shooting activity may not use weapons propelling projectiles faster than 1000 ft./sec.

ii) a participant may not discharge any weapon while driving a vehicle or holding a spotlight.

(ii) ~~from, upon, or across any highway:~~ from, upon, or across any interstate, paved highway, principle road, or an improved road, or within 600 feet of other persons or vehicles occupied by persons not participating in the same shooting activity as the person discharging the firearm or dangerous weapon; and the shooting activity must be in compliance with all other state laws and city ordinances.

I invite members of various archery associations to propose reasonably safe changes under this code section relating to archery, including the use of crossbows. I see no reason why archery equipment could not be used to spotlight various varmints and predators. In fact, archery equipment could be the weapon of choice for predator control near more populated areas. Several eastern state cities have permitted bow hunting of white tail deer which have become overpopulated and pose a serious safety risk to city residents. The State of Utah's Department of Wildlife Resources could obtain a wealth of information from such cities.

Pancho's Wisdom
To the EPA with Love . . . "Shoot Lead Bullets!"

U.C.A. 76-10-509. Possession of dangerous weapon by minor.

"Plain Talk"

GUNS, MINORS AND JUVENILES --- Utah State gun laws refer to persons under 18 years of age as "minors." Federal gun laws call them "juveniles." This Utah statute creates two categories of minors. Minors 14 to 18 years of age can possess a dangerous weapon if their parents give permission. Minors under 14 years of age must be accompanied by a responsible adult to have a dangerous weapon in their possession. Remember, "dangerous weapon" could mean anything that could kill or cause severe injury, such as a pocket knife, a blow gun, or a slingshot.

Without referring to our "Youngsters, Guns and Ammo" chart, Appendix F, it is almost impossible for anyone, including attorneys, peace officers and even BATF agents, to keep straight all the state and federal laws placing age limitations on firearms use. Don't rely on U.C.A. 76-10-509 without referring to Appendix F.

ACTUAL TEXT

(1) A minor under 18 years of age may not possess a dangerous weapon unless he:

  (a) has the permission of his parent or guardian to have the weapon; or

(b) is accompanied by a parent or guardian while he has the weapon in his possession.

(2) Any minor under 14 years of age in possession of a dangerous weapon shall be accompanied by a responsible adult.

(3) Any person who violates this section is guilty of:

      (a) a class B misdemeanor upon the first offense; and

      (b) a class A misdemeanor for each subsequent offense.

U.C.A. 76-10-509

Commentary

Federal law goes a step further than state law when it comes to juveniles possessing handguns for legitimate purposes. Under state law, the parent can give oral permission, accompany the child or ask another person 21 or older to accompany the minor. Federal law requires WRITTEN PERMISSION [a piece of paper] which must be kept on the juvenile at all times, even if the parent or guardian accompanies the juvenile in possession of the handgun (see 18 U.S.C. 922(x)(1) which we cover at length in Chapter XIII). The form in "Appendix A" may be used by parents to give written permission to their children to possess a handgun for the purposes referred to on the form. The juvenile should keep the consent form with him at all times while possessing the pistol or revolver.

U.C.A. 76-10-509.4. Prohibition of possession of certain weapons by minors.

"Plain Talk"

Section (1) says minors cannot possess a handgun. But there are several exceptions found in Section 512 below, including target shooting at amusement parks, attending a firearm safety course, practicing at a shooting range or other place where the discharge of a firearm is not prohibited by state or local law (outside all city limits and off of all highways and at least 600 feet from any person or building or enclosure where domestic animals are kept). Section 512 also permits minors to hunt with handguns.

Minors cannot possess sawed-off shotguns or rifles or fully automatic weapons "except as provided under federal law." The only exceptions under federal law seem to be in connection with military service.

ACTUAL TEXT

(1) A minor under 18 years of age may not possess a handgun.

(2) Except as provided by federal law, a minor under 18 years of age may not possess the following:

(a) a sawed-off rifle or sawed-off shotgun; or

(b) a fully automatic weapon.

(3) Any person who violates Subsection (1) is guilty of:

(a) a class B misdemeanor upon the first offense; and

(b) a class A misdemeanor for each subsequent offense.

(4) Any person who violates Subsection (2) is guilty of a third degree felony.

U.C.A. 76-10-509.5. Penalties for providing certain weapons to a minor.

> **"Plain Talk"**
> This section penalizes anyone assisting minors to obtain the weapons prohibited above.

ACTUAL TEXT

(1) Any person who provides a handgun to a minor when the possession of the handgun by the minor is a violation of Section 76-10-509.4 is guilty of:

(a) a class B misdemeanor upon the first offense; and

(b) a class A misdemeanor for each subsequent offense.

(2) Any person who transfers in violation of applicable state or federal law a sawed-off rifle, sawed-off shotgun, or fully automatic weapon to a minor is guilty of a third degree felony.

U.C.A. 76-10-509.6. Parent or guardian providing firearm to violent minor.

> **"Plain Talk"**
> It is a Class A Misdemeanor for a parent or guardian to knowingly allow a minor, convicted of a violent felony, as defined in U.C.A. 76-10-501(18) and U.C.A.. 76-3-203.5 above, to possess a firearm. The parent or guardian commits a third degree felony for every additional violation of this code section. ~~Strikeout~~ and underlining indicate changes for 2000.

ACTUAL TEXT

(1) A parent or guardian may not intentionally or knowingly provide a firearm to, or permit the possession of a firearm by, any minor who has been convicted of a [~~crime of violence~~] _violent felony as defined in Section 76-3-203.5_ or any minor who has been adjudicated in juvenile court for an offense which would constitute a [~~crime of violence~~] _violent felony_ if the minor were an adult.

(2) Any person who violates this section is guilty of:

(a) a class A misdemeanor upon the first offense; and

(b) a third degree felony for each subsequent offense.

U.C.A. 76-10-509.7. Parent or guardian knowing of minor's possession of dangerous weapon.

"Plain Talk"

A parent who knows a minor illegally possesses a dangerous weapon or a firearm (meaning without the parent's or guardian's permission or outside his or her presence) and fails to make reasonable efforts to take the weapon or handgun away from the minor, is guilty of a Class B Misdemeanor.

ACTUAL TEXT

Any parent or guardian of a minor who knows that the minor is in possession of a dangerous weapon in violation of Section 76-10-509 or a firearm in violation of Section 76-10-509.4 and fails to make reasonable efforts to remove the firearm from the minor's possession is guilty of a class B misdemeanor.

U.C.A. 76-10-509.9. Sales of firearms to juveniles.

"Plain Talk"

No one can sell a firearm to a minor outside the presence of his parent or guardian. To do so is a third degree felony.

ACTUAL TEXT

(1) A person may not sell any firearm to a minor under 18 years of age unless the minor is accompanied by a parent or guardian.

(2) Any person who violates this section is guilty of a third degree felony.

U.C.A. 76-10-509.9

Commentary

Caution gun dealers! This code section suggests it's legal to sell handguns to minors accompanied by a parent or guardian. However, federal law states, "It shall be unlawful for a person to sell . . .[a handgun] to a person who the transferor knows or has reasonable cause to believe is a juvenile" (see 18 U.S.C.§ 922(x)(1), covered in Chapter XIII of this book). The only exceptions are "temporary" transfers of handguns to minors for farming, ranching, target practicing, hunting and serving in the military. I told you this stuff is complicated. It would be extremely unfortunate for a gun dealer, relying on state law, to lose his dealer's license for violating federal law. This Utah code section should be amended to conform with federal law, 18 U.S.C. § 922(x)(1).

U.C.A. 76-10-510. Repealed.

> **"Plain Talk"**
>
> This code section has been repealed, meaning it doesn't exist in the law books anymore. We put the title here to inform you we didn't inadvertently skip this code section.

U.C.A. 76-10-511.   Possession of loaded firearm at residence authorized.

> **"Plain Talk"**
>
> Hallelujah! This is one of the good gun laws. The good guys (and gals, of course) can legally protect themselves and their families with a loaded gun in their homes, hotel rooms, trailers, tents, and sleeping bags while camping. This should include dormitories if a student is 18 years of age or older.

ACTUAL TEXT

Except for persons described in Section 76-10-503, **[convicted felons, mentally defective persons, drug addicts etc.]** a person may have a loaded firearm at his place of residence, including any temporary residence or camp.

> U.C.A. 76-10-511
>
> **Commentary**
>
> In my "mind's eye," I see campus administrators biting their nails at the suggestion that students 18 years of age and older should be able to have the same privileges as adult students living off campus. We draft 18 year olds, slap M-16s in their hands, and expect them to sleep together in crowded, wet foxholes in hostile lands. If they are mature enough to do that, they are mature enough to be able to defend their temporary homes if need be, whether on or off campus. It's all about trusting the good guys, isn't it? If our laws hold people criminally and civilly ACCOUNTABLE for injuries caused by firearms, we shouldn't have to place PRIOR RESTRAINTS on the rights of law-abiding citizens to bear arms.

U.C.A. 76-10-512. Target concessions, shooting ranges, competitions, and hunting excepted from prohibitions.

"Plain Talk"

Thanks to this code section, we can teach our kids to shoot and hunt with a handgun. Subsection (3) is pretty broad. It says minors can practice using a handgun in ANY place where discharging a firearm is NOT PROHIBITED by state or local law. This means that if a minor has written permission from his parent or guardian to practice shooting a handgun in a remote area, outside city limits, off of highways, at least 600 feet from buildings or enclosures where domestic animals are kept, the minor may legally possess a handgun. Minors under 14 must be accompanied by an adult to possess any dangerous weapon (see U.C.A. 76-10-509(2) above) even if they have written permission. WORDS OF CAUTION: This law must be read in context with several other state laws and the federal law governing juveniles and firearms. Without seeing all these laws in one location and comparing them, they are IMPOSSIBLE to decipher. To help, we compiled a table summarizing them in Appendix F. DON'T LEAVE HOME WITHOUT APPENDIX F (or the consent form in Appendix A, for that matter) anytime you MIX KIDS and GUNS. Otherwise, you could get an "F" which stands for FELONY! ~~Strikeout~~ and underlining indicate changes for 2000.

ACTUAL TEXT

The provisions of [~~Sections 76-10-503,~~] Section 76-10-509 [~~;~~] and Subsection 76-10-509.4 (1) regarding possession of handguns by minors shall not apply to any of the following:

(1) Patrons firing at lawfully operated target concessions at amusement parks, piers, and similar locations provided that the firearms to be used are firmly chained or affixed to the counters.

(2) Any person in attendance at a hunter's safety course or a firearms safety course.

(3) Any person engaging in practice or any other lawful use of a firearm at an established range or any other area where the discharge of a firearm is not prohibited by state or local law.

(4) Any person engaging in an organized competition involving the use of a firearm, or participating in or practicing for such competition.

(5) Any minor under 18 years of age who is on real property with the permission of the owner, licensee, or lessee of the property and who has the permission of a parent or legal guardian or the owner, licensee, or lessee to possess a firearm not otherwise in violation of law.

(6) Any resident or nonresident hunters with a valid hunting license or other persons who are lawfully engaged in hunting.

(7) Any person traveling to or from any activity described in Subsection (2), (3), (4), (5), or (6) with an unloaded firearm in his possession.

U.C.A. 76-10-513 to 519 have either been repealed or renumbered (replaced by other code sections).

U.C.A. 76-10-520. Number or mark assigned to pistol or revolver by Department of Public Safety.

"Plain Talk"

Sometimes "low-lifers" file the serial numbers off of guns they intend to use in a crime. As Section 522 below states, this is a crime. Code Section 520 gives the Department of Public Safety the authority to issue a new number to someone who, through legal means, ends up with a pistol or revolver with no serial number.

ACTUAL TEXT

The Department of Public Safety upon request may assign a distinguishing number or mark of identification to any pistol or revolver whenever it is without a manufacturer's number, or other mark of identification or whenever the manufacturer's number or other mark of identification or the distinguishing number or mark assigned by the Department of Public Safety has been destroyed or obliterated.

U.C.A. 76-10-521. Unlawful marking of pistol or revolver.

"Plain Talk"

If you end up with a handgun without a serial number, you can't just stamp one on without getting permission from the Department of Public Safety (DPS).

ACTUAL TEXT

(1) Any person who places or stamps on any pistol or revolver any number except one assigned to it by the Department of Public Safety is guilty of a class A misdemeanor.

U.C.A. 76-10-522. Alteration of number or mark on pistol or revolver.

"Plain Talk"

It's against the law to grind serial numbers and other I.D. marks off of pistols and revolvers.

ACTUAL TEXT

Any person who changes, alters, removes, or obliterates the name of the maker, the model, manufacturer's number, or other mark of identification, including any distinguishing number or mark assigned by the Department of Public Safety, on any pistol or revolver, without first having secured written permission from the Department of Public Safety to make the change, alteration, or removal, is guilty of a class A misdemeanor.

U.C.A. 76-10-523. Persons exempt from weapons laws.

"Plain Talk"

The following persons are exempt from all of the weapon laws referenced in this "part," (part 5), sections 500 to 531:

Federal marshals, federal officials required to carry guns, police officers, judges, freight companies transporting firearms as merchandise, non-residents traveling through the state (as long as the gun is unloaded and securely encased as defined in Section 501).

The 2001 Utah Legislature made several changes in this code section making it easier for Utahns and CWP holders from other states to carry concealed weapons for self defense. The 2001 changes are indicated by the ~~strikeout key~~ and underlining. Briefly, the 2001 changes authorize federal marshals, police officers and other federal officials that carry guns as part of their work duties, to carry concealed weapons off duty. The law now recognizes permits from all other states and counties even though the rules for getting a permit in those places are less restrictive than in Utah. Out-of-stater's permits are only valid for 60 days, however. This means Utah residents will not be able to circumvent Utah's CWP law by qualifying under less stringent standards in another state e.g. a Utahn gets a Washington state permit without taking a concealed carry certification class and uses it as his Utah permit because Utah recognizes Washington's permit. A Utahn could do so, but his Washington permit would be valid for only 60 days. The 2001 changes will increase the number of states that recognize Utah's permit because there are states that will not recognize our permit unless we recognize theirs. Now that we recognize all permits, many states will recognize ours, although no one is quite sure what affect the 60 day limitation will have on other states honoring Utah's CWPs.

Concealed Weapon Holders - This section also gives concealed weapon holders several privileges not enjoyed by those who do not have a concealed weapon permit. Concealed weapon holders can carry a concealed dangerous weapon (such as a knife) as well as a loaded firearm, (U.C.A. 76-10-504(1)(a)). They can carry a loaded gun in their vehicles (U.C.A. 76-10-505(1)(a)) and on public streets (U.C.A. 76-10-505(1)(b)). They cannot, however, conceal a sawed-off shotgun or sawed-off rifle. Permit holders cannot legally carry their weapons into secured areas within the courts, airports, correctional facilities (jails, prisons, reform schools), and mental health facilities (see sections 523.5 and 529 below).

Subsection (2)(b) refers to the other states whose concealed weapon permits Utah recognizes. As of 2001, Utah recognizes the permits of all states and counties.

The only states with which Utah has a written reciprocal agreement are Arizona, Arkansas and Kentucky. (See Bureau of Criminal Identification Web page at www.bci.state.ut.us.) However, unofficial sources claim that in addition to these states, the following states recognize Utah's permit (See www.packing.org) They are Idaho, Florida, Indiana, Michigan, Montana, Oklahoma, South Carolina and Wyoming. At one time the NRA reported that Alaska recognized Utah's permit. Now that Utah recognizes all other states' permits, we anticipate there will be other states that reciprocate by recognizing Utah's. We suggest permit holders traveling out of state call in advance to verify. In Appendix E you will find the telephone number of every state attorney general. Keep in mind some states don't have a uniform law provision like Utah's UCA 76-10-500. Therefore, there may be cities and counties within a state that accepts our permit, that have unusual restrictions on concealed weapon permit holders. For example, some states don't authorize permit holders to carry their weapons into school zones, churches or private businesses that post signs. You will not know this unless you call ahead and ask about carrying a concealed weapon in the cities and counties in which you intend to travel. See also www.packing.org for UNOFFICIAL info about what states accept other state's permits.

ACTUAL TEXT

(1) This part and Title 53, Chapter 5, Part 7, Concealed Weapon Act, do not apply to any of the following:

(a) a United States marshal ~~while engaged in the performance of his official duties~~;

(b) a federal official required to carry a firearm ~~while engaged in the performance of his official duties~~;

(c) a peace officer of this or any other jurisdiction ~~while engaged in the performance of his official duties~~;

(d) a law enforcement official as defined and qualified under Section 53-5-711;

(e) a judge as defined and qualified in Section 53-5-711;

(f) a common carrier while engaged in the regular and ordinary transport of firearms as merchandise; or

(g) a nonresident traveling in or through the state, provided that any firearm is:

(i) unloaded; and

(ii) securely encased as defined in Section 76-10-501.

(2) The provisions of Subsections 76-10-504(1)(a), (1)(b), and Section 76-10-505 do not apply to any person to whom a permit to carry a concealed firearm has been issued:

(a) pursuant to Section 53-5-704; or

(b) ~~by another state whose requirements for issuance of a concealed firearm permit have been determined annually by the Department of Public Safety to meet or exceed the requirements for issuance of a concealed firearm permit in this state.~~ by another state or county.

(3)(a) Notwithstanding Subsection (2), a concealed firearm permit issued by another state or county is only valid in this state for 60 consecutive days.

(b) in order to carry a concealed firearm, a person that remains in the state for longer than 60 consecutive days shall obtain a permit pursuant to section U.C.A. 53-5-70 4.

U.C.A. 76-10-523.5. Compliance with rules for secure facilities.

"Plain Talk"

This section makes no sense without knowing what Sections 76-8-311.1, 76-8-311.3, and 78-7-6 say, so we combined them all together here. In short, it is a third degree felony for persons, including those who have concealed weapon permits, to take firearms into secured areas in jails, mental health facilities and the courts. It is a second degree felony to give them to inmates. Section 529 below gives airports the authority to establish secured areas where even concealed weapon holders may not take firearms.

ACTUAL TEXT

Any person, including a person licensed to carry a concealed firearm under Title 53, Chapter 5, Part 7, Concealed Weapons, shall comply with any rule established for secure facilities pursuant to Sections 76-8-311.1, 76-8-311.3, and 78-7-6 and shall be subject to any penalty provided in those sections.

U.C.A. 76-8-311.1. Secure areas -- Items prohibited -- Penalty.

"Plain Talk"

> Obviously, taking explosives, firearms or other weapons into a jail or mental institution could create an extremely dangerous situation. The weapon holder could be overpowered by an inmate resulting in death, serious bodily injury or escape. Therefore, Utah law authorizes such facilities to create "secure areas" where such weapons are banned. The facility creating a secure area must post a sign explaining the prohibitions. Facilities having secure areas MUST PROVIDE A STORAGE AREA for weapons, and its employees are responsible for the weapons while gun owners visit the facility. Remember, even concealed weapon permit holders may not enter a secured area without checking their weapons. See "Plain Talk" explanation for section 76-10-523.5 above.

ACTUAL TEXT

(1) In addition to the definitions in Section 76-10-501, as used in this section:

(a) "Correctional facility" has the same meaning as defined in Section 76-8-311.3.

(b) "Explosive" has the same meaning as defined for "explosive, chemical, or incendiary device" defined in Section 76-10-306.

(c) "Law enforcement facility" means a facility which is owned, leased, or operated by a law enforcement agency.

(d) "Mental health facility" has the same meaning as defined in Section 62A-12-202.

(e)(i) "Secure area" means any area into which certain persons are restricted from transporting any firearm, ammunition, dangerous weapon, or explosive.

(ii) A "secure area" may not include any area normally accessible to the public.

(2) A person in charge of a correctional, law enforcement, or mental health facility may establish secure areas within the facility and may prohibit or control by rule any firearm, ammunition, dangerous weapon, or explosive.

(3) At least one notice shall be prominently displayed at each entrance to an area in which a firearm, ammunition, dangerous weapon, or explosive is restricted.

(4) Provisions shall be made to provide a secure weapons storage area so that persons entering the secure area may store their weapons prior to entering the secure area. The entity operating the facility shall be responsible for weapons while they are stored in the storage area.

(5) It is a defense to any prosecution under this section that the accused, in committing the act made criminal by this section, acted in conformity with the facility's rule or policy established pursuant to this section.

(6) Any person who knowingly or intentionally transports into a secure area of a facility any firearm, ammunition, dangerous weapon, or explosive is guilty of a third degree felony.

U.C.A. 76-8-311.3. Items prohibited in correctional and mental health facilities -- Penalties.

"Plain Talk"

See "Plain Talk" explanation for section 76-10-523.5 above.

ACTUAL TEXT
(1) As used in this section:
. . .
    (c) "Correctional facility" means:
        (i) any facility operated by the Department of Corrections to house offenders in either a secure or nonsecure setting;
        (ii) any facility operated by a municipality or a county to house or detain criminal offenders;
        (iii) any juvenile detention facility; and
        (iv) any building or grounds appurtenant to the facility or lands granted to the state, municipality, or county for use as a correctional facility.

. . .
    (e) "Mental health facility" has the same meaning as defined in Section 62A-12-202.
    (f) "Offender" means a person in custody at a correctional facility.
    (g) "Secure area" has the same meaning as provided in Section 76-8-311.1.
(2) Notwithstanding any other statute to the contrary, including Subsection 76-10-501(b), a correctional or mental health facility may provide by rule that no firearm, ammunition, dangerous weapon, . . . may be:
    (a) transported to or upon a correctional or mental health facility;
    (b) sold or given away at any correctional or mental health facility;
    (c) given to or used by any offender at a correctional or mental health facility; or
    (d) knowingly or intentionally possessed at a correctional or mental health facility.
(3) It is a defense to any prosecution under this section if the accused in committing the act made criminal by this section:
    (a) with respect to a correctional facility operated by the Department of Corrections, acted in conformity with departmental rule or policy;
    (b) with respect to a correctional facility operated by a municipality,
    (c) with respect to a correctional facility operated by a county, acted in conformity with the policy of the county; or

(d) with respect to a mental health facility, acted in conformity with the policy of the mental health facility.

(4)(a) Any person who transports to or upon a correctional facility, or into a secure area of a mental health facility, any firearm, ammunition, dangerous weapon, explosive, or implement of escape with intent to provide or sell it to any offender, is guilty of a second degree felony.

(b) Any person who provides or sells to any offender at a correctional facility, or any detainee at a secure area of a mental health facility, any firearm, ammunition, dangerous weapon, explosive, or implement of escape is guilty of a second degree felony.

(c) Any offender who possesses at a correctional facility, or any detainee who possesses at a secure area of a mental health facility, any firearm, ammunition, dangerous weapon, explosive, or implement of escape is guilty of a second degree felony.

(d) Any person who, without the permission of the authority operating the correctional facility or the secure area of a mental health facility, knowingly possesses at a correctional facility or a secure area of a mental health facility any firearm, ammunition, dangerous weapon, implement of escape, or explosive is guilty of a third degree felony. . . .

U.C.A. 78-7-6. Rules -- Right to make -- Limitation -- Security.

"Plain Talk"
See "Plain Talk" explanation for section 76-10-523.5 above.

ACTUAL TEXT. . .

(2) The judicial council may provide, through the rules of judicial administration, for security in or about a courthouse or courtroom, or establish a secure area as prescribed in Section 76-8-311.1.

(3) Unless authorized by the rules of judicial administration, any person who knowingly or intentionally possesses a firearm, ammunition, dangerous weapon, or explosive within a secure area established by the judicial council under this section is guilty of a third degree felony.

U.C.A. 78-7-6

Commentary

Restricting a civil right should never be taken lightly. A person disarming another, making him or her vulnerable to attack, takes on a new responsibility, that of protecting the disarmed citizen from assault. Jails, airports, and courts who deprive citizens of this right, should be required to guarantee the safety of such citizens who are no longer armed to protect themselves. Courts throughout the country have held that grocery stores, apartments, hotels, banks with ATMs may be held liable for failing to prevent criminal attacks upon their patrons. Airlines have been held responsible to their passengers for failing to prevent bombings. Civil law (see discussion in Chapter X below) should impose liability for depriving others of a right to defend themselves. There was a great deal of controversy over what to do about the 2002 Winter Olympics and concealed weapon permit holders. Personally, I see no reason why Utah concealed weapon permit holders, who pose no threat to the public, should not be able to conceal on an Olympic venue. What would the "Duke" have done? He'd 've posted signs every 25 yards around Olympic venues stating:

"Warning to Terrorists: The State of Utah has invited its 40,000 concealed weapon permit holders to come to the Games to help keep the peace. Terrorists enter at Your Own Risk!"

U.C.A. 76-10-524. Purchase of firearms in contiguous states pursuant to federal law.

"Plain Talk"

This state law, coupled with Section 922(b)(3) of the Federal Gun Control Act of 1968[24] authorizes gun dealers to sell rifles and shotguns to residents of other states if the sale is legal in Utah and the home state of the buyer. The buyer has to buy the gun in person at the dealer's place of business. The dealer has to be "darn sure" the sale is legal in both Utah and the customer's home state. Federal law presumes the dealer knows the laws of both states.

ACTUAL TEXT of U.C.A. 76-10-524.

This part will allow purchases of firearms and ammunition by residents in contiguous states pursuant to the Federal Fire Arms Gun Control Act of 1968, section 922, paragraph B[sic], no. 3.

ACTUAL TEXT of 18 U.S.C. § 922(b)(3) [of the Federal Gun Control Act of 1968]

(b) It shall be unlawful for any licensed importer, licensed manufacturer, licensed dealer, or licensed collector to sell or deliver--

. . .

---

[24] We have included the relevant portions of 922(b)3 just below the text of U.C.A. 76-10-524 for your convenience.

(3) any firearm to any person who the licensee knows or has reasonable cause to believe does not reside in (or if the person is a corporation or other business entity, does not maintain a place of business in) the State in which the licensee's place of business is located, except that this paragraph (A) shall not apply to the sale or delivery of any rifle or shotgun to a resident of a State other than a State in which the licensee's place of business is located if the transferee meets in person with the transferor to accomplish the transfer, and the sale, delivery, and receipt fully comply with the legal conditions of sale in both such States (and any licensed manufacturer, importer or dealer shall be presumed, for purposes of this subparagraph, in the absence of evidence to the contrary, to have had actual knowledge of the State laws and published ordinances of both States), and (B) shall not apply to the loan or rental of a firearm to any person for temporary use for lawful sporting purposes;

U.C.A. 76-10-524

Commentary

This Utah code section and section 922(b)(3) of the Federal Gun Control Act do not mirror each other and thus, create confusion. The Utah law allows the sale of "firearms" which includes handguns, while federal law only refers to "rifles and shotguns." The Utah law talks about "ammunition:" the corresponding section of the federal law does not limit the sale of ammo to residents. Federal law allows sales to residents of "other states" while the Utah law refers only to "contiguous" (states next to Utah like Colorado, Nevada, Wyoming and Arizona). What does this all mean? I DON'T KNOW! DOES ANYONE KNOW? To be safe, gun dealers should probably only sell shotguns and rifles, not pistols, to buyers from adjacent states. The Bureau of Alcohol, Tobacco and Firearms (BATF) publishes a "blue book" which contains state laws and local ordinances related to the sale of firearms. Dealers should consult this manual to find out if the sale of a shotgun or rifle to a nonresident is legal in the buyer's home state.

Pancho's Wisdom

It's an insult to every American patriot to have a federal agency entitled the Bureau of Alcohol, Tobacco and Firearms (ATF). Gun ownership isn't a VICE, it's the CORNERSTONE of our LIBERTY! Disband the firearms division of ATF and put those agents to work

> **enforcing a 5 day waiting period on Cuban cigars and Canadian whiskey!**

U.C.A. 76-10-525. Disposition of weapons after use for court purposes.

> **"Plain Talk"**
> If your weapon is used as evidence in a legal case, you will probably get it back after the case is over. But if you committed a crime with it, kiss your Kimber goodbye. Handguns owned AND used by criminals to commit crimes get a "Terminator 2" bubble bath (otherwise known as Sarah Brady Stew). It's not what the Founding Fathers had in mind when they envisioned America as a "melting pot!"

ACTUAL TEXT
All police departments and/or sheriff's departments which have in their possession a weapon after it has been used for court purposes shall determine the true owner of the weapon and return it to him; however, if unable to determine the true owner of the weapon, or if the true owner is the person committing the crime for which the weapon was used as evidence, the department shall confiscate it and it shall revert to that agency for their use and/or disposal as the head of the department determines.

> U.C.A 76-10-525
> **Commentary**
> This law has a horrible conflict of interact built into it. It allows police agencies to use the weapons they seize. This tempts police to arrest gun owners on "trumped up" charges to "get their guns." This law should be amended so that the arresting agency has no financial interest whatever in confiscating a gun. Furthermore, guns should be forfeited only after conviction felonies, not misdemeanors.

U.C.A. 76-10-526. Criminal background check prior to purchase of a firearm -- Fee -- Exemption for concealed firearm permit holders.

> **"Plain Talk"**
> In other words, it now takes an "Act of Congress" and you go through the "Third Degree" to buy a gun. This code section was

passed to comply with federal requirements under the Brady Act (see our discussion of the Brady Act in Chapter XIII). You have to show the dealer a photo I.D. on a card issued by a government, and one other documentation of residence with the same address as on the photo I.D. The second form of I.D. may be a personal check, a bill, an insurance document or other document with the same address as the photo I.D. Until further notice, the fee for the "Brady check" is $7.50. Denials may be appealed. Old gun owners never die, their firearm-purchase-transaction numbers just eventually (hopefully) fade from the FBI computer. 2000 changes give the Utah Bureau of Criminal Investigation (BCI) the right to research juvenile court records and to deny firearm purchases to persons who were convicted of offenses that would have been felonies had they been adults at the time the offense was committed (See also U.C.A. 76-10-503 above). The 2000 Legislature also took steps to ensure that other records, including those containing pleas of insanity, findings of mental incompetence to stand trial, and orders of civil commitment are accessible to BCI (U.C.A. 53-10-208 and 208.1, not included in this book). Shootings at the Triad Center and the Genealogical Library of the LDS Church raised concerns that BCI did not have sufficient access to records to prevent mentally ill persons from purchasing firearms. The 2000 Legislature intended to remedy this problem and appease public outcry to prevent such persons from having guns. Utah law does not expressly address how those adjudicated mentally deficient may regain their right to possess a firearm in the event they recover from their mental deficiency.

Because concealed weapon holders have already gone through the "third degree" to get their permits (this rule does not apply to temporary permits), they do not have to go through it again. Dealers can sell them a gun upon proof that their concealed weapon permits are still valid. The Utah Department of Public Safety computers are sophisticated enough to check whether CWPs are valid on a daily basis. CWPs are exempt from the Brady fee and pay no fee for the computer check to see if their permits are valid.

Even though the proponents of the Brady Act PUBLICIZED it as a law restricting the sale of HANDGUNS (The Brady HANDGUN Violence Prevention Act), as of November 30, 1998, it regulates the sale of RIFLES and SHOTGUNS too. Call it "creeping

> infringement" which has nearly worn out Pancho's patience and that of every other true Westerner.

ACTUAL TEXT

(1) A criminal background check required by this section shall only apply to the purchase of a handgun until federal law requires the background check to extend to other firearms.

(2) At the time that federal law extends the criminal background check requirement to other firearms, the division shall make rules to extend the background checks required under this section to the other firearms.

(3) For purposes of this section, "valid permit to carry a concealed firearm" does not include a temporary permit issued pursuant to Section 53-5-705.

(4) To establish personal identification and residence in this state for purposes of this part, a dealer shall require any person receiving a firearm to present:

    (a) one photo identification on a form issued by a governmental agency of the state; and

    (b) one other documentation of residence which must show an address identical to that shown on the photo identification form.

(5) A criminal history background check is required for the sale of a firearm by a licensed firearm dealer in the state.

(6) Any person, except a dealer, purchasing a firearm from a dealer shall consent in writing to a criminal background check, on a form provided by the division. The form shall also contain the following information:

    (a) the dealer identification number;

    (b) the name and address of the person receiving the firearm;

    (c) the date of birth, height, weight, eye color, and hair color of the person receiving the firearm; and

    (d) the Social Security number or any other identification number of the person receiving the firearm.

(7)(a) The dealer shall send the form required by Subsection (6) to the division immediately upon its completion.

    (b) No dealer shall sell or transfer any firearm to any person until the dealer has provided the division with the information in Subsection (6) and has received approval from the division under Subsection ~~(8)~~ *(9)*.

(8) The dealer shall make a request for criminal history background information by telephone to the division and shall receive approval or denial of the inquiry by telephone.

(9) When the dealer calls for or requests a criminal history background check, the division shall:

    (a) review the criminal history files, *including juvenile court records,* to determine if the person is prohibited from purchasing, possessing, or transferring a firearm by state or federal law;

    (b) inform the dealer that:

(i) the [criminal record indicates] *records indicate* the person is so prohibited; or

(ii) the person is approved for purchasing, possessing, or transferring a firearm;

(c) provide the dealer with a unique transaction number for that inquiry; and

(d) provide a response to the requesting dealer during the call for a criminal background, or by return call, or other electronic means, without delay, except in case of electronic failure or other circumstances beyond the control of the division, the division shall advise the dealer of the reason for [such] *the* delay and give the dealer an estimate of the length of [such] *the* delay.

(10) The division shall not maintain any records of the criminal history background check longer than 20 days from the date of the dealer's request if the division determines that the person receiving the gun is not prohibited from purchasing, possessing, or transferring the firearm under state or federal law. However, the division shall maintain a log of requests containing the dealer's federal firearms number, the transaction number, and the transaction date for a period of 12 months.

(11) If the criminal history background check discloses information indicating that the person receiving the firearm is prohibited from purchasing, possessing, or transferring a firearm, the division shall inform the chief law enforcement officer in the jurisdiction where the person resides.

(12) If a person is denied the right to purchase a firearm under this section, the person may review his criminal history information and may challenge or amend the information as provided in Section 53-10-108.

(13) The division shall make rules as provided in Title 63, Chapter 46a, Utah Administrative Rulemaking Act, to ensure the identity, confidentiality, and security of all records provided by the division pursuant to this part are in conformance with the requirements of the Brady Handgun Violence Prevention Act, Pub. L. No. 103-159, 107 Stat. 1536 (1993).

(14)   (a) All dealers shall collect a fee established by the division in accordance with Section 63-38-3.2 for every criminal history background check done pursuant to this part. Until changed by the division through this process, the fee shall be $7.50.

(b) The dealer shall forward at one time all fees collected for criminal history background checks performed during the month to the division by the last day of the month following the sale of a firearm. The division may retain the fees as dedicated credits to cover the cost of administering and conducting the criminal history background check program.

(15) A person with a concealed firearm permit issued pursuant to Title 53, Chapter 5, Part 7, Concealed Weapon Act, shall be exempt from the

background check and corresponding fee required in this section for the purchase of a firearm if:

(a) the person presents his concealed firearm permit to the dealer prior to purchase of the firearm; and

(b) the dealer verifies with the division that the person's concealed firearm permit is valid.

U.C.A. 76-10-527. Penalties.

"Plain Talk"

DEALERS, you're in a heap o' trouble if you sell handguns without doing a criminal background check. GUN BUYERS, if you lie to buy a handgun, you'll be singin' the "Jail House Rock." PURCHASERS, it's a felony to use your "squeaky clean" criminal background to buy handguns for ineligible persons such as convicted felons, those who have been convicted of acts of domestic violence, illegal aliens, mental incompetents, minors, citizens from other states[25] and other "undesirables." Young adults, 18 or older, but younger than 21, cannot buy handguns or handgun ammo from a dealer. They can, however, buy a handgun and handgun ammo from a "non-dealer," as long as the non-dealer did not purchase the handgun or ammo from a dealer, having the INTENT AT THE TIME OF PURCHASE, to turn around and sell to the young adult. See Appendix F entitled "Youngsters, Guns and Ammo."

ACTUAL TEXT

(1) A dealer is guilty of a class A misdemeanor who willfully and intentionally:

(a) requests, obtains, or seeks to obtain criminal history background information under false pretenses; or

(b) disseminates criminal history background information.

(2) A person who purchases or transfers a handgun is guilty of a felony of the third degree who willfully and intentionally makes a false statement of the information required in Subsection 76-10-526(3).

(3) A dealer is guilty of a felony of the third degree if the dealer willfully and intentionally sells or transfers a handgun in violation of this part.

(4) A person is guilty of a felony of the third degree who purchases a handgun with the intent to:

---

[25] You'd think this would violate the Privileges and Immunities Clause of the United States Constitution.

(a) resell or otherwise provide a handgun to any person who is ineligible to purchase or receive from a dealer a handgun; or

(b) transport a handgun out of this state to be resold to an ineligible person.

U.C.A. 76-10-528. Carrying a dangerous weapon while under influence of alcohol or drugs unlawful.

> **"Plain Talk"**
> SIX-GUNS and SIXERS don't mix!

ACTUAL TEXT

(1) Any person who carries a dangerous weapon while under the influence of alcohol or a controlled substance as defined in Section 58-37-2 is guilty of a class B misdemeanor. Under the influence means the same level of influence of blood or breath alcohol concentration as provided in Section 41-6-44.

(2) It is not a defense to prosecution under this section that the person:

(a) is licensed in the pursuit of wildlife of any kind; or

(b) has a valid permit to carry a concealed firearm.

U.C.A. 76-10-529. Possession of dangerous weapons, firearms, or explosives in airport secure areas prohibited -- Penalty.

> **"Plain Talk"**
> Nobody, including concealed weapon permit holders, can carry a gun, bomb (uh, how come?) or other dangerous weapon past the metal detectors (in other words into the "secure area") at an airport. If you do it intentionally, it's a class B misdemeanor, but if you forget you have the weapon,[26] the penalty is an infraction (in other words, a class C misdemeanor without a jail sentence). But don't be too anxious to pack your PPK onto the plane just because Utah calls it a misdemeanor. Under the guise of deterring terrorism, the feds just beefed up the penalty from 1 year in the slammer to 10 for taking or attempting to take a dangerous weapon onto any aircraft (49 U.S.C. 46505).

ACTUAL TEXT

(1) As used in this section:

---

[26] Don't laugh, it's easy to do if you carry a concealed weapon all the time and get used to it!

(a) "Airport authority" is the same as defined in Section 17A-2-1502.

(b) "Dangerous weapon" is the same as defined in Section 76-10-501.

(c) "Explosive" is the same as defined for "explosive, chemical, or incendiary device" in Section 76-10-306.

(d) "Firearm" is the same as defined in Section 76-10-501.

(2)   (a) Within a secure area of an airport established pursuant to this section, a person, including a person licensed to carry a concealed firearm under Title 53, Chapter 5, Part 7, Concealed Weapons Act, is guilty of:

(i) a class B misdemeanor if the person knowingly or intentionally possesses any dangerous weapon, firearm, or explosive; or

(ii) an infraction if the person recklessly or with criminal negligence possesses any dangerous weapon, firearm, or explosive.

(b) Subsection (2)(a) does not apply to:

(i) persons exempted under Section 76-10-523; and

(ii) members of the state or federal military forces while engaged in the performance of their official duties.

(3) An airport authority, county, or municipality regulating the airport may:

(a) establish any secure area located beyond the main area where the public generally buys tickets, checks and retrieves luggage; and

(b) use reasonable means, including mechanical, electronic, x-ray, or any other device, to detect dangerous weapons, firearms, or explosives concealed in baggage or upon the person of any individual attempting to enter the secure area.

(4) At least one notice shall be prominently displayed at each entrance to a secure area in which a dangerous weapon, firearm, or explosive is restricted.

(5) Upon the discovery of any dangerous weapon, firearm, or explosive, the airport authority, county, or municipality, the employees, or other personnel administering the secure area may:

(a) require the individual to deliver the item to the air freight office or airline ticket counter;

(b) require the individual to exit the secure area; or

(c) obtain possession or retain custody of the item until it is transferred to law enforcement officers.

THE FEDERAL COUNTERPART CARRYING A MINIMUM 10 YEAR SENTENCE SAYS:

49 U.S.C. 46505. Carrying a weapon or explosive on an aircraft

(a) Definition. In this section, "loaded firearm" means a starter gun or a weapon designed or converted to expel a projectile through an explosive, that has a cartridge, a detonator, or powder in the chamber, magazine, cylinder, or clip.

(b) General criminal penalty. An individual shall be fined under title 18, imprisoned for not more than 10 years, or both, if the individual--

(1) when on, or attempting to get on, an aircraft in, or intended for operation in, air transportation or intrastate air transportation, has on or about the individual or the property of the individual a concealed dangerous weapon that is or would be accessible to the individual in flight; **[as is typical of the feds, this is overkill; it doesn't seem to require proof of intent - forget your pistola in your carpet bag and you'll rot in the federal pen! And check out the following provision which gives you 10 years if you forget to unload your piece and check it in your luggage. Forget the fact it ain't even accessible to you in flight! Doesn't anyone in Washington love gun owners?]**

(2) has placed, attempted to place, or attempted to have placed a loaded firearm on that aircraft in property not accessible to passengers in flight; or

(3) has on or about the individual, or has placed, attempted to place, or attempted to have placed on that aircraft, an explosive or incendiary device.

(c) Criminal penalty involving disregard for human life. An individual who willfully and without regard for the safety of human life, or with reckless disregard for the safety of human life, violates subsection (b) of this section, shall be fined under title 18, imprisoned for not more than 15 years, or both.

(d) Nonapplication. Subsection (b)(1) of this section does not apply to--

(1) a law enforcement officer of a State or political subdivision of a State, or an officer or employee of the United States Government, authorized to carry arms in an official capacity;

(2) another individual the Administrator of the Federal Aviation Administration by regulation authorizes to carry a dangerous weapon in air transportation or intrastate air transportation; or

(3) an individual transporting a weapon (except a loaded firearm) in baggage not accessible to a passenger in flight if the air carrier was informed of the presence of the weapon.

76-10-530. Trespass with a firearm in a house of worship or private residence — Notice — Penalty.

"Plain Talk"

New in 1999, U.C.A. 76-10-530 clarifies the criminal trespass statute (U.C.A. 76-6-206). The criminal trespass statute gives a resident on private property who has not invited the public to enter, the right to prohibit access to anyone for any reason. Some were concerned that the language of the concealed weapons statute giving Utahns the right to carry concealed weapons "throughout the state without restriction" might prevent property owners or residents from ousting a gun totin' guest. UCA 76-10-530 unambiguously gives residents the right to ask anyone to leave the resident's home for any reason including the fact that he or she does not want them on the property with a firearm. The same goes for houses of worship. The prohibition may be communicated orally or by posting a sign. Notice that a violation of this code section is an infraction which will not cause the violator to lose his or her concealed weapon permit. Also, the prosecutor will have a tough burden of proving the accused guilty if the defendant claims he didn't know of the restriction. Section (1) requires proof that the defendant "knowingly and intentionally" violated the law. Thus, if the concealed weapon holder carelessly fails to observe a sign prohibiting concealed weapons on the premises, he has a defense because he did not transport his firearm onto the prohibited premises "knowingly and intentionally."

Although it is clear under Subsection 3 of this new code section that a landlord may not prohibit a renter or lessee from lawfully possessing a firearm on the rented premises, the issue arises as to whether landlord may post a notice in an apartment complex prohibiting guests of the tenants from transporting their legal concealed weapons into the facility. This could be remedied by adding "or invitee" to the phrase "to restrict the renter or lessee from lawfully . . . ."

The Legislature made a distinction between houses of worship, which are only open to "welcome visitors," as opposed to private businesses which invite the public at large. The owners or mangers of businesses such as grocery or video stores CANNOT prohibit concealed weapon holders from entering their premises.

ACTUAL TEXT

(1) A person, including a person licensed to carry a concealed firearm pursuant to Title 53, Chapter 5, Part 7, Concealed Weapon Act, after having received notice as provided in Subsection (2) that firearms are prohibited, may not knowingly and intentionally:
    (a) transport a firearm into:
        (i) a house of worship; or
        (ii) a private residence; or
    (b) while in possession of a firearm, enter or remain in:

(i) a house of worship; or

(ii) a private residence.

(2) Notice that firearms are prohibited may be made by:

(a) personal communication to the actor by:

(i) the church or organization operating the house of worship;

(ii) the owner, lessee, or person with lawful right of possession of the private residence; or

(iii) a person with authority to act for the person or entity in Subsections (2)(a)(i) and (ii); or

(b) posting of signs reasonably likely to come to the attention of persons entering the house of worship or private residence.

(3) Nothing in this section permits an owner who has granted the lawful right of possession to a renter or lessee to restrict the renter or lessee from lawfully possessing a firearm in the residence.

(4) A violation of this section is an infraction.

U.C.A. 76-10-531. Restricting dangerous weapons and explosives in Olympic venue secure areas — Penalty — Defense.

> ### "Plain Talk"
> As mentioned earlier U.C.A. 76-10-531 makes Olympic venues secured areas and prohibits concealed firearms as well as other dangerous weapons.

ACTUAL TEXT

(1) A person, including a person licensed to carry a concealed firearms pursuant to Title 53, Chapter 5, Part 7, Concealed Weapon Act, may not knowingly and intentionally transport into an Olympic venue secure area, designated by rule pursuant to Section 53-12-301.1:

(a) a firearm, ammunition, or dangerous weapon; or

(b) an explosive, chemical, or incendiary device, as those terms are defined in Section 76-10-306.

(2) A violation of this section is:

(a) a class B misdemeanor if the violation is with a firearm, ammunition, or dangerous weapon; or

(b) a first degree felony if the violation is with an explosive, chemical, or incendiary device.

(3) It is a defense to any prosecution under this section that the accused, in committing the act made criminal by this section, acted in conformity with the rules authorized by Section 53-12-301.1.

. . . . . AND WHILE WE'RE TALKING ABOUT COMMON CARRIERS LIKE AIRLINES, WHAT ABOUT BUSES?

U.C.A. 76-10-1504 Bus hijacking -- Assault with intent to commit hijacking -- Use of a dangerous weapon or firearm -- Penalties.

"Plain Talk"

It's a second degree felony to get on a commercial bus carrying a concealed dangerous weapon. This law does not apply to cops, security guards, concealed weapon permit holders or people who have the consent of the bus company to carry a weapon.

ACTUAL TEXT

(4)(a) Any person who boards a bus with a concealed dangerous weapon
or firearm upon his person or effects is guilty of a second degree felony.

(b) The prohibition of Subsection (4)(a) does not apply to elected or appointed peace officers or commercial security personnel who are in possession of weapons or firearms used in the course and scope of their employment, or a person licensed to carry a concealed weapon; nor shall the prohibition apply to persons in possession of weapons or firearms with the consent of the owner of the bus or his agent, or the lessee or bailee of the bus.

U.C.A. 76-10-1504

Commentary

TRANSFORMATION INTO A FELON AS SOON AS YOU STEP INTO THE BUS TERMINAL OR ONTO THE BUS - The preceding and following code sections could pose a real problem for citizens who are not concealed weapon permit holders, but who assume that concealing is only a misdemeanor (and it is under most circumstances, see U.C.A. 76-10-504 above). The requirements for a concealed carry permit are very strict and not all law-abiding citizens qualify. Riding the bus can be a frightening experience depending upon the time of day and the area. These two statutes make felons out of people who feel the need to protect themselves with a concealed weapon on the bus or in a bus depot. However, if they conceal a firearm in the grocery store, they are only guilty of a misdemeanor. These statutes do not require bus companies to warn citizens of the step-up penalty for riding the bus or entering a bus terminal. Some bus companies warn that no weapons are allowed, but do not mention the penalty. This statute should be amended:

> (4) (a) Any person who boards a bus with a concealed dangerous weapon or firearm upon his person or effects is guilty of a ~~second degree felony~~ class B misdemeanor unless the dangerous weapon is possessed with the intent to assault or harm another without legal jurisdiction, in which case the person is guilty of a second degree felony.

U.C.A. 76-10-1507. Exclusion of persons without bona fide business from terminal -- Firearms and dangerous materials -- Surveillance devices and seizure of offending materials -- Detention of violators -- Private security personnel.

> **"Plain Talk"**
> It's a felony to set foot in a bus terminal if you're carrying a concealed weapon, whether or not it's loaded. This is more restrictive than the law regulating airlines. If they ultimately inform ticket agents of the weapon, airline passengers may carry unloaded firearms in their suitcases into airline terminals (see discussion in Chapter XIII).

ACTUAL TEXT

(2) Any person who carries a concealed dangerous weapon, firearm, or any explosive, highly inflammable or hazardous materials or devices into a terminal or aboard a bus shall be guilty of a third degree felony. The bus company may employ reasonable means, including mechanical, electronic or x-ray devices to detect such items concealed in baggage or upon the person of any passenger. Upon the discovery of any such item, the company may obtain possession and retain custody thereof until it is transferred to a peace officer.

> U.C.A. 76-10-1507
> **Commentary**
> Interestingly, this code section does not contain an exception for concealed weapon permit holders and police officers like 1504 does. It's doubtful the Legislature intended to let concealed weapon permit holders RIDE THE BUS with a concealed weapon, but not to ENTER THE BUS TERMINAL. Section 1507 should be amended to include the same exceptions as 1504 as follows:

(5) The prohibitions contained in Subsection (2) do not apply to elected or appointed peace officers or commercial security personnel who are in possession of weapons or firearms used in the course and scope of their employment, or persons licensed to carry concealed weapons; nor shall the prohibition apply to persons in possession of weapons or firearms with the consent of the owner of the bus or his agent, or the lessee or bailee of the bus.

Paragraph (6) below should be added to parallel federal law allowing passengers to carry unloaded firearms in baggage not accessible to passengers in flight, provided they have informed the airline of the presence of the weapon, 49 U.S.C. 46505 subsection (d) (We talk about this in Chapter VII under the discussion of U.C.A. 76-10-529).

(6) Subsection (2) of this section does not apply to an individual transporting a weapon (except a loaded firearm) in baggage not accessible to a passenger on the bus, if the bus company was informed of the presence of the weapon.

CHAPTER VIII:
CONCEALED WEAPON PERMITS

Pancho's Wisdom
If you ain't packin', you ain't fully dressed.

U.C.A. 53-5-701. Short title

"Plain Talk"

Sections 701 through 711 together with the regulations discussed below, govern the actions of concealed weapon permit holders (hereinafter "CWPs"). (Notice the state code does not hyphenate "concealed weapon" when used as an adjective.)

ACTUAL TEXT

This part is known as the "Concealed Weapon Act."

U.C.A. 53-5-702. Definitions.

"Plain Talk"

These definitions are simple, so we won't bore you by simply restating them. However, please take note that a plea of "nolo contendere" (no contest) and pleas held in abeyance are still considered a "conviction" for purposes of disqualifying a person for a concealed weapon permit (CWP). This also applies to "diversions" (essentially a continuance followed by a dismissal) during the time the diversion is pending, but not after the dismissal is granted.

ACTUAL TEXT

(1) As used in this part:

(a) "Board" means the Concealed Weapon Review Board created in Section 53-5-703;

(b) "Commissioner" means the commissioner of the Department of Public Safety; and

(c) "Conviction" means criminal conduct where the filing of a criminal charge has resulted in:

(i) a finding of guilt based on evidence presented to a judge or jury;

(ii) a guilty plea;

(iii) a plea of nolo contendere;

(iv) a plea of guilty or nolo contendere which is held in abeyance pending the successful completion of probation;

(v) a pending diversion agreement; or

(vi) a conviction which has been reduced pursuant to Section 76-3-402.

(2) The definitions in Section 76-10-501 apply to this part.

U.C.A. 53-5-703. Board -- Membership -- Compensation -- Terms -- Duties.

"Plain Talk"

There is a "review board" to review denials or revocations of CWPs when requested by an unsuccessful applicant. The board can have no more than five members. One member of the board must have some connection to law enforcement, one must represent sporting interests (presumably shooting sports), and the third is just an ordinary citizen. This means YOU, as a citizen, can have input into the decision making process, if you serve on the board.

ACTUAL TEXT

(1) There is created within the division the Concealed Weapon Review Board.

(2)   (a) The board is comprised of not more than five members appointed by the commissioner on a bipartisan basis.

(b) The board shall include a member representing law enforcement and at least two citizens, one of whom represents sporting interests.

(3)   (a) Except as required by Subsection (b), as terms of current board members expire, the commissioner shall appoint each new member or reappointed member to a four-year term.

(b) Notwithstanding the requirements of Subsection (a), the commissioner shall, at the time of appointment or reappointment, adjust the length of terms to ensure that the terms of board members are staggered so that approximately half of the board is appointed every two years.

(4) When a vacancy occurs in the membership for any reason, the replacement shall be appointed for the unexpired term.

(5)(a)(i) Members who are not government employees shall receive no compensation or benefits for their services, but may receive per diem and expenses incurred in the performance of the member's official duties at the rates established by the Division of Finance under Sections 63A-3-106 and 63A-3-107.

(ii) Members may decline to receive per diem and expenses for their service.

(b)(i) State government officer and employee members who do not receive salary, per diem, or expenses from their agency for their service may receive per diem and expenses incurred in the performance of their official duties from the board at the rates established by the Division of Finance under Sections 63A-3-106 and 63A-3-107.

(ii) State government officer and employee members may decline to receive per diem and expenses for their service.

(6) The board shall meet at least quarterly, unless the board has no business to conduct during that quarter.

(7) The board, upon receiving a timely filed petition for review, shall review within a reasonable time the denial, suspension, or revocation of a permit or a temporary permit to carry a concealed firearm.

U.C.A. 53-5-704. Division duties -- Permit to carry concealed firearm -- Requirements for issuance -- Violation -- Denial, suspension, or revocation -- Appeal procedure.

"Plain Talk"

Utah is a "shall issue" state meaning the "good guys and gals" with clean criminal records qualify for a CWP without having to give a reason for having one. (There are now 33 "shall issue" states in the U.S. the newest of which are Michigan and New Mexico.) Before Utah became a "shall issue" state, applicants had to have a good reason to get a permit like having received a death threat. The permit is valid throughout the state "without restriction" (see discussion under "Commentary" below.)

The things that can disqualify you from getting a CWP are:

- having been convicted of a felony (see Chapter V for examples),

- a crime of violence, **["crime of violence" has been deleted from the definitions in U.C.A. 76-10-501 - the term has been changed to "violent felony" (see U.C.A. 76-10-501(18))]**

- an offense involving alcohol (like driving under the influence of alcohol),

- drug offenses (for example, possession of marijuana or cocaine),

- offenses involving moral turpitude (crimes of dishonesty such as theft, embezzlement, passing bad checks and crimes involving immorality such as prostitution, adultery and lewd behavior),

- domestic violence (physically abusing your spouse or children - careful, this statute is extremely broad and could include breaking a dish or other object in the presence of a spouse or child),
- having been judged mentally incompetent, or
- having a history which shows you could be a threat to yourself or others (threats of suicide or violence against others).

The division can look at juvenile records and expunged records (records which have been sealed by order of the court to wipe your record clean - see discussion below) even though such records are generally confidential. If you were "bbbbbad to the bone" as a teenager, the Division of Public Safety may find out, even though your juvenile records are sealed.

If you are charged with a violent felony in Utah or any other state, the division must suspend your CWP immediately. However, if you are acquitted or the charge is dropped, the division has to reinstate your suspended permit. **["crime of violence" has been deleted from the definitions in U.C.A. 76-10-501 - the term has been changed to "violent felony" (see U.C.A. 76-10-501(18))]**

Former police officers with honorable discharges must be issued a concealed weapon permit within 5 years, unless they have a criminal record.

You may be able to get a permit although you have a criminal record. The division can consider "mitigating circumstances," meaning reasons why you should be issued a permit anyway. Several years without an arrest could be a "mitigating circumstance."

Concealed weapon permit applications require:

a.   letters of character reference,

b.   two recently dated photographs,

c.   two sets of fingerprints,

d.   a five year employment history,

e.   a five year residential history,

f.   evidence of familiarity with the type of firearm to be concealed.

Familiarity with a firearm means you know how to safely load, unload, store and carry it. You should also understand the law of self defense including where and when you can use deadly force (see Chapter XI). You must know how to transport and conceal your gun safely and legally. You can satisfy the "general familiarity" requirement by completing a national, state or local firearms training course approved by the division or by being certified by a person who has been approved by the division. This could include a police officer, military firearms instructor, a civilian firearms instructor or a hunter safety instructor. You can also satisfy the requirement by showing that you have equivalent experience by having participated in an organized shooting competition. If you have worked in law enforcement or military service, this could also satisfy the requirement. All permits issued and renewed after May 1, 1998 are valid for 5 years unless suspended or revoked.

The State of Utah is not "vicariously" liable for damages caused by a permit holder. This means that a permit holder may be held civilly liable for causing injury or death (see Chapter X), but the State of Utah is not liable for simply issuing a permit.

If you intentionally give false information to get a permit, you are guilty of a class B misdemeanor and your application may be denied or your permit suspended or revoked when the licensing agency finds out. Your permit may not be denied, suspended or revoked for a single infraction conviction under the weapon laws. If you are denied a concealed weapon permit, you have 60 days from the date of the denial, suspension or revocation to appeal. The denial has to be in writing and must give the general reasons why the permit was denied, suspended or revoked. You have the right to see the information upon which the agency based its decision to revoke, suspend or deny. At the appeal, the agency has the burden of proving by a preponderance of the evidence (meaning more likely than not), that you are not qualified for a concealed weapon permit. The division has to issue an order within 30 days. Once that 30 days is up, the applicant can appeal to a court of law (See Utah Administrative Procedure Act, U.C.A. 63-46b-5 to U.C.A. 63-46b-15).

Instead of making a peace officer submit the mountain of paperwork ordinary citizens have to provide to get a concealed weapon permit, subsection (7) permits a peace officer to simply get a letter of "good standing" from his commanding officer. This eliminates the need for letters of character reference, five year employment history, five year residential history and evidence of general familiarity of the types of firearms to be concealed.

The changes to this code section in the year 2000 are shown as ~~deletions~~ and additions. The most significant change to this code section requires concealed weapon permit instructors to give students a written outline of the course and a certificate of completion. Instructors are now "certified" to teach the CWP course of instruction rather than "approved." Recognizing most people who defend themselves with a firearm never shoot the gun, and if they do, it's from a very short distance, the Legislature astutely refused to require an applicant to demonstrate "proficiency" with a firearm. The applicant must still show "general familiarity" with the type(s) of firearms to be concealed. Legislators who held the line on this issue should be reelected.

ACTUAL TEXT

(1) The division or its designated agent shall issue a permit to carry a concealed firearm for lawful self defense to an applicant who is 21 years of age or older within 60 days after receiving an application and upon proof that the person applying is of good character. The permit is valid throughout the state, without restriction except as provided by Section 53-5-710:

(a) for two years; or

(b) for five years for permits issued or renewed on or after May 1, 1998.

(2) An applicant satisfactorily demonstrates good character if he:

(a) has not been convicted of a felony;

(b) has not been convicted of any crime of violence **["crime of violence" has been deleted from the definitions in U.C.A. 76-10-501 - the term has been changed to "violent felony" (see U.C.A. 76-10-501(18))]**;

(c) has not been convicted of any offenses involving the use of alcohol;

(d) has not been convicted of any offense involving the unlawful use of narcotics or other controlled substances;

(e) has not been convicted of any offenses involving moral turpitude;

(f) has not been convicted of any offense involving domestic violence;

(g) has not been adjudicated by a court of a state or of the United States as mentally incompetent, unless the adjudication has been withdrawn or reversed; and

(h) is qualified to purchase and possess a dangerous weapon and a handgun pursuant to Section 76-10-503 and federal law.

(3) (a) The division may deny, suspend, or revoke a concealed firearm permit if the licensing authority has reasonable cause to believe that the

applicant has been or is a danger to self or others as demonstrated by evidence including, but not limited to:

(i) past pattern of behavior involving unlawful violence or threats of unlawful violence;

(ii) past participation in incidents involving unlawful violence or threats of unlawful violence; or

(iii) conviction of any offense in violation of Title 76, Chapter 10, Part 5, Weapons.

(b) The division may not deny, suspend, or revoke a concealed firearm permit solely for a single conviction for an infraction violation of Title 76, Chapter 10, Part 5, Weapons.

(c) In determining whether the applicant has been or is a danger to self or others, the division may inspect:

(i) expunged records of arrests and convictions of adults as provided in Section 77-18-15; and

(ii) juvenile court records as provided in Section 78-3a-206.

(d) (i) If a person granted a permit under this part has been charged with a crime of violence in Utah or any other state, the division shall suspend the permit.**["crime of violence" has been deleted from the definitions in U.C.A. 76-10-501 - the term has been changed to "violent felony" (see U.C.A. 76-10-501(18))]**

(ii) Upon notice of the acquittal of the person charged, or notice of the charges having been dropped, the division shall immediately reinstate the suspended permit.

(4) A former peace officer who departs full-time employment as a peace officer, in an honorable manner, shall be issued a concealed firearm permit within five years of that departure if the officer meets the requirements of this section.

(5) In assessing good character under Subsection (2), the licensing authority shall consider mitigating circumstances.

(6) Except as provided in Subsection (7), the licensing authority shall also require the applicant to provide:

(a) address of applicant's permanent residence;

[(a)] *(b)* letters of character reference;

[(b)] *(c)* two recent dated photographs;

[(c)] *(d)* two sets of fingerprints;

[(d)] *(e)* a five-year employment history;

[(e)] *(f)* a five-year residential history; and

[(f)] *(g)* evidence of general familiarity with the types of firearms to be concealed as defined in Subsection (8).

(7) An applicant who is a law enforcement officer under Section 53-13-103 may provide a letter of good standing from the officer's commanding officer in place of the items required by Subsections (6)[(a)]*(b)*, [(d),] (e), [and] (f), *and (g)*.

(8) (a) General familiarity with the types of firearms to be concealed

includes training in:

(i) the safe loading, unloading, storage, and carrying of the types of firearms to be concealed; and (ii) current laws defining lawful use of a firearm by a private citizen, including lawful self-defense, use of *force by a private citizen including use of* deadly force, transportation, and concealment.

(b) Evidence of general familiarity with the types of firearms to be concealed may be satisfied by one of the following:

(i) completion of a course of instruction conducted by any national, state, or local firearms training organization approved by the division;

(ii) certification of general familiarity by a person who has been [approved] *certified* by the division, which may include a law enforcement officer, military or civilian firearms instructor, or hunter safety instructor; or

(iii) equivalent experience with a firearm through participation in an organized shooting competition, law enforcement, or military service.

(9) An applicant for certification as a Utah concealed firearms instructor shall:

(a) be at least 21 years of age; and

(b) be currently eligible to possess a firearm under Section 76-10-503 and federal law.

(10) Each certified concealed firearms instructor shall provide for his students the required course of instruction outline approved by the division.

(11) All concealed firearms instructors are required to provide a signed certificate to persons completing the course of instruction, which certificate shall be provided by the applicant to the division.

(12) The division may deny, suspend, or revoke the certification of a concealed firearms instructor if the licensing authority has reason to believe the applicant has:

(a) become ineligible to possess a firearm under Section 76-10-503 or federal law; or

(b) knowingly and willfully provided false information to the division.

(13) A concealed firearms instructor has the same appeal rights as set forth in Subsection (16).

[(9)] *(14)* In issuing a permit under this part, the licensing authority is not vicariously liable for damages caused by the permit holder.

[(10)] *(15)* If any person knowingly and willfully provides false information on an application filed under this part, he is guilty of a class B misdemeanor, and his application may be denied, or his permit may be suspended or revoked.

[(11)] *(16)* (a) In the event of a denial, suspension, or revocation by the agency, the applicant may file a petition for review with the board within 60 days from the date the denial, suspension, or revocation is received by the applicant by certified mail, return receipt requested.

(b) The denial of a permit shall be in writing and shall include the general reasons for the action.

(c) If an applicant appeals his denial to the review board, the applicant may have access to the evidence upon which the denial is based in accordance with Title 63, Chapter 2, Government Records Access and Management Act.
(d) On appeal to the board, the agency shall have the burden of proof by a preponderance of the evidence.
(e) Upon a ruling by the board on the appeal of a denial, the division shall issue a final order within 30 days stating the board's decision. The final order shall be in the form prescribed by Subsection 63-46b-5 (1)(i). The final order is final agency action for purposes of judicial review under Section 63-46b-15 .
[(12)] (17) The commissioner may make rules in accordance with Title 63, Chapter 46a, Utah Administrative Rulemaking Act, necessary to administer this chapter.

U.C.A. 53-5-704

Commentary

Utah law says the permits are valid throughout the state without restriction. Unfortunately, certain university administrators and the Governor's staff are breaking this law by refusing to honor the permits of adult students and state employees. This could result in civil rights lawsuits (See Chapter XIV).[27] During the past three years, the governor's office and the media have tried to bully the Legislature into passing a law to invalidate the permits in schools, churches and public buildings. The Legislature, with clear marching orders from their constituents, by letter, fax and telephone, has refused to fix what isn't broken. Restricting the rights of Utah's 40,000 concealed weapon permit holders is as logical as telling drivers with clean driving records that they can't drive their kids to school or church, because drunk drivers cause accidents. Restricting the rights of good drivers will not reduce the number of injuries and deaths related to drunk driving. Likewise, restricting the rights of law-abiding citizens will not keep criminals from committing violent crimes. Legislators should be praised for refusing to pass a law that broadcasts to would-be mass murderers that they can shoot up our schools, churches and public office buildings without fear of armed resistance. I, for one, want criminals to believe that some of my kids' teachers and principals may be carrying concealed weapons.

---

[27] I'm your Huckleberry! (Doc Holiday, *Tombstone*)

U.C.A. 53-5-705. Temporary permit to carry concealed firearm -- Denial, suspension, or revocation -- Appeal.

"Plain Talk"

TEMPORARY PERMITS - It could take several weeks before a permanent permit is issued. This could be discomforting to a woman being stalked by an x-con-x-boyfriend who has a fetish for Bowie knives. If her record is clean and the division agrees that "stalking" is an "extenuating circumstance" ("extenuating" is not defined in the code), she will get a temporary permit. If the temporary permit is denied, there is no appeal to the review board - applicants just have to wait to get the "Real McCoy."

ACTUAL TEXT

(1) The division or its designated agent may issue a temporary permit to carry a concealed firearm to a person who:

(a) has applied for a permit under Section 53-5-704;

(b) has applied for a temporary permit under this section; and

(c) meets the criteria required in Subsections (2) and (3).

(2) To receive a temporary permit under this section, the applicant shall:

(a) demonstrate good character by the same requirements as in Section 53-5-704; and

(b) demonstrate in writing to the satisfaction of the licensing authority extenuating circumstances that would justify issuing a temporary permit.

(3) A temporary permit may not be issued under this section until preliminary record checks regarding the applicant have been made with the National Crime Information Center and the division to determine any criminal history.

(4) A temporary permit is valid only for a maximum of 90 days or any lesser period specified by the division, or until a permit under Section 53-5-704 is issued to the holder of the temporary permit, whichever period is shorter.

(5) The licensing authority may deny, suspend, or revoke a temporary permit prior to expiration if the commissioner determines:

(a) the circumstances justifying the temporary permit no longer exist;

(b) the holder of the permit has knowingly and willfully provided false information regarding his character; or

(c) the holder of the temporary permit does not meet the requirements for a permit under Section 53-5-704.

(6)   (a) The denial, suspension, or revocation of a temporary permit shall be in writing and shall include the reasons for the action.

(b) The licensing authority's decision to deny, suspend, or revoke a temporary permit may not be appealed to the board.

(c) Denial, suspension, or revocation under this subsection is final action for purposes of judicial review under Section 63-46b-15.

U.C.A. 53-5-706. Permit -- Fingerprints transmitted to division -- Report from division.

U.C.A. 53-5-706

"Plain Talk"

Big Brother AND Santa Claus are both STILL watching you! You have to pass a fingerprint search and a criminal background check in both the state and FBI computers to get a concealed weapons permit.

ACTUAL TEXT

(1)(a) Except as provided in Subsection (2), the fingerprints of each applicant shall be taken on two copies of forms prescribed by the division and shall be forwarded to the division.

(b) Upon receipt of the fingerprints and the fee prescribed in Section 53-5-707, the division shall conduct a search of its files for criminal history information pertaining to the applicant, and shall request the Federal Bureau of Investigation to conduct a similar search through its files.

(c) The division shall promptly furnish the forwarding licensing authority a report of all data and information pertaining to any applicant of which there is a record in its office, or of which a record is found in the files of the Federal Bureau of Investigation.

(d) A permit may not be issued by any licensing authority until receipt of the report from the division.

(2) If the permit applicant has previously applied to the same licensing authority for a permit to carry concealed firearms and the applicant's fingerprints and fee have been previously forwarded within one year to the division, the licensing authority shall note the previous identification numbers and other data which would provide positive identification in the files of the division on the copy of any subsequent permit submitted to the division in accordance with this section, and no additional application form, fingerprints, or fee are required.

U.C.A. 53-5-707. Permit -- Fee -- Disposition.

"Plain Talk"

It's $35 smackers for the original permit and $10 for the renewal.

ACTUAL TEXT

(1) Each applicant for a permit shall pay a fee of $35 at the time of filing an application. The initial fee shall be waived for an applicant who is a law enforcement officer under Section 53-13-103.

(2) The renewal fee for the permit is $10.

(3) The replacement fee for the permit is $10.

(4) The late fee for the renewal permit is $7.50.

(5) All fees shall promptly be deposited in the state treasury and credited to the General Fund.

(6) The division may collect any fees charged by an outside agency for additional services required by statute as a prerequisite for issuance of a permit. The division shall promptly forward any fees collected to the appropriate agency.

U.C.A. 53-5-708. Permit -- Names private.

"Plain Talk"

Although the state keeps a record of your personal information when issuing a permit, your name, address, telephone number, date of birth and Social Security Number are confidential, and the state will not disclose this information to anyone else.

ACTUAL TEXT

(1) When any permit is issued, a record shall be maintained in the office of the licensing authority. Notwithstanding the requirements of Subsection 63-2-301(1)(b), the names, addresses, telephone numbers, dates of birth, and Social Security numbers of persons receiving permits are protected records under Subsection 63-2-304(9).

(2) Copies of each permit issued shall be filed immediately by the licensing authority with the division.

U.C.A. 53-5-709. Repealed.

U.C.A. 53-5-710. Cross-references to concealed firearm permit restrictions.

> **"Plain Talk"**
>
> CWPs, don't be totin' yo' guns into the secured areas of no airports, jails, prisons, or reform schools, or d'man'l be haulin' YOUR butt to jail (English don't get no plainer than that)! The 1999 Legislature made churches and private residences off limits to CWPs when authorized clergy or residents give them sufficient notice by telling them or posting a sign. An Olympic venue is now a secured area similar to an airport.[For a more scholarly (less plain) explanation of the "secure area" laws, see the "Plain Talk" boxes for code sections U.C.A. 76-10-523.5 and U.C.A. 76-10-529.]

ACTUAL TEXT

A person with a permit to carry a concealed firearm may not carry a concealed firearm in the following locations:

(1) any secure area prescribed in Section 76-10-523.5 in which firearms are prohibited and notice of the prohibition posted;

(2) in any airport secure area as provided in Section 76-10-529;

(3) in any house of worship or in any private residence where dangerous weapons are prohibited as provided in Section 76-10-530; or

(4) at an Olympic venue secure area in violation of Section 76-10-531.

U.C.A. 53-5-711. Law enforcement officials and judges -- Training requirements -- Qualification -- Revocation.

> **"Plain Talk"**
>
> Judges, criminal prosecutors and police officers spend most of their professional careers offending hundreds, if not thousands, of dysfunctional people. It's conceivable that some might try to get even. This section invites these state and local officials to get special concealed weapon permits (sometimes referred to as "super permits") if they pass a criminal background check and pay the fee. If they step out of line, their permits will be revoked, just like for anyone else. A "super permit" ("certificate of qualification") allows permit holders to pack in secured areas established by state law (as opposed to federal law). See U.C.A. 76-10-523, U.C.A. 53-5-711 and R724-4-8 through 11 (Applications for a Certificate of Qualification).

ACTUAL TEXT

(1) For purposes of this section and Section 76-10-523:

(a) "Judge" means a judge or justice of a court of record or court not of record, but does not include a judge pro tem or senior judge.

(b) "Law enforcement official of this state" means:

(i) a member of the Board of Pardons and Paroles;

(ii) a district attorney, deputy district attorney, county attorney or deputy county attorney of a county not in a prosecution district;

(iii) the attorney general;

(iv) an assistant attorney general designated as a criminal prosecutor; or

(v) a city attorney or a deputy city attorney designated as a criminal prosecutor.

(2) To qualify for the exemptions enumerated in Section 76-10-523, a law enforcement official or judge shall complete the following training requirements:

(a) meet the requirements of Sections 53-5-704, 53-5-706, and 53-5-707; and

(b) successfully complete an additional course of training as established by the commissioner of public safety designed to assist them while carrying out their official law enforcement and judicial duties as agents for the state or its political subdivisions.

(3) Annual requalification requirements for law enforcement officials and judges shall be established by the:

(a) Board of Pardons and Paroles by rule for its members;

(b) Judicial Council by rule for judges; and

(c) the district attorney, county attorney in a county not in a prosecution district, the attorney general, or city attorney by policy for prosecutors under their jurisdiction.

(4) The division may:

(a) issue a certificate of qualification to a judge or law enforcement official who has completed the requirements of Subsection (1), which certificate of qualification is valid until revoked;

(b) revoke the certificate of qualification of a judge or law enforcement official who fails to meet the annual requalification criteria established pursuant to Subsection (3); and

(c) certify instructors for the training requirements of this section.

U.C.A. 53-12-301.1. Olympic venue secure areas — Restrictions — Rulemaking authority — Notice — Responsibilities — Liability.

> **"Plain Talk"**
>
> In 1999 the Utah Legislature enacted 53-12-301.1 to define the perimeters of Olympic secured areas and the responsibilities of the Olympic law enforcement commander. It gives the commander authority to define the penalty for taking a dangerous weapon into an Olympic venue.[28] Okay, so our Legislature got a little carried away giving the Olympic commander the power over life and death. They made up for it by enacting subsection (5) that says that when the state deprives a law abiding citizen of an important civil right, like the right to bear arms, and he or she is injured, that the state is LIABLE![29] The burden of proof is by "clear and convincing" evidence. This is less of a burden than "beyond a reasonable doubt," but more of a burden than by a "preponderance of evidence" (more likely than not).
>
> The legislators who helped to enact this section deserve a hero's reception at the Pioneer Days Parade and should have rose petals cast before their feet for "hanging tough" and "walking tall" and insisting on this important provision. It establishes a magnificent legal basis for a civil rights lawsuit against a political subdivision for depriving a person of the right to bear arms! Congratulations to Woody Powell, Republican Party Chairman Rob Bishop and others at the Utah Shooting Sports Council (USSC) who drafted and insisted upon this important provision!

ACTUAL TEXT

(1) For purposes of this section and Section 76-10-531, "Olympic venues" means a specific location:

    (a) that is secured by a perimeter and public access is controlled; and

    (b) where spectators view Olympic events; or

---

[28] I don't see any limitations on the commander's power to define a penalty. When Olympic "riggers" or "roadies" start erecting gallows we'll know what El Commandante has in mind!

[29] The word "liable" brings music to the ears of a plaintiff's attorney. "I work hard for the money.... ♫ hard for the money ♫......"

(c) designated for media or official athlete housing not open to the general public.

(2) In accordance with Title 63, Chapter 46a, Utah Administrative Rulemaking Act, the Olympic law enforcement commander designated in Section 53-12-301 shall make rules:

(a) designating the locations of secure areas within Olympic venues where a firearm, ammunition, dangerous weapon, or explosive, chemical, or incendiary device is prohibited between January 25, 2002 and April 1, 2002;

(b) providing notice that a reasonable person would understand regarding:

(i) the locations of the Olympic venue secure areas where the items in Subsection (1)(a) are prohibited;

(ii) the locations of public access entrances and exits to the Olympic venue secure areas; and;

(iii) the locations of secure weapons storage areas;

(iv) the penalty for violating Section 76-10-531, restriction of dangerous weapons in Olympic venue secure areas; and

(c) designating persons authorized to carry weapons into Olympic venues, including those persons exempted by Subsection 76-10-523(1).

(3) The notice in Subsection (1)(b) shall include:

(a) written notice provided to a person at the time the person receives tickets to events at Olympic venue secure areas; and

(b) at least one notice prominently displayed at each entrance to every Olympic venue secure area in which a dangerous weapon or explosive is prohibited.

(4) The Olympic law enforcement commander:

(a) shall use reasonable means, which may include mechanical, electronic, x-ray, or any other device to detect dangerous weapons or explosives concealed in or upon the person of any individual attempting to enter an Olympic venue secure area;

(b) may provide secure weapons storage areas so that persons may store their weapons prior to entering an Olympic venue secure area; and

(c) shall provide instructions to personnel operating an Olympic venue secure area that, upon discovery of a firearm possessed by a person licensed to carry a concealed firearm, the personnel may:

(i) require the person to deliver the firearm to a secure weapons storage area permitted by Subsection (3)(b); or

(ii) require the person to exit the Olympic venue secure area.

(5) A cause of action may be maintained against the state for any injury where an individual can establish by clear and convincing evidence that:

(a) if a person licensed to carry a concealed firearm had been able to access the concealed firearm the injury would not have occurred to that individual or others; and

(b) the individual suffered damages as a consequence.

(6) Nothing in Subsection (5) modifies or amends Title 63, Chapter 30, Governmental Immunity Act.

Commentary

U.C.A. 53-12-301.1 exempts those persons described in U.C.A. 76-10-523(1) from the prohibition of taking weapons into Olympic venues. It is not surprising that this group of individuals includes federal marshals, and other federal officials acting within the scope of their employment. It <u>IS</u> surprising, however, that 76-10-523(1) permits non-residents to carry unloaded weapons which are securely encased (don't forget, an unloaded weapon could be a weapon which contains ammunition but does not have a bullet in the chamber). Thus, this Olympic bill gives non-residents privileges that residents do not have. Ain't that a dandy! So instead of bringing your gun to the Games, bring an out-of-stater with a securely-encased firearm containing ammunition!

63-55b-153. Repeal date — Title 53.

"Plain Talk"

The Senate wanted to make sure that this distasteful restriction on concealed weapon holders didn't continue after the Olympics. Therefore they enacted <u>two</u> statutes to repeal the law after the Olympics are over. U.C.A. 63-55b-153 and 63-55b-176 both repeal the statute on April 1, 2002.

ACTUAL TEXT

(1) Subsection 53-5-710(4) pertaining to restrictions at Olympic venue secure areas is repealed April 1, 2002.

(2) Section 53-12-301.1 is repealed April 1, 2002.

63-55b-176. Repeal date — Title 76.

Section 76-10-531 is repealed April 1, 2002.

R724-4-1. Purpose.

> **"Plain Talk"**
> Concealed weapon permits are not only governed by state statute, but also by a truckload of "regulations" appearing below.

ACTUAL TEXT
The purpose of this rule is to set forth the process whereby the Division of Law Enforcement and Technical Services **[Division of Criminal Investigation and Technical Services - it's been renamed]** administers the Concealed Weapons Act in accordance with Title 53, Chapter 5, Part 7.

R724-4-2. Authority.

> **"Plain Talk"**
> The Legislature gives state agencies authority to "promulgate" (think up and write) regulations. This can be dangerous, because regulations are enforced like any other law, but the bureaucrats that write them are not accountable to voters. For an ugly example, see some of the regulations promulgated by the Environmental Protection Agency.

ACTUAL TEXT
This rule is authorized by Subsection 53-5-704(12)**[Should be 17]**.

R724-4-3. Definitions.

> **"Plain Talk"**
> These definitions are quite helpful, because they contain definitions of words and phrases used, but not defined, in the Utah Code. Unfortunately, many of the definitions involve multiple references to other code sections. This reminds us of the impossible-to-read federal tax code -- by the time you get to the fourth reference, you forget what the first and second references said. To keep you from constantly turning pages to check references, we have inserted the text **[using brackets and bold print]** of a few of the most important code sections and regulations referred to in these regulations.
>
> A very disturbing change shows how bureaucrats can "tighten the noose" on the rights of law-abiding citizens without the blessings

of our elected officials or by carelessly interpreting the intent of legislators. To qualify for a concealed weapon permit a person must be of "good character." One way to demonstrate good character is never to have been convicted of a crime of moral turpitude (basically immoral). Because the term is not of common daily usage, BCI defines it in this regulation. Before this year it included "firearms violations involving a crime of violence" (**R724-4-3** M. 15.) But the Legislature replaced the term "crime of violence" with the term "violent felony" (see U.C.A. 76-10-503 above). Instead of making the same substitution in this regulation, BCI simply dropped the ending of M.15. as follows, "firearms violations~~involving a crime of violence~~." The only thing that keeps a bureaucrat from denying a permit to a person with a petty firearm violation is U.C.A. 53-10-704(3)(b) that prevents denying, suspending or revoking a permit for a single conviction for an infraction under the weapons code. Unfortunately this allows them to revoke a permit for two infractions or for an infraction of the hunting code rather than the weapons code (e.g. shooting 30 minutes and 30 seconds after sundown), or for a petty misdemeanor (e.g. shooting from a pickup at a coyote decimating a flock of sheep). Furthermore, the definition suggests that such violations are immoral and should result in denying or yanking of your permit, which is absurd. M.15. should be changed to read, "firearms violations involving a violent felony." This would conform to legislative intent (and Pancho's peace of mind).

ACTUAL TEXT

Terms used in this rule shall be defined as follows:

A. "Affidavit" means a written statement made under oath before a notary public.

B. "Approved **[Certified]** firearms instructor" means a person approved by the Division who can certify that an applicant meets the general firearm familiarity requirement of Subsection 53-5-704(7)**[should be (8)]**and is an instructor who is certified pursuant to Sections R724-4-13 and 14 **[should say 14 and 15]**.

C. "Board" means the Concealed Weapons Review Board referred to in Section 53-5-703.

D. "Concealed" means that which is covered, hidden, or secreted in a manner that the public would not be aware of its presence and is readily accessible for immediate use.

E. "Crime of violence" means any crime defined as such in Subsection 76-10-501(2)(b). **["crime of violence" has been deleted from the definitions in U.C.A. 76-10-501 - the term has been changed to** "violent felony" (see U.C.A. 76-10-501(18) and the several references to the term in Chapter VII e.g. U.C.A. 76-10-509.6..)]

F. "Division" means the Division of Law Enforcement [Criminal Investigations] and Technical Services of the Utah Department of Public Safety.

G. "Domestic violence" means any of the crimes listed in Subsection 77-36-1(2) when committed by one co-habitant against another.[any criminal offense involving violence or physical harm or threat of violence or physical harm, or any attempt, conspiracy, or solicitation (like "I'll give you 25 bucks to beat up my wife") to commit a criminal offense involving violence or physical harm. This includes assault (an attempt or a threat, accompanied by a show of immediate force or violence, to do bodily injury to another or an act that causes or creates a risk of bodily injury to another), aggravated assault (intentionally causing bodily injury to another or using a dangerous weapon likely to produce death or serious bodily injury), criminal homicide, harassment (a written or recorded threat to commit a violent felony), kidnaping, child kidnaping, or aggravated kidnaping (kidnaping while using or threatening to a dangerous weapon, holding for ransom, taking hostage, afflicting bodily injury, interfering with the performance of a governmental institution, or committing a sexual offense)[30], mayhem (cutting off or disabling a member of the body, putting out an eye, slitting the nose, ear, or lip), sexual offenses (see description below under "unlawful sexual conduct"), stalking (repeatedly maintaining a visual or physical proximity to a person that would make that person fear for himself or a member of his immediate family) unlawfully detaining a person against his or her will, violating a protective order not to contact the person, destroying a person's property by fire or otherwise, possessing a deadly weapon with an intent to assault, discharging a firearm from a vehicle.]

H. "Equivalent experience with a firearm through participation in law enforcement" means experience showing that the applicant has within the last five years met the firearms requirement of his/her department as evidenced by verifiable documentation from his/her department.

I. "Equivalent experience with a firearm through participation in the military" means experience showing that the applicant has within the last five years successfully met the firearms requirements of his/her military organization as evidenced by verifiable documentation from

---

[30] Pardon me for asking, but why hasn't the Legislature made kidnaping a child a mandatory death penalty offense (excluding, of course, kidnaping by a non-custodial parent)?

his/her military organization, provided that such training meets the requirements of Subsection 53-5-704(7)(a)**[should be (8)(a)]**.

    J.   "Equivalent experience with a firearm through participation in an organized shooting competition" means experience showing that the applicant has within the last five years competed in an organized shooting competition as evidenced by verifiable documentation from the organization sanctioning or conducting the organized shooting competition, provided the organized shooting competition meets the requirements of Subsection 53-5-704(7)(a)**[should be (8)(a)] [If not NRA or P.O.S.T. person must submit outline to show the course satisfies the requirements]**.

    K. "Felony" means any criminal conduct other than those crimes defined as misdemeanors or infractions by the statutes of this state. It also includes any criminal conduct that is punishable by more than one year in prison by a federal statute, or by the statute of some other state.

    L.   "Mitigating circumstances" means circumstances which reduce culpability for purposes of assessing good character.

    M. "Moral turpitude" means a conviction for criminal conduct under the statutes of this state or any other jurisdiction involving any of the following offenses:

1. theft;
2. fraud;
3. tax evasion;
4. issuing bad checks;
5. robbery;
6. aggravated robbery;
7. bribery;
8. perjury;
9. extortion;
10. arson or aggravated arson;
11. criminal mischief;
12. falsifying government records;
13. forgery;
14. receiving stolen property;
15. firearms violations; **[should say . . . "involving a violent felony" - see "Plain Talk" for this section.]**
16. burglary or aggravated burglary;
17. vandalism;
18. kidnaping, aggravated kidnaping, or child kidnaping;

19.   crimes involving unlawful sexual conduct as described in Title 76, Chapter 5, Part 4[31], Chapter 5a, Chapter 7, Part 1 **[engaging in activities related to child pornography]**, and Chapter 10, Part 13 **[engaging in activities related to prostitution]**[32]; and

20.   violations of the pornographic and harmful materials and performances act, as defined in Title 76, Chapter 10, Part **[engaging in a host of activities related to the blight of pornography]**.

N.   "Offenses involving the use of alcohol" means any of the following offenses:

1. Any violation of Sections 41-6-44 through 41-6-44.20 **[driving under the influence of alcohol or illegal drugs or having an open container in the passenger compartment of a motor vehicle]**;

2. Violations of Title 32A, Chapter 12, Part 2 **[offenses involving the unlawful distribution and consumption of alcoholic beverages such as the sale to intoxicated persons or minors]** involving the illegal use or consumption of an alcoholic beverage, and

3. a violation of 76-10-528.

O.   "Offenses involving the use of narcotics" means any offense involving the use, possession, manufacturing or distribution of any narcotic or drug as defined in Title 58, Chapter 37, 37a, 37b, 37c, 37d, and 37e or a violation of 76-10-528. **[the improper use of controlled drugs]**.

P.   ""Past pattern of behavior" means verifiable incidents, with or without an arrest or conviction, **[do these words worry anyone besides Pancho?]** that would lead a reasonable person to believe that an individual has a violent nature and would be a danger to themselves or others **[like, uh, you spank your kids?]**.

---

[31]   Unlawful sexual intercourse, rape, rape of a child, object rape (don't ask), object rape of a child (rightfully a first degree felony with a possible life sentence), sodomy, forcible sodomy, sodomy on a child (deserving a life sentence), forcible sexual abuse of adults and children, sexual assault, etc.

[32]   Do you think Former President Bill Clinton would qualify for a concealed weapon license in Utah? Who needs one when you're surrounded by a myriad of secret agents with machine guns, right?

R724-4-4. Application For a Concealed Firearm Permit.

> **"Plain Talk"**
>
> To qualify for a concealed weapon permit, an applicant must be at least 21 years old. Other requirements include familiarity with the types of firearms to be concealed, a five-year employment history, a five-year residential history, two letters of character reference, two color passport photos, and fingerprints. Of the $59 for the application fee, $24 goes to the FBI to process fingerprints. The Bureau of Criminal Identification does a background check that includes verifying the accuracy of the information on the application, checking the applicant's criminal history through local and state computer files, a search of the National Crime Information Center computer database, a search of juvenile justice files, and even a search for expunged records.[33] Beginning in 2000 the courts must also make records available to BCI showing a plea of insanity, or incompetence to stand trial, an adjudication of mental incompetence, or an involuntary commitment. Once an applicant qualifies for a permit, the permit is good for five years (even though this regulation says two years). See U.C.A. 53-5-704 above. Renewal fees are really $10 although this reg says $5.

ACTUAL TEXT

A. Application for a permit to carry a concealed firearm shall be made in writing to the Division on forms provided by the Division. An application package shall include:

1. a completed application form;

2. proof that the applicant is 21 years of age or older at the time application is made;

3. evidence of general familiarity with the types of firearms to be concealed, verified by a signed certificate from an approved firearms instructor;

4. a five-year employment history;

---

[33] After many years of good behavior, a person convicted of a crime may have his criminal record expunged (cleansed) by court order (see discussion of U.C.A. 77-18-10 through 77-18-12 in Chapter XII). A person with an expunged criminal record can legally declare, on all applications, EXCEPT THE APPLICATION FOR A CONCEALED WEAPON PERMIT, that he has never been convicted of a crime. This emphasizes how difficult it is for anyone ever convicted of a crime, to qualify for a concealed weapon permit in Utah.

5. a five-year residential history;

6. two letters of character reference;

7. two recent color photographs of passport quality, measuring 2" x 2"; and

8. two completed fingerprint cards.

B. An applicant shall pay a non-refundable processing fee of $59.00 at the time the application is filed. This fee consists of $35.00 mandated by Section 53-5-707 and a $24.00 Federal Bureau of Investigation finger print processing fee. Payment shall be in the form of cash, cashier's check, or money order. The Division is not responsible for cash lost in the mail.

C. An applicant may request an interview prior to submitting the application. The Division may require an interview subsequent to the submission of the application.

D. A background investigation shall be conducted on all applicants to determine if they are of good character as required by Section 53-5-704. The background investigation shall consist of:

1. verifying the accuracy of the application information;

2. checking the applicant's criminal history through local, state and national computer files which include:

a. Utah computerized criminal history;

b. national crime information center;

c. Utah law enforcement information network;

d. drivers license information;

e. statewide warrants file;

f. criminal justice juvenile files;

g. criminal history expungement system; and

h. national instant check system (when available).

[and beginning in 2000 records showing a plea of insanity, or incompetence to stand trial, an adjudication of mental incompetence, or an involuntary commitment.]

3. The fingerprint cards will be sent to the FBI for a review of the applicant's criminal history record pursuant to Sections 53-5-704 and 706.

E. The Division will review all the above information and approve or deny the application.

1. Notice of approval may be given by telephone or in writing.

2. Notice of denial shall be given in writing and shall state the reasons for denial.

F. Renewal of a permit to carry a concealed firearm is required every two years.

1. The renewal form is available from the Division.

2. A renewal applicant shall pay a non-refundable fee of $5.00 as required by Section 53-5-707 **[707 says ten bucks, but if they only charge you $5, buy a box of reloads!]**. Payment shall be made in the form of

cash, cashier's check or money order. The Division is not responsible for cash lost in the mail.

G. A peace officer who has honorably retired from full-time employment within five years of making application shall be exempt from the following requirements:

    1. two letters of character reference; and

    2. two sets of fingerprints.

R724-4-5. Temporary Concealed Firearm Permit.

> **"Plain Talk"**
> See discussion in U.C.A. 53-5-705 above.

ACTUAL TEXT

A. To be eligible to obtain a temporary permit to carry a concealed firearm, as provided for in Section 53-5-705, an applicant must:

    1. apply for a permit under Section 53-5-704;

    2. apply for a temporary permit under Section 53-5-705;

    3. demonstrate good character; and

    4. prove to the satisfaction of the Division extenuating circumstances justifying the need for a temporary permit.

B. Provisions regarding denial, suspension or revocation of a temporary permit are set forth in Subsection R724-4-18(F).

R724-4-6. Out-of-State Concealed Firearm Permit Applicants.

> **"Plain Talk"**
> Citizens of other states may apply for a Utah permit by going through the same process as Utah citizens. This would be too much of a hassle for someone simply passing through the state; but someone who consistently visits Utah on business or for pleasure may want to suffer the inconvenience and expense of applying for a permit.

ACTUAL TEXT

Out-of-state applicants for a concealed firearm permit will be subject to the same application process as in-state applicants.

R724-4-7. Out-of-State Concealed Firearm Permits.

> **"Plain Talk"**
> As of 2001 Utah recognizes the permits of all other states and counties. Therefore, the Bureau of Criminal Identification (BCI) will have to update this regulation.

ACTUAL TEXT

A. In accordance with Subsection 76-10-523(2)(b) the Division will conduct research annually to determine which states have requirements for the issuance of a concealed firearm permit that meet or exceed the requirements for issuance of a concealed firearm permit in this state.

B. A list of the out of state permits that will be honored in this state will be maintained by the Division. The list will be available to the public upon request.

R724-4-8. Application for a Certificate of Qualification.

> **"Plain Talk"**
> Law enforcement officials (see definition in U.C.A. 53-5-711 above) and judges get to have a "super permit" that lets them pack in court houses and other state-established (as opposed to federal) secured areas. (See also U.C.A. 76-10-523 in Chapter VII.)

ACTUAL TEXT

A. Application for a certificate of qualification shall be made in writing to the Division on forms provided by the Division and will be subject to the same application requirements as concealed firearm permit applicants set forth in Section R724-4-4. The applicant must also provide proof to the satisfaction of the Division that they are a law enforcement official or judge as defined in Section 53-5-711.

B. A certificate of qualification will act as identification to verify that the holder is exempt from weapons laws in accordance with Section 76-10-523.

R724-4-9. Additional Training Requirements for Obtaining a Certificate of Qualification.

> **"Plain Talk"**
> With greater freedom comes greater responsibility. "Super Permit" holders must comply with training requirements that exceed those of the typical concealed weapon permit holder.

ACTUAL TEXT

Training requirements for obtaining a certificate of qualification, as set forth in Subsection 53-5-711(2)(b), will be established by the commissioner. A copy of the training requirements will be available in the Division office upon request. The commissioner may make changes or additions to the training requirements as needed. It is the responsibility of the applicant to acquire the training through their agency.

R724-4-10. Annual Requalification Requirement for Obtaining a Certificate of Qualification.

"Plain Talk"

These requirements are established by the "Commish" (a bureaucrat himself). I am told by BCI officials that presently they are required to qualify yearly at the shooting range.

ACTUAL TEXT

Proof of annual requalification must be submitted to the Division, in writing, no earlier than November 1 and no later than November 30 of each year. If an applicant has received an initial certificate of qualification after August 1, requalification will not be required until the following year. Failure to provide proof of annual requalification by November 30 of each year will result in revocation of the certificate of qualification.

R724-4-11. Duty of Certificate of Qualification Holder to Notify the Division Upon Termination of Status as a Law Enforcement Official or Judge.

"Plain Talk"

When da judge tells 'em to "take this job and shove it" she's got to inform the folks at BCI within 6 months so they can issue a regular, as opposed to a "super" permit.

ACTUAL TEXT

A certificate of qualification holder who resigns or is terminated from their position must notify the Division within six months after leaving their position. If the holder obtains other employment as a Law Enforcement Official or Judge within the month period, the Division will allow the certificate of qualification to remain current provided the holder has not committed an offense that is grounds for revocation under Title 53 Chapter 5 Part 7. If a holder of a certificate of qualification has not obtained another position as a Law Enforcement Official or Judge, the certificate of qualification will be revoked and a concealed firearm permit will be issued provided the holder has not committed an offense that is grounds for revocation under Title 53 Chapter 5 Part 7.

R724-4-12. Denial, Suspension, or Revocation of a Concealed Firearm Permit or Certificate of Qualification.

"Plain Talk"

Super permit and regular CWP holders must maintain "good character" (see definition in U.C.A. 53-5-704) or lose their permits.

ACTUAL TEXT

A concealed firearm permit or certificate of qualification may be denied, suspended or revoked for any of the reasons set forth in Subsections 53-5-704 (3)(a) and (c), or for failure to maintain good character as defined in Subsection 53-5-704(2).

R724-4-13. Requirement to Notify Peace Officer When Stopped.

"Plain Talk"

"BY THE WAY, OFFICER, I'M PACKING." - When stopped for questioning by a police officer, a permit holder possessing a concealed firearm must inform the officer of the weapon and the permit. As the following regulation mandates, these should be the first words out of the permit holder's mouth.

ACTUAL TEXT

When a concealed firearm permit holder or certificate of qualification holder is stopped for questioning by a peace officer based on reasonable suspicion in accordance with Section 77-7-15[34] and the holder has a concealed firearm in his/her possession, the holder shall immediately advise the peace officer that he/she is a lawful holder and has a concealed firearm in his/her possession.

---

[34] **U.C.A. 77-7-15. Authority of peace officer to stop and question suspect - Grounds.** "A peace officer may stop any person in a public place when he has a reasonable suspicion to believe he has committed or is in the act of committing or is attempting to commit a public offense and may demand his name, address and an explanation of his actions."

R724-4-14. Concealed Firearm Permit Instructors.

> **"Plain Talk"**
>
> PROCESS FOR BECOMING A CONCEALED FIREARMS INSTRUCTOR - Applicants for a concealed weapon permit must prove that they are familiar with the firearm they will conceal and know how to handle it safely. To do so they meet with a certified instructor who conducts such an investigation. The firearms instructor must have completed a program sponsored by the National Rifle Association or Peace Officer Standards and Training (POST) or equivalent. The instructor should file a copy of his written course of instruction to BCI. He must maintain "good character" as that term is defined above in U.C.A. 53-5-704 (in this chapter - Chapter VIII.)

ACTUAL TEXT

A. The Division will certify concealed firearm permit instructors as provided for in Subsection 53-5-704(7)(b)(ii) **[should say 704(8)(b)(2)]**.

B. Application to become a concealed firearm permit instructor shall be made in writing to the Division on forms provided by the Division. The application shall include:

1. a completed application form;

2. evidence that the applicant has completed a firearms instructor training program sponsored by the National Rifle Association, or Peace Officer Standards and Training, or a program equivalent thereto; and

3. a notarized release of information form.

C. A concealed firearm permit instructor applicant shall pay a non-refundable fee of $5.00. Payment shall be made in the form of cash, cashier's check or money order. The Division is not responsible for cash lost in the mail.

D. The applicant must submit with the application a copy of a course of instruction that meets the course content requirements established by the Division as required by Subsection 53-5-704(7)(a)**[should say 704(8)(a)]**.

E. The applicant must meet the good character requirements set forth in Subsections 53-5-704(2)(a) through (g)**[should say (h)]**.

R724-4-15. Certificate of Qualification Instructors.

> **"Plain Talk"**
>
> "Super Permit" instructors have to be "POST" (Peace Officers Standards and Training) certified. They must show proof of good character. The Division can limit the number of instructors needed to fill the demand for these special CWPs.

ACTUAL TEXT

A. The Division will certify certificate of qualification instructors as provided for in Subsection 53-5-711(4)(c). An applicant for a certificate of qualification instructor shall:

1. be certified as a firearms instructor by Peace Officer Standards and Training;

2. make a written request to the Division for approval;

3. meet the good character requirements set forth in Subsections 53-5-704(2)(a) through(g)**[h]**; and

4. demonstrate to the satisfaction of the Division that their approval would provide a benefit to the training program.

B. The number of certificate of qualification instructors approved by the Division will be limited to the needs of the program.

R724-4-16. Denial, Suspension, or Revocation of Approval as a Concealed Firearm Permit Instructor or Certificate of Qualification Instructor.

> **"Plain Talk"**
>
> Instructors must teach from an approved course of instruction (presumably approved when the instructor submits his course outline to BCI). Firearm safety instructors must abide by the same legal and ethical standards as concealed weapon permit holders, to preserve their teaching privileges. They must also keep accurate records concerning their students. Of course, he or she will be denied or deprived of a certificate of instruction if he or she gives false information to the Division.

ACTUAL TEXT

Approval as a concealed firearm permit instructor or certificate of qualification instructor may be denied, suspended or revoked for any of the following reasons:

1. failing to meet the requirements of Sections R724-4-14 or 15;

2. failing to teach from an approved course of instruction;

3. failing to maintain records verifying that an applicant has passed a required course of instruction; or

4. knowingly and wilfully providing false information to the Division.

R724-4-17. Records Access.

> **"Plain Talk"**
> The division cannot release information about a permit applicant to other agencies. Even the applicant cannot access the file, unless the division denies the permit. If an application is denied, the applicant may then review the file to find out what records formed the basis of the denial.

ACTUAL TEXT

A. The purpose of this section is to define access to concealed firearm permit and certificate of qualification records in accordance with Title 63, Chapter 2, and Subsection 53-5-708(1).

B. Except as provided in Subsection 53-5-708(1), information supplied to the Division by an applicant shall be considered "private" in accordance with Subsection 63-2-302(2)(d).

C. Information gathered by the Division and placed in the applicant's file shall be considered "protected" in accordance with Subsections 63-2-304(8)and(9). However, if such information is used as the basis for denial of a concealed firearm permit or certificate of qualification, such information shall be considered "private" in accordance with Subsection 63-2-302(2)(d) and the applicant shall have access to it in accordance with Subsection 53-5-704(10)(c).

R724-4-18. Adjudicative Procedures.

> **"Plain Talk"**
> If your permit to carry a concealed weapon or to instruct, has been denied, suspended or revoked, you can appeal within 60 days of the notice of the suspension, denial or revocation. You can't appeal to a court of law, though, until you "exhaust" (complete) all administrative appeals.

ACTUAL TEXT

A. Any applicant denied a concealed firearm permit or certificate of qualification may request a hearing before the board by filing an appeal to the Division within 60 days from the date the notice of denial is issued. This appeal process also applies to a concealed firearm permit holder or certificate of qualification holder whose concealed firearm permit or certificate of qualification has been suspended or revoked.

B. Board hearings will be conducted informally in accordance with Section 63-46b-5.

C. Board decisions shall be issued within 30 days from the date of the hearing in accordance with Subsection 53-5-704(10)(E) and shall comply with the requirements of Subsection 63-46b-5(1)(i).

D. In accordance with Section 63-46b-11 the board may enter a default order against any party who fails to participate in a hearing.

E. Judicial review of all final actions resulting from informal adjudicative proceedings is available pursuant to Section 63-46b-15.

F. Denial, suspension, or revocation of a temporary permit is not appealable to the board.

G. A concealed firearm permit instructor or certificate of qualification instructor has the same appeal rights as set forth in this section for concealed firearm permit holders and certificate of qualification holders.

SUMMARY OF CONCEALED WEAPON LAWS

There are so many interrelated state and federal code sections governing concealed weapons that it may be difficult for the reader to understand exactly where he or she can or cannot carry a concealed weapon. The following summary is a SIMPLIFICATION. Grey areas are specifically discussed in Chapters VII, VIII and XIII.

A. A CWP holder can carry a concealed weapon "throughout the state without restriction" EXCEPT the following places:

1. Secured areas of airports, courthouses, jails, mental institutions, and Olympic Venues.

2. Private residences or churches if the permit holder is told orally or in writing that firearms are not allowed,

3. Federal facilities and buildings including post offices (see possible defenses in Chapter XIII).

4. In the passenger compartments of airlines and other INTERSTATE modes of travel such as trains (e.g. AMTRAK) and buses (e.g. Greyhound). However, permit holders may carry concealed weapons in INTRASTATE mass transit vehicles such as UTA buses and TRAX.

5. In national parks and monuments.

6. In states not recognizing Utah's permit.

B. States that recognize Utah's permit.

The only states that Utah has formal reciprocal agreement with are Arizona and Arkansas. (See Bureau of Criminal Identification Web page at www.bci.state.ut.us.) However, unofficial sources claim that in addition to Arizona and Arkansas, the following states recognize Utah's permit (See www.packing.org) They are Idaho, Florida, Indiana, Kentucky, Michigan, Montana, Oklahoma, South Carolina and Wyoming. At one time the NRA reported that Alaska recognized Utah's permit. Now that Utah recognizes all other states' permits, we anticipate there will be other states that reciprocate by recognizing Utah's. We suggest permit holders traveling out of state call in advance to verify. In Appendix E you will find the telephone number of every state attorney general. Keep in mind some states don't have a uniform law provision like Utah's UCA 76-10-500. Therefore, there may be cities and counties within a state that accepts our permit, that have unusual restrictions on concealed weapon permit holders. For example, some states don't authorize permit holders to carry their weapons into school zones, in churches or into private business that post signs. You will not know this unless you call ahead and ask about carrying a concealed weapon in the cities and counties in which you intend to travel (see Attorney General listings in Appendix E).

C. Areas of Controversy

Several state and private institutions claim they can prohibit citizens from defending themselves with a concealed weapon despite clear intent of the Legislature to the contrary. Only the Legislature has the authority to regulate the use of firearms. Policies enacted by political subdivisions that are contrary to state law are unenforceable (see Chapter VII, U.C.A. 76-10-500). Therefore, concealed weapon permit holders may carry firearms for self defense in the following places:

1. In public places, including state libraries and office buildings.

2. On the premises of private businesses where the public has free access.

3. In public schools and on university campuses, despite school board and university policies to the contrary.

D. Hot issue - "No Weapons Policies" at work.

Many employers have adopted policies prohibiting concealed weapon permit holders from taking their firearms to work for self defense. This is particularly true of businesses with home offices in states that do not have laws permitting the carrying of lawful concealed weapons. These employers intimidate employees who are permit holders, telling them they will be fired if they bring their guns to work. What these employers don't realize is that although Utah is an "employment-at-will" state (your employer can terminate you for any reason), that it is still a "wrongful termination" to fire an employee in violation of an express Utah public policy. Utah has a strong public policy of deterring violent crime by encouraging more people to have concealed weapon permits. Our Legislature has enacted laws based upon the conclusion that "more guns mean less crime" and the greater number of concealed weapon permit holders, the less violent crime. "Gun-free zones" frustrate the deterrent effect of the laws passed by the Legislature. In the past several years lobbyists representing employers have petitioned the Utah Legislature to pass a law which would allow private businesses to prohibit CWPs on the premises. The Legislature has refused, recognizing Gun Free Zones are really "Free Kill Zones" that attract mass murderers. For these reasons, employers who terminate employees who have valid concealed weapon permits and who bring their weapons to work for self defense, take a significant chance of being sued for wrongful termination. Keep your eye on the case *Hansen et. al. v. America On Line* (AOL) currently pending in the Weber County Court. "Yours Truly" is one of the attorneys handling the case. As far as we know, it is the only wrongful termination case in the country involving employees who were fired for having guns in a public parking lot leased by an employer.

Another word of caution about "no weapon policies." They prevent innocent employees from protecting customers from an armed assault. If a customer is injured during such an attack, and the injured person can show he or she would not have been injured by the assailant if the store had not enforced its "no weapons policy," the business enforcing the policy should be held partially liable for the injury. The state of Utah has agreed to hold itself strictly liable for injuries and death shown to be caused by the disarming of CWPs at the Olympics. Likewise, business owners should be held accountable for foolish business policies that leave customers defenseless. Business owners, in the event of a shooting at your business, do you think you have a greater risk of being held liable by OBEYING the law and allowing your CWP employees to carry weapons, or by DISOBEYING the law?

Pancho's Wisdom

In the next few years dozens of school children, teachers and employees will die because of the foolish concept of "gun free" [free kill] zones, coupled with inadequate security. Their blood will be on the heads of politicians and employers who institute such ineffective and foolish policies, NOT upon the heads of innocent gun manufactures, dealers or gun owners. Either protect the innocent with secured areas and armed guards or let them arm themselves, if they so choose, for their own protection.

Pancho's Angels

CHAPTER IX:
HUNTING LAWS AND REGULATIONS
(As they relate to the use of firearms)

Pancho's Wisdom
If liberals knew what they were missing, they'd give up drugs, sex and rock-n-roll for hunting and shooting. . .but then the rest of us would never draw an elk tag. . . so to Hell with 'em!

INTRODUCTION

There are hundreds of code sections and regulations that govern hunting in the State of Utah. Only a few of them, however, dictate where, when and what types of firearms hunters can use. We omitted code sections and regulations that deal with hunting and fishing in general. They are outside the scope of this book and can be found in State hunting proclamations. We have included the laws regulating the types of firearms that can be used for hunting various species, restricting where guns can be discharged and defining what violations can result in felony convictions and confiscation of property.

In this chapter you will notice hunting regulations that appear to conflict with state code sections. When state code sections conflict with hunting regulations, the code sections govern. For example, several of the following hunting regulations that prohibit firearms while bow hunting, hunting with a muzzle loader or pursuing bear or cougar conflict with and are invalidated by the concealed weapon laws (Chapter VIII. See R651-612-1 and Commentary). Of course, bow hunters with concealed weapon permits cannot kill wild animals with their handguns unless they do it in legitimate self defense.

There appear to be no hunting codes or regulations that say you can kill an animal in "self defense" (compare the code sections in Chapter XI, discussing the use of deadly force to counter an attack by another human being). Fortunately, even without a code section spelling it out, under the common law (case law as opposed to statutory law), for every criminal act there is always the defense of "justification." A hunter would certainly be justified in killing an attacking bear or cougar without a license to kill that species, if he reasonably believed he was in immediate danger of serious bodily harm or death.

U.C.A. 10-8-47. [The authority of Cities and Towns to Regulate] Firearms.

> **"Plain Talk"**
>
> This code section gives Utah CITIES AND TOWNS the authority to regulate the use of firearms. No similar law exists that authorizes COUNTIES to control the use of firearms. However, U.C.A. 23-13-17, the state spotlighting statute (see discussion below) gives counties the right to enact ordinances governing night hunting of predators and varmints with spotlights.

ACTUAL TEXT

They [cities and towns] . . . **they may regulate and prevent the discharge of firearms,** rockets, powder, fireworks or any other dangerous or combustible material: . . . **(emphasis added).**

U.C.A. 23-13-2. Definitions.

> **"Plain Talk"**
>
> Although most of the definitions used in Title 23 are quite understandable, two of the terms, "feral" and "protected wildlife," invite further discussion. Feral animals are those that were once domestic, like cats, dogs, and pigeons, but have run off or flown away and become wild. Feral animals are not protected wildlife. And speaking of protected wildlife, notice that everything that has a back bone except coyote, field mouse, gopher, ground squirrel, jack rabbit, muskrat, and raccoon, is protected. Interestingly, rats, were omitted from this exception, hopefully an oversight. This makes RATS, if you can believe it, PROTECTED WILDLIFE![35]

ACTUAL TEXT

§ **23-13-2.** Definitions [Effective January 1, 2001]
    As used in this title:

---

[35] Elsewhere in Utah law, rats are excluded the definition of "game animal" and are listed as "non controlled." This provides a strong argument that they may be hunted in the daytime without a permit or certificate of registration. However, because they are defined as "protected wildlife," they are probably illegal to hunt at night with a spotlight (see state spotlighting statute, U.C.A. 23-13-17, below). These kinds of ambiguities in the gun laws and hunting regulations leave shooters and hunters nervous and frustrated.

(1) "Activity regulated under this title" means any act, attempted act, or activity prohibited or regulated under any provision of Title 23 or the rules, and proclamations promulgated thereunder pertaining to protected wildlife including:
  (a) fishing;
  (b) hunting;
  (c) trapping;
  (d) taking;
  (e) permitting any dog, falcon, or other domesticated animal to take;
  (f) transporting;
  (g) possessing;
  (h) selling;
  (i) wasting;
  (j) importing;
  (k) exporting;
  (l) rearing;
  (m) keeping;
  (n) utilizing as a commercial venture; and
  (o) releasing to the wild.
(2) "Aquatic animal" has the meaning provided in Section 4-37-103.
(3) "Aquatic wildlife" means species of fish, mollusks, crustaceans, aquatic insects, or amphibians.
(4) "Aquiculture facility" has the meaning provided in Section 4-37-103.
(5) "Bag limit" means the maximum limit, in number or amount, of protected wildlife that one person may legally take during one day.
(6) "Big game" means species of hoofed protected wildlife.
(7) "Carcass" means the dead body of an animal or its parts.
(8) "Certificate of registration" means a document issued under this title, or any rule or proclamation of the Wildlife Board granting authority to engage in activities not covered by a license, permit, or tag.
(9) "Closed season" means the period of time during which the taking of protected wildlife is prohibited.
(10) "Conservation officer" means a full-time, permanent employee of the Division of Wildlife Resources who is POST certified as a peace or a special function officer.
(11) "Dedicated hunter program" means a program that provides:
  (a) expanded hunting opportunities;
  (b) opportunities to participate in projects that are beneficial to wildlife; and
  (c) education in hunter ethics and wildlife management principles.
(12) "Division" means the Division of Wildlife Resources.
(13) (a) "Domicile" means the place:
  (i) where an individual has a fixed permanent home and principal establishment;

(ii) to which the individual if absent, intends to return; and

(iii) in which the individual and the individual's family voluntarily reside, not for a special or temporary purpose, but with the intention of making a permanent home.

(b) To create a new domicile an individual must:

(i) abandon the old domicile; and

(ii) be able to prove that a new domicile has been established.

(14) "Endangered" means wildlife designated as such pursuant to Section 3 of the federal Endangered Species Act of 1973.

(15) "Fee fishing facility" has the meaning provided in Section 4-37-103.

(16) "Feral" means an animal which is normally domesticated but has reverted to the wild.

(17) "Fishing" means to take fish or crayfish by any means.

(18) "Furbearer" means species of the Bassariscidae, Canidae, Felidae, Mustelidae, and Castoridae families, except coyote and cougar.

(19) "Game" means wildlife normally pursued, caught, or taken by sporting means for human use.

(20) (a) "Guide" means a person who receives compensation or advertises services for assisting other person to take protected wildlife.

(b) Assistance under Subsection (20)(a) includes the provision of food, shelter, or transportation, or any combination of these.

(21) "Guide's agent" means a person who is employed by a guide to assist another person to take protected wildlife.

(22) "Hunting" means to take or pursue a reptile, amphibian, bird, or mammal by any means.

(23) "Intimidate or harass" means to physically interfere with or impede, hinder, or diminish the efforts of an officer in the performance of the officer's duty.

(24) "Nonresident" means a person who does not qualify as a resident.

(25) "Open season" means the period of time during which protected wildlife may be legally taken.

(26) "Pecuniary gain" means the acquisition of money or something of monetary value.

(27) "Permit" means a document, including a stamp, which grants authority to engage in specified activities under this title or a rule or proclamation of the Wildlife Board.

(28) "Person" means an individual, association, partnership, government agency, corporation, or an agent of the foregoing.

(29) "Possession" means actual or constructive possession.

(30) "Possession limit" means the number of bag limits one individual may legally possess.

. . .

(32) "Private wildlife farm" means an enclosed place where privately owned birds or furbearers are propagated or kept and which restricts the birds or furbearers from:

(a) commingling with wild birds or furbearers; and

(b) escaping into the wild.

(33) "Proclamation" means the publication used to convey a statute, rule, policy, or pertinent information as it relates to wildlife.

. . .

(35) (a) "Protected wildlife" means wildlife as defined in Subsection (49), except as provided in Subsection (35)(b).

(b) "Protected wildlife" does not include coyote, field mouse, gopher, ground squirrel, jack rabbit, muskrat, and raccoon. **[See, what did I tell ya? Do you see the word "rat" in this sentence anywhere?]**

(36) "Released to the wild" means to turn loose from confinement.

(37) (a) "Resident" means a person who:

(i) has been domiciled in the state of Utah for six consecutive months immediately preceding the purchase of a license; and

(ii) does not claim residency for hunting, fishing, or trapping in any other state or country.

(b) A Utah resident retains Utah residency if that person leaves this state:

(i) to serve in the armed forces of the United States or for religious or educational purposes; and

(ii) complies with Subsection (37)(a)(ii).

(c) (i) A member of the armed forces of the United States and dependents are residents for the purposes of this chapter as of the date the member reports for duty under assigned orders in the state if the member:

(A) is not on temporary duty in this state; and

(B) complies with Subsection (37)(a)(ii).

(ii) A copy of the assignment orders must be presented to a wildlife division office to verify the member's qualification as a resident.

(d) A nonresident attending an institution of higher learning in this state as a full-time student may qualify as a resident for purposes of this chapter if the student:

(i) has been present in this state for 60 consecutive days immediately preceding the purchase of the license; and

(ii) complies with Subsection (37)(a)(ii).

(e) A Utah resident license is invalid if a resident license for hunting, fishing, or trapping is purchased in any other state or country.

(f) An absentee landowner paying property tax on land in Utah does not qualify as a resident.

(38) "Sell" means to offer or possess for sale, barter, exchange, or trade, or the act of selling, bartering, exchanging, or trading.

(39) "Small game" means species of protected wildlife:

(a) commonly pursued for sporting purposes; and

(b) not classified as big game, aquatic wildlife, or furbearers and excluding cougar and bear.

(40) "Spoiled" means impairment of the flesh of wildlife which renders it unfit for human consumption.

(41) "Spotlighting" means throwing or casting the rays of any spotlight, headlight, or other artificial light on any highway or in any field, woodland, or forest while having in possession a weapon by which protected wildlife may be killed.

(42) "Tag" means a card, label, or other identification device issued for attachment to the carcass of protected wildlife.

(43) "Take" means to:

(a) hunt, pursue, harass, catch, capture, possess, angle, seine, trap, or kill any protected wildlife; or

(b) attempt any action referred to in Subsection (43)(a).

(44) "Threatened" means wildlife designated as such pursuant to Section 3 of the federal Endangered Species Act of 1973.

(45) "Trapping" means taking protected wildlife with a trapping device.

(46) "Trophy animal" means an animal described as follows:

(a) deer -- any buck with an outside antler measurement of 24 inches or greater;

(b) elk -- any bull with six points on at least one side;

(c) bighorn, desert, or rocky mountain sheep -- any ram with a curl exceeding half curl;

(d) moose -- any bull;

(e) mountain goat -- any male or female;

(f) pronghorn antelope -- any buck with horns exceeding 14 inches; or

(g) bison -- any bull.

(47) "Waste" means to abandon protected wildlife or to allow protected wildlife to spoil or to be used in a manner not normally associated with its beneficial use. . . .

(48) "Wildlife" means:

(a) crustaceans, including brine shrimp and crayfish;

(b) mollusks; and

(c) vertebrate animals living in nature, except feral animals.

Pancho's Wisdom

If Steve Erwin (the Crocodile Hunter) thinks crocodiles are beautiful, he should see some of Pancho's handguns. What GORGEOUS CREATURES! They're not crocs mate; they're Glocks! But because of "Eeeeevil government hunters" like Senators Schumer, Kennedy, Clinton, and Feinstein, they have become an endangered species.

The Endangered Species Act

"Plain Talk"

Because the preceding definitions include the terms "endangered" and "threatened" species, and because later code sections make you a felon if you happen to "drill" one of these creatures, we had better discuss the state and federal Endangered Species Acts right here and right now. After I had searched the state and federal codes for hours failing to find a "list" of endangered species, I began to wonder if the list vanished with the last unicorn. But believing that you can find anything and everything on the Internet, I finally searched there and Wallah!

First, let me say that this book ain't long enough to contain the complete endangered and threatened species list. Second, even if it was, I'd have to publish a new book every day because the list is subject to DAILY CHANGES (just to keep you hunters on yer toes, or is it to bring you to your knees?)! The list contains every endangered and threatened plant and animal in the world and can be found at http://endangered.fws.gov. Fortunately, the list is broken down by country and further by state. The state of Utah keeps its own list at http://yechaw.state.ut.us. When you get there search for "Utah Sensitive Species List." Inasmuch as these lists are subject to change every day, it won't surprise you that they are not the same. Uhhhh, so which one do I include below? How about both, so you can see for yourself how they differ? Notice how the state website says the federal list includes peregrine falcon as an endangered species when it doesn't. According to Federal Register, the American peregrine falcon was taken off the endangered and threatened species lists in August of 1999.

The federal Endangered Species <u>Act</u> is found in the United States Code at 16 U.S.C. 1531-1543, but it's not included in this book because it doesn't contain the <u>list</u> of endangered species. 16 U.S.C. 1540 contains civil penalties up to $25,000, criminal fines up to $50,000 and prison terms up to 1 year, for ramming a Ruger to its Rareness. And then the state prosecutes Desert Tortoise connoisseurs as felons (see U.C.A. 23-20-4).

ACTUAL TEXT (Subject to daily changes)

Utah State Endangered and Threatened Species (scientific classifications [*Latinus bulshiticus*] omitted - the number "1" indicates species is federally listed as endangered and "2" as threatened)

> **Endangered Birds:** American Peregrine Falcon 1, Southwestern Willow Flycatcher 1
>
> **Threatened Birds:** Bald Eagle 2, Ferruginous Hawk, Yellow-billed Cuckoo, Mexican Spotted Owl 2
>
> **Endangered Mammal:** Black-footed Ferret 1
>
> **Threatened Mammals:** Utah Prairie Dog 2, Wolverine
>
> **Endangered Reptiles:** Banded Gila Monster, Desert Tortoise 2
>
> **Endangered Fish:** Bonytail 1, Colorado Squawfish 1, Humpback Chub 1, Razorback Sucker 1, Woundfin 1, Virgin River Chub 1, June Sucker 1
>
> **Threatened Fish:** Lahontan Cutthroat Trout 2, Roundtail Chub
>
> **Endangered Invertebrates:** Kanab Ambersnail 1, Fish Springs Pond Snail, Utah Valvatasnail 1
>
> **Threatened Invertebrates:** California Floater, Thickshell Pondsnail [Utah Band Snail] (Stagnicola [Pepsi or Coke?] utahensis)

Federal Endangered and Threatened Species list for Utah (E=Endangered, T = Threatened and I have no clue what XN or T(S/A) mean)

Status	Listing
E	Ambersnail, Kanab
E	Chub, bonytail
E	Chub, humpback
E	Chub, Virgin River
E	Crane, whooping (except where XN)
XN	Crane, whooping [XN]
T	Eagle, bald (lower 48 States)
E	Ferret, black-footed (except where XN)
XN	Ferret, black-footed [XN]
E	Flycatcher, southwestern willow
T	Lynx, Canada (lower 48 States)
T	Owl, Mexican spotted
E	Pikeminnow, Colorado (except Salt and Verde R. drainages, AZ)
T	Prairie dog, Utah

E	Snail, Utah valvata
E	Sucker, June
E	Sucker, razorback
T(S/A)	Tortoise, desert (outside/taken from Sonoran Desert)
T	Tortoise, desert (U.S.A., except in Sonoran Desert)
T	Trout, Lahontan cutthroat
E	Woundfin (except Gila R. drainage, AZ, NM)

Commentary

Maybe I was daydreamin' 'bout shootin' my Colts when we discussed ecology in biology class, but haven't hundreds of thousands of species become extinct since the dinosaurs? Would we have oil if they hadn't? So why hyperventilate 'bout a couple of snails or suckers goin' the way of the dodo? Aren't we messin' with Mother Nature trying to keep 'em around anyhow? And shouldn't a few Nimrods snag a couple of HEAD MOUNTS before they're gone? Gimme a BUCK TAG for a T-REX . . .YEAH BABY!

Pancho's Wisdom
Human hunters always have been and always will be part of the earth's "ecosystem." Jason Vilos

U.C.A. 23-13-17. Spotlighting of coyote, red fox, striped skunk, and raccoon -- County ordinances -- Permits.

"Plain Talk"

SURPRISE! Spotlighting[36] is legal in some counties.[37] In counties with spotlighting ordinances, you can hunt coyote, red fox,[38] striped skunk and raccoon at night with a spotlight. If the county fails to enact an ordinance, then the general public, excepting persons protecting their crops and domestic animals, may not spotlight. The good ol' spotlights you used to plug into your car's cigarette lighter aren't legal anymore. Spotlights must be portable, like a flashlight, rather than using a vehicle as a power source. There are several rechargeable models available on the market, but my experience has been that the batteries last no longer than 20 to 30 minutes and it takes hours to recharge them. Unless a hunter owns four or more portable spotlights, his night hunt could be rather short. Hunters cannot occupy or ride in the back of a motor vehicle when spotlighting. The Utah Code definition of "motor vehicle" includes ATV's, Jeeps, motorcycles, snowmobiles and dune buggies. This is a BIG CHANGE from spotlighting in the good old days.

The state statute gives counties broad powers to control night hunting and spotlighting within their boundaries. They can prohibit spotlighting altogether, except for persons protecting their crops or livestock. Counties can control the time of day and seasons spotlighting is allowed, , create "safety zones" by closing areas in the county to spotlighting, control the type of weapons allowed, dictate the penalties for violating the ordinance, restrict the number of hunters spotlighting by limiting the number of permits issued, and require hunters to notify the county sheriff of where and when they will be

---

[36] "Spotlighting" means "throwing or casting the rays of any spotlight, headlight, or other artificial light on any highway or in any field, woodland, or forest while having in possession a weapon by which protected wildlife may be killed," U.C.A. 23-13-2(41).

[37] It should go without saying, that you CANNOT hunt big game animals, upland game or migratory birds at night with or without a spotlight.

[38] Many people are surprised you can even hunt red fox, let alone shoot them at night.

spotlighting. The counties may charge a fee for the permit to cover the costs of administering the ordinance, but surplus revenues must be turned over to the Division of Wildlife Resources. The ordinance does not apply to animal damage control agents (you know, those government guys who get paid by taxpayers to kill the predators that we're all itchin' to shoot!).[39]

Because every county has the authority to tailor its spotlighting ordinance to its own needs, it takes an entire book to adequately cover the topic of spotlighting. My book *The Utah Spotlighting and Night Hunting Manual*, explains the state spotlighting law and analyzes each county's spotlighting ordinance. It reveals how, when, and where you can legally spotlight in the various counties. It covers additional topics including:

1. spotlighting "unprotected wildlife" (partially addressed in next section),

2. the use of night vision equipment,

3. vague areas in state and county spotlighting laws and ordinances that may be unenforceable against hunters,

4. county ordinances that are unenforceable because they conflict with state law,

5. the full text of each county ordinance,

6. recommendations for change in both state law and county ordinances, and

7. a comparison chart showing the differences in the various county ordinances.

Appendix B contains order forms for *The Utah Spotlighting and Night Hunting Manual*, if you are interested in doing a little spotlighting.

ACTUAL TEXT

(1) Spotlighting may be used to hunt coyote, red fox, striped skunk, or raccoon where allowed by a county ordinance enacted pursuant to this section.

(2) The ordinance shall provide that:

(a) any artificial light used to spotlight coyote, red fox, striped skunk, or raccoon must be carried by the hunter;

---

[39] How do those guys get these dream jobs? I wonder if DWR would consider "deputizing" a cantankerous old lawyer?

(b) a motor vehicle headlight or light attached to or powered by a motor vehicle may not be used to spotlight the animal; and

(c) while hunting with the use of an artificial light, the hunter may not occupy or operate any motor vehicle.

(3) For purposes of the county ordinance, "motor vehicle" shall have the meaning as defined in Section 41-6-1.

(4) The ordinance may specify:

(a) the time of day and seasons when spotlighting is permitted;

(b) areas closed or open to spotlighting within the unincorporated area of the county;

(c) safety zones within which spotlighting is prohibited;

(d) the weapons permitted; and

(e) penalties for violation of the ordinance.

(5)   (a) A county may restrict the number of hunters engaging in spotlighting by requiring a permit to spotlight and issuing a limited number of permits.

(b)   (i) A fee may be charged for a spotlighting permit.

(ii) Any permit fee shall be established by the county ordinance.

(iii) Revenues generated by the permit fee shall be remitted to the Division of Wildlife Resources for deposit into the Wildlife Resources Account, except the Wildlife Board may allow any county that enacts an ordinance pursuant to this section to retain a reasonable amount to pay for the costs of administering and enforcing the ordinance, provided this use of the permit revenues does not affect federal funds received by the state under 16 U.S.C. Sec. 669 et seq., Wildlife Restoration Act and 16 U.S.C. Sec. 777 et seq., Sport Fish Restoration Act.

(6) A county may require hunters to notify the county sheriff of the time and place they will be engaged in spotlighting.

(7) The requirement that a county ordinance must be enacted before a person may use spotlighting to hunt coyote, red fox, striped skunk, or raccoon does not apply to:

(a) a person or his agent who is lawfully acting to protect his crops or domestic animals from predation by those animals; or

(b) an animal damage control agent acting in his official capacity under a memorandum of agreement with the division.

R657-11-13. Spotlighting

"Plain Talk"

You cannot hunt "protected wildlife" at night with a spotlight. Guns, "protected wildlife" and artificial light do not mix. If you get caught with a gun while using artificial light, which could be interpreted to mean a flashlight, this is "prima facie" evidence against you and gives law enforcement officers sufficient authority to make an arrest. This is troubling because, when "nature calls" in bear and cougar country, most hunters I know take a flashlight and gun into the night. Under this code section, a vindictive wildlife officer could arrest someone for spotlighting for merely using the bathroom. Fortunately, subsection (2) requires arresting authorities to prove specific intent to hunt protected wildlife and it recognizes other lawful uses of artificial light near protected wildlife.

Notice that neither U.C.A. 23-13-17 nor the related regulations contain the term "unprotected wildlife." If you recall, coyote, field mouse, gopher, ground squirrel, jack rabbit, muskrat, and raccoon are excepted from the definition of protected wildlife. Except for coyote and raccoon, both of which are specifically included in the spotlighting statute, the spotlighting of unprotected wildlife is nether controlled nor prohibited. So if you are hunting jack rabbits at night in the unincorporated area of a county, just remember to take your gun, ammo, a legal spotlight and your attorney! This interpretation is discussed at length in my book about spotlighting.

ACTUAL TEXT

(1)(a) Except as provided in Subsection (3), a person may not use or cast the rays of any spotlight, headlight, or other artificial light to locate protected wildlife while having in possession a firearm or other weapon or device that could be used to take or injure protected wildlife.

(b) The use of a spotlight or other artificial light in a field, woodland, or forest where protected wildlife are generally found is prima facie evidence of attempting to locate protected wildlife.

(2) The provisions of this section do not apply to the use of the headlight of a motor vehicle or other artificial light in a usual manner where there is no attempt or intent to locate protected wildlife.

. . .

[The remainder of this regulation says exactly the same thing as the preceding spotlighting statute, U.C.A. 23-13-17.]

U.C.A. 23-20-1. Enforcement authority of conservation officers -- Seizure and disposition of property.

"Plain Talk"

This is the doozy of a statute you have heard about that permits wildlife officers to take away your car, guns, ammunition, camping gear, camper, boat, airplane or whatever you have used to poach protected wildlife. Wait until you see some of the fines for poaching trophy animals in the sections below! If the fines and forfeitures don't discourage poachers, nothing will, short of the death penalty.

This code section gives wildlife officers the authority to "seize" the wildlife you have shot and the "materials and devices" (guns, tree stands, trailers, tents, etc.) used to hunt them with. Poaching a species of wildlife given an arbitrary value of $5 can result in the forfeiture of a several-thousand-dollar gun. If the poaching of a particular species results in a felony conviction (see section U.C.A. 23-20-4 below), the division can confiscate all the property, including very expensive vehicles, used to commit the felony. If the poaching offense is a misdemeanor, vehicles must be returned to the owner within 30 days.

ACTUAL TEXT

(1) Conservation officers of the division shall enforce the provisions of this title with the same authority and following the same procedures as other law enforcement officers.

(2)   (a) Conservation officers shall seize any protected wildlife illegally taken or held.

(b)(i) Upon determination of a defendant's guilt by the court, the protected wildlife shall be confiscated by the court and sold or otherwise disposed of by the division.

(ii) Proceeds of the sales shall be deposited in the Wildlife Resources Account.

(iii) Migratory wildfowl may not be sold, but must be given to a charitable institution or used for other charitable purposes.

(3)(a) Materials and devices used for the unlawful taking or possessing of protected wildlife shall be seized, and upon a finding by the court that they were used in the unlawful taking or possessing of protected wildlife, the materials and devices shall be:

(i) confiscated by the court;

(ii) conveyed to the division; and

(iii) upon the expiration of time for appeal, sold at a public auction or otherwise disposed of by the division.

(b) Any proceeds from the sale of the material or device shall be deposited into the Wildlife Resources Account.

(4)   (a)(i) As used in Subsection (4), "owner" means a person, other than a person with a security interest, having a property interest in or title to a vehicle and entitled to the use and possession of a vehicle.

(ii) "Owner" includes a renter or lessee of a vehicle.

(b)(i) Conservation officers may seize and impound a vehicle used for the unlawful taking or possessing of protected wildlife for any of the following purposes:

(A) to provide for the safekeeping of the vehicle, if the owner or operator is arrested;

(B) to search the vehicle as provided in Subsection (2)(a) or as provided by a search warrant; or

(C) to inspect the vehicle for evidence that protected wildlife was unlawfully taken or possessed.

(ii) The division shall store any seized vehicle in a public or private garage, state impound lot, or other secured storage facility.

(iii) A seized vehicle shall be released to the owner no later than 30 days after the date the vehicle is seized, unless the vehicle was used for the unlawful taking or possessing of wildlife by a person who is charged with committing a felony under this title.

(c)(i) Upon a finding by a court that the person who used the vehicle for the unlawful taking or possessing of wildlife is guilty of a felony under this title, the vehicle may be:

(A) confiscated by the court;

(B) conveyed to the division; and

(C) upon expiration of time for appeal, sold at a public auction or otherwise disposed of by the division.

(ii) Any proceeds from the sale shall be deposited into the Wildlife Resources Account.

(iii) If the vehicle is not confiscated by the court, it shall be released to the owner.

(d)(i) The owner of a seized vehicle is liable for the payment of any impound fee if the person who used the vehicle for the unlawful taking or possessing of wildlife is found by a court to be guilty of a violation of this title.

(ii) The owner of a seized vehicle is not liable for the payment of any impound fee or, if the fees have been paid, is entitled to reimbursement of the fees paid, if:

(A) no charges are filed or all charges are dropped which involve the use of the vehicle for the unlawful taking or possessing of wildlife; or

(B) the person charged with using the vehicle for the unlawful taking or possessing of wildlife is found by a court to be not guilty.

U.C.A. 23-20-4

Commentary

This forfeiture statute is subject to the sweeping limitations on forfeiture recently passed in a November 2000 ballot initiative. The new law ensures that innocent owners do not lose their property without due process of law. It also provides that an innocent property owner who has to pay an attorney to get his property back may recover his attorney fees. The entire code section is too lengthy to include in this book. Because it relates to all property forfeitures, not just those relating to guns and hunting, we did not include the law in this book. For some reason, Utah Attorney General Mark Shurtleff is challenging the new law limiting forfeitures. Maybe readers of this book should call him and ask, "Why?" Under the old law, DWR sells confiscated guns back to the owner. Does this mean that wildlife officers get a raise if they write enough tickets and confiscate enough valuable property? Isn't there some sort of a conflict hidden in this procedure?

U.C.A. 23-20-3. Taking, transporting, selling, or purchasing protected wildlife illegal except as authorized -- Penalty.

"Plain Talk"

The long and short of this code section means that you cannot kill protected wildlife without a valid hunting license. If they catch you in possession of protected wildlife without a valid license, tag or "certificate of registration,"[40] it is presumed that you killed it illegally. If you unintentionally kill the wrong animal, you are guilty of a class B misdemeanor. But if the animal you kill has an arbitrary value of over $500 (e.g. moose, elk or trophy deer), you will probably be charged with a felony (see "Plain Talk" of next code section).

ACTUAL TEXT

(1) Except as provided in this title or a rule, proclamation, or order of the Wildlife Board, a person may not:

    (a) take or permit his dog to take:

        (i) protected wildlife or their parts;

        (ii) an occupied nest of protected wildlife; or

        (iii) an egg of protected wildlife;

    (b) transport, ship, or cause to be shipped protected wildlife or their parts;

    (c) sell or purchase protected wildlife or their parts; or

    (d) possess protected wildlife or their parts unaccompanied by a valid license, permit, tag, certificate of registration, bill of sale, or invoice.

---

[40] A certificate of registration is what you need to hunt certain species of non-game animals like prairie dogs. It can be a long, drawn-out process to get a certificate.

(2) Possession of protected wildlife without a valid license, permit, tag, certificate of registration, bill of sale, or invoice is prima facie evidence that the protected wildlife was illegally taken and is illegally held in possession.
(3) A person is guilty of a class B misdemeanor if he:
    (a) violates any provision of Subsection (1); and
    (b) does so with criminal negligence as defined in Subsection 76-2-103(4).

U.C.A. 23-20-4. Wanton destruction of protected wildlife -- Penalties.

"Plain Talk"

Gun owners and hunters, please read this law with fear and trembling. This code section assigns an arbitrary (plucked out of the air) value to every species of protected wildlife to determine whether poaching these animals is a misdemeanor or a felony. It is a felony to poach a trophy deer or antelope, an elk, moose or an animal classified as endangered.

Most people don't equate poaching with shooting a big game animal in the wrong area as long as the hunter has a proper tag. Think Again! DWR has been charging hunters with a felony for shooting animals that have an arbitrary value over $500 (elk, moose, trophy deer etc.) while in the wrong area, after hours, or an animal of the wrong sex even if the hunter didn't realize he was in the wrong. I got a call from one elderly gentleman who was charged with a felony for taking a shot at a spike elk and hitting a mature bull by mistake. State law says a hunter doesn't have to know he or she was breaking the law, if his or her actions were reckless. Lawmakers should either change this to require a proof of intent by clear and convincing evidence or DWR should do a better job of defining areas and warning hunters of potential felony charges in the hunting proclamations. Otherwise, it's just a matter of time before a hunter who hunts elk and trophy animals regularly will unintentionally violate the law and be charged with a felony. A felony conviction will, of course, result in a permanent loss of the right to bear arms. Pancho believes that there are groups who want to make it so risky for gun owners to shoot and hunt that we'll all just hang up our Peacemakers. . . but Pancho's got news fer 'em . . . He ain't NEVER hangin' up his!!!! Ya hear that Sarah . . . and the rest of you weasels at Handgun [Confiscation] Inc. NEVER!!!!!!!!!!!!!!!!!!!!!!!!!!!!!!!!!!!!

ACTUAL TEXT

(1) A person is guilty of wanton destruction of protected wildlife if he:

(a) commits an act in violation of Section 23-13-4,[41] 23-13-5,[42] 23-13-13,[43] 23-15-6[44] through 23-15-9,[45] 23-16-5,[46] or Subsection 23-20-3(1);[47]
(b) captures, injures, or destroys protected wildlife; and
(c)(i) does so with intentional, knowing, or reckless conduct as defined in Section 76-2-103;[48]

---

[41] Capturing and keeping protected wildlife is illegal, except under certain circumstances (such as owning a private wildlife farm, U.C.A. 23-13-8).

[42] Importing or exporting wildlife in and out of Utah or releasing exotic wildlife into the wilds of Utah without written permission from the Division of Wildlife Resources is prohibited. Like the person who released the cayman into Utah Lake!

[43] You can't make money buying or selling wildlife, like owning a private wildlife farm, except as otherwise provided by law.

[44] It's illegal to pollute waters containing protected aquatic wildlife (game fish) and certain bugs (I'll have a bug light!) that fish eat.

[45] Unless you own a fish farm, you can't transport live game fish.

[46] Sportsmen cannot hunt and kill more than one species of big game during any year, regardless of how many licenses or permits you purchase, except as otherwise provided in the code for proclamations of the Board of Big Game Control (there are many exceptions to this, particularly regarding antlerless hunts).

[47] This is the code section that covers shooting and killing protected wildlife without a valid license, permit, tag, or certificate of registration (for non-game, protected wildlife such as prairie dogs).

[48] **U.C.A. 76-2-103. Definitions of "intentionally, or with intent or willfully";"knowingly, or with knowledge"; "recklessly, or maliciously"; and "criminal negligence or criminally negligent."**
A person engages in conduct:
(1) Intentionally, or with intent or willfully with respect to the nature of his conduct or to a result of his conduct, when it is his conscious objective or desire to engage in the conduct or cause the result.

(2) Knowingly, or with knowledge, with respect to his conduct or to circumstances surrounding his conduct when he is aware of the nature of his conduct or the existing circumstances. A person acts knowingly, or with knowledge, with respect to a result of his conduct when he is aware

           (ii) intentionally abandons protected wildlife or a carcass;

           (iii) commits the offense at night with the use of a weapon;

           (iv) is under a court or division revocation of a license, tag, permit, or certificate of registration; or

           (v) acts for pecuniary gain.

(2) Subsection (1) does not apply to actions taken which are in accordance with the following:

           (a) Title 4, Chapter 14, Utah Pesticide Control Act;[49]

           (b) Title 4, Chapter 23, Agriculture and Wildlife Damage Prevention Act;[50] or

           (c) Section 23-16-3.[51]

(3) Wanton destruction of wildlife is punishable:

           (a) as a third degree felony if:

                (i) the aggregate value of the protected wildlife determined by the values in Subsection 23-20-4(4) is more than $500; or

---

that his conduct is reasonably certain to cause the result.

    (3) Recklessly, or maliciously, with respect to circumstances surrounding his conduct or the result of his conduct when he is aware of but consciously disregards a substantial and unjustifiable risk that the circumstances exist or the result will occur. The risk must be of such a nature and degree that its disregard constitutes a gross deviation from the standard of care that an ordinary person would exercise under all the circumstances as viewed from the actor's standpoint.

    (4) With criminal negligence or is criminally negligent with respect to circumstances surrounding his conduct or the result of his conduct when he ought to be aware of a substantial and unjustifiable risk that the circumstances exist or the result will occur. The risk must be of such a nature and degree that the failure to perceive it constitutes a gross deviation from the standard of care that an ordinary person would exercise in all the circumstances as viewed from the actor's standpoint.

[49] You can kill certain "pests" with poison, U.C.A. 4-14-2 (20), (21), which includes rats and snails even though they are "protected wildlife" (see definition on protected wildlife in U.C.A. 23-13-1(35)(a)(b) above). [Sorry for all of the confusing cross references, but I didn't write the code or regs, THEY did!]

[50] The Department of Wildlife Resources, as well as property owners under certain conditions, can kill predators and even protected wildlife to protect domestic livestock and crops.

[51] Authority for farmers to kill big game animals destroying their crops under certain conditions.

          (ii) a trophy animal was captured, injured, or destroyed;

    (b) as a class A misdemeanor if the aggregate value of the protected wildlife, other than any trophy animal, determined by the values established in Subsection 23-20-4(4) is more than $250, but does not exceed $500;

    (c) as a class B misdemeanor if the aggregate value of the protected wildlife determined by the values established in Subsection 23-20-4(4) is $250 or less.

(4) Regardless of the restitution amounts imposed under Subsection 23-20-4.5(2), the following values shall be assigned to protected wildlife for the purpose of determining the offense for wanton destruction of wildlife:

    (a) $1,000 per animal for:

        (i) bison;

        (ii) bighorn sheep;

        (iii) rocky mountain goat;

        (iv) moose;

        (v) bear; or

        (vi) endangered species; [including Desert Tortoise eggs; it's okay to abort a human embryo, however, during the first three months of pregnancy.]

    (b) $750 per animal for:

        (i) elk; or

        (ii) threatened species;

    (c) $500 per animal for:

        (i) cougar;

        (ii) golden eagle;

        (iii) river otter; or

        (iv) Gila monster;

    (d) $400 per animal for:

        (i) pronghorn antelope; or

        (ii) deer;

    (e) $350 per animal for bobcat;

    (f) $100 per animal for:

        (i) swan;

        (ii) sandhill crane;

        (iii) turkey;

        (iv) pelican;

        (v) loon;

        (vi) egrets;

        (vii) herons;

        (viii) raptors, except those that are threatened or endangered;

        (ix) Utah milk snake; or

        (x) Utah mountain king snake;

    (g) $35 per animal for furbearers, except:

        (i) bobcat;

(ii) river otter; and

(iii) threatened or endangered species;

(h) $15 per animal for game birds, except:

(i) turkey;

(ii) swan; and

(iii) sandhill crane;

(i) $10 per animal for game fish;

(j) $8 per pound dry weight of processed brine shrimp including eggs;

and

(k) $5 per animal for protected wildlife not listed. **["Poach" a rat or crawfish and lose your new Marlin MR-7 30-.06, if BOTH the wildlife officer AND the judge (unlikely, but possible) don't like your looks.]**

(5) For purposes of sentencing for a wildlife violation, a person who has been convicted of a third degree felony under Subsection (3)(a) is not subject to the mandatory sentencing requirements prescribed in Subsection 76-3-203(4).

(6) As part of any sentence imposed, the court shall impose a sentence of incarceration of not less than 20 consecutive days for any person convicted of a third degree felony under Subsection (3)(a)(ii) who captured, injured, or destroyed a trophy animal for pecuniary gain.

(7) If a person has already been convicted of a third degree felony under Subsection (3)(a)(ii) once, each separate further offense under Subsection (3)(a)(ii) is punishable by, as part of any sentence imposed, a sentence of incarceration of not less than 20 consecutive days.

(8) The court may not sentence a person subject to Subsection (6) or (7) to less than 20 consecutive days of incarceration or suspend the imposition of the sentence unless the court finds mitigating circumstances justifying lesser punishment and makes that finding a part of the court record.

U.C.A. 23-20-4

Commentary

Let's just go through a couple of examples to show you how easy it could be to commit a felony under this law. While deer hunting, you see what appears to be the most magnificent buck deer you have ever seen partially hidden in the trees. After you shoot it, you discover it was an awesome 6 X 7 BULL ELK instead of a buck deer! A game warden arrests you for poaching. At your trial, a jury of your peers will decide whether or not the kill was intentional (you meant to kill an elk rather than a deer, a felony), reckless (really stupid, also a felony), or simply negligent (stupid, but truly a mistaken identity, not a felony). If you are lucky enough to have a few hunters on the jury who understand "buck fever," they will hopefully find you were negligent (stupid), but not guilty of intending to kill or recklessly killing an elk, a felony.

> But what if you shoot a bull moose? Moose are almost black and their antlers look nothing like a deer's. If you do something extremely stupid like that, even the most sympathetic jury might find you guilty of a felony for intentionally poaching a trophy animal. MAKE SURE OF YOUR TARGET!
>
> And don't forget, intentionally or recklessly shooting an animal classified as endangered or threatened is a felony.

U.C.A. 23-20-4.5. Illegal taking, possession, or wanton destruction of protected wildlife -- Restitution -- Reimbursable damages -- Assessment by magistrates --Disposition of monies.

> ### "Plain Talk"
>
> This code section gives guidelines to the courts to impose fines for poaching different species of wildlife. The code section begins by suggesting a fine of $1,000 per animal for bison, big horn sheep, etc. This section does not allow judges to reduce the fines for killing trophy animals. Section 23-13-1 (see discussion above) defines trophy animal. Generally, a trophy big horn is a ram with a greater than ½ curl, a trophy deer is a buck having antlers with at least a 24-inch spread, and a trophy elk has six points on one of its antlers. The fine for killing a desert or rocky mountain big horn sheep is a whopping $30,000 (You could buy a DODGE RAM for that kind of money)!
>
> The fines go to the Division of Wildlife Resources to help set up programs to help stop poaching. When a hunter is found guilty of poaching and these fines are imposed, the judgment becomes a lien on any real estate the hunter owns in the county where he is convicted. These are severe penalties, but they are needed to deter poachers who make big money selling animal parts, including antlers and mounted heads, overseas.

ACTUAL TEXT

(1) When a person is adjudged guilty of illegal taking, illegal possession, or wanton destruction of protected wildlife, other than any trophy animal, the court may order the defendant to pay restitution as set forth in Subsection (2), or a greater or lesser amount, for the value of each animal taken, possessed, or destroyed, unless the court finds that restitution is inappropriate.

(2) Suggested minimum restitution values for protected wildlife are as follows:

    (a) $1,000 per animal for:

        (i) bison;

    (ii) bighorn sheep;
    (iii) rocky mountain goat;
    (iv) moose;
    (v) bear; or
    (vi) endangered species;
  (b) $750 per animal for:
    (i) elk; or
    (ii) threatened species;
  (c) $500 per animal for:
    (i) cougar;
    (ii) golden eagle;
    (iii) river otter; or
    (iv) Gila monster;
  (d) $400 per animal for:
    (i) pronghorn antelope; or
    (ii) deer;
  (e) $350 per animal for bobcat;
  (f) $100 per animal for:
    (i) swan;
    (ii) sandhill crane;
    (iii) turkey;
    (iv) pelican;
    (v) loon;
    (vi) egrets;
    (vii) herons;
    (viii) raptors, that are threatened or endangered;
    (ix) Utah milk snake; or
    (x) Utah mountain king snake;
  (g) $35 per animal for furbearers, except:
    (i) bobcat;
    (ii) river otter; and
    (iii) threatened or endangered species;
  (h) $15 per animal for game birds, except:
    (i) turkey;
    (ii) swan; and
    (iii) sandhill crane;
  (i) $10 per animal for game fish;
  (j) $8 per pound dry weight of processed brine shrimp including eggs; and
  (k) $5 per animal for protected wildlife not listed.
(3) If the court finds that restitution is inappropriate or if the value imposed is less than the suggested minimum value as provided in Subsection (2), the court shall make the reasons for the decision part of the record.
(4) The court shall order any person convicted of a third degree felony under Subsection 23-20-4(3)(a)(ii) to pay restitution. Minimum restitution values for trophy animals are as follows:

[ANYONE TEMPTED TO POACH A TROPHY ANIMAL SHOULD SEAR THESE DOLLAR AMOUNTS INTO THE CROSS HAIRS OF HIS MEMORY!]

(a) $30,000 per animal for bighorn, desert, or rocky mountain sheep;

(b) $8,000 per animal for deer;

(c) $8,000 per animal for elk;

(d) $6,000 per animal for moose or mountain goat;

(e) $6,000 per animal for bison; and

(f) $2,000 per animal for pronghorn antelope.

(5) Any restitution shall be remitted to the division and deposited in the Wildlife Resources Account.

(6) Restitution monies shall be used by the division for activities and programs to help stop poaching, including:

(a) educational programs on wildlife crime prevention;

(b) acquisition and development of wildlife crime detection equipment;

(c) operation and maintenance of anti-poaching projects; and

(d) wildlife law enforcement training.

(7) If restitution is required it shall be in addition to:

(a) any other fine or penalty imposed for a violation of any provision of this title; and

(b) any remedial action taken to revoke or suspend a person's license, permit, tag, or certificate of registration.

(8) A judgment imposed under this section constitutes a lien when recorded in the judgment docket and shall have the same effect and is subject to the same rules as a judgment for money in a civil action.

U.C.A. 23-20-12. Airplanes or terrestrial or aquatic vehicles -- Use in taking wildlife unlawful -- Exceptions.

"Plain Talk"

You can't hunt with an airplane[52] or any other motorized vehicle including hang gliders, ultra light aircraft, 4-wheelers and snowmobiles. However, people who are paralyzed or permanently required to use a wheelchair or crutches may be authorized to hunt from a vehicle.

ACTUAL TEXT

It is unlawful for any person to take any wildlife from an airplane or any other airborne vehicle or device or any motorized terrestrial or aquatic vehicle, including snowmobiles and other recreational vehicles, except as provided by this code or in the rules and regulations of the Wildlife Board. Provided, however, that an individual validly licensed to hunt who is a paraplegic, or otherwise permanently disabled so as to be permanently confined to a wheelchair or the use of crutches, may be authorized to hunt from a vehicle under terms and conditions specified by the Wildlife Board.

U.C.A. 23-20-13. Signs or equipment -- Damage or destruction unlawful.

"Plain Talk"

Don't "Westernize" (blast holes through) signs erected by the Division of Wildlife Resources, even if you don't like what the signs say.

ACTUAL TEXT

A person may not:

(1) shoot at, shoot, deface, damage, remove, or destroy any division signs or placards located in any part of this state; or

(2) damage, destroy, remove, or cause to be damaged, destroyed, or removed any equipment or devices owned, controlled, or operated by the Division of Wildlife Resources.

---

[52] If your hunting buddy is a helicopter pilot who spots elk herds for you at night with infrared equipment, stop it, you're cheating.

U.C.A. 23-20-14. Definitions -- Posted property -- Hunting by permission -- Entry on private land while hunting or fishing -- Violations -- Penalty -- Prohibitions inapplicable to officers -- Promotion of respect for private property.

"Plain Talk"

Before the 2000 Legislature, property owners had to make it clear to hunters that they could not trespass. They did this by painting their fence posts with bright yellow or fluorescent paint at all corners, where fishing streams cross property lines, at roads, gates and other rights of way entering the land. The 2000 Legislature changed this by making all cultivated land the same as land posted "no trespassing." Hunting on posted land is a class B misdemeanor (U.C.A. 23-20-3.5[not included in book]), but a subsequent conviction within 5 years could cause trespassing hunters to lose their right to hunt for up to 5 years.

ACTUAL TEXT [strikeout and underlining show new changes in 2000]

(1) As used in this section:

      (a) "Division" means the Division of Wildlife Resources.

      (b) "Cultivated land" means land which is readily identifiable as:

            (i) land whose soil is loosened or broken up for the raising of crops;

            (ii) land used for the raising of crops; or

            (iii) pasturage which is artificially irrigated.

      [(b)] (c) "Permission" means written authorization from the owner or person in charge to enter upon private land that is either cultivated or properly posted, and must include:

            (i) the signature of the owner or person in charge;

            (ii) the name of the person being given permission;

            (iii) the appropriate dates; and

            (iv) a general description of the property.

      [(c)] (d) "Properly posted" means that "No Trespassing" signs or a minimum of 100 square inches of bright yellow, bright orange, or fluorescent paint are displayed at all corners, fishing streams crossing property lines, roads, gates, and rights-of-way entering the land. If metal fence posts are used, the entire exterior side must be painted.

      (2) (a) While taking wildlife or engaging in wildlife related activities, a person may not:

            (i) without the permission of the owner or person in charge, enter upon privately owned [and properly posted] land [of any other person, firm, or corporation] that is cultivated or properly posted;

            (ii) refuse to immediately leave the private land if requested to do so by the owner or person in charge; or

            (iii) obstruct any entrance or exit to private property.

(b) "Hunting by permission cards" will be provided to landowners by the division upon request.

(c) A person may not post:

(i) private property he does not own or legally control: or

(ii) land that is open to the public as provided by Section 23-21-4.

(3) (a) A person convicted of violating any provision of Subsection (2) may have his license, tag, certificate of registration, or permit, relating to the activity engaged in at the time of the violation, revoked by a hearing officer.

(b) A hearing officer may construe any subsequent conviction which occurs within a five-year period as a flagrant violation and may prohibit the person from obtaining a new license, tag, certificate of registration, or permit for a period of up to five years.

(4) Subsection (2)(a) does not apply to peace or conservation officers in the performance of their duties.

(5) (a) The division shall provide information regarding owners' rights and sportsmen's duties:

(i) to anyone holding licenses, certificates of registration, tags, or permits to take wildlife: and

(ii) by using the public media and other sources.

(b) The restrictions in this section relating to trespassing shall be stated in all hunting and fishing proclamations issued by the Wildlife Board.

(6) Any person who violates any provision of Subsection (2) is guilty of a class B misdemeanor.

U.C.A. 23-20-15. Destruction of signs or inclosure on private land unlawful.

> **"Plain Talk"**
> Stop giving "NO TRESPASSING" signs the "Bonnie and Clyde" treatment.

ACTUAL TEXT

It is unlawful for any person, without the consent of the owner or person in charge of any privately owned land, to tear down, mutilate, or destroy any sign, signboard or other notice which regulates trespassing for purposes of hunting, trapping, or fishing on this land: or to, without such consent, tear down, deface, or destroy any fence or other inclosure on this privately owned land, or any gate or bars belonging to any such fence or inclosure.

U.C.A. 23-20-20. Children accompanied by adults while hunting with weapon.

"Plain Talk"

This code section explains when adults must accompany kids who are hunting. But it does not give you the "full picture." For a complete analysis of all of the state and federal laws placing restrictions on minors using firearms, carefully study Appendix F, at the end of this book. It is entitled "Youngsters, Guns and Ammo" and it compares, in table format, all of the laws and regulations relating to juveniles, firearms, hunting and possession of ammunition. Don't take your kids hunting without it.

"Accompany" means being close enough to see and talk to the minor (the rule doesn't tell us whether communicating by walkie talkie satisfies the "verbal communication" requirement). When hunting big game, kids 14 and older but less than 16, must be accompanied by a parent or guardian, or by an adult, 21 or older who is approved of by the parent. When these same kids are hunting small game, the accompanying adult must be 21 or older, but doesn't need to be a parent or guardian, or approved by a parent or guardian. Kids under 14 must always be accompanied by a parent or guardian, or by an adult, 21 or older who is approved of by the parent, while hunting.

Children under 12 cannot hunt protected wildlife, and I'm not aware of any exceptions.[53]

ACTUAL TEXT

(1) As used in this section, "accompanied" means at a distance within which visual and verbal communication is maintained for the purposes of advising and assisting.

(2) A person under the age of 14 years must be accompanied by his parent or legal guardian, or other responsible person of the age of 21 years or older and approved by his parent or guardian, while hunting with any weapon.

(3) A person of at least 14 years of age and under 16 years of age must be accompanied by his parent or legal guardian, or other responsible person of the age of 21 years or older and approved by his parent or guardian, while hunting big game with any weapon.

(4) A person of at least 14 years of age and under 16 years of age must be accompanied by a person of the age of 21 years or older while hunting wildlife, other than big game, with any weapon.

---

[53] This means they can't hunt rats, but they can hunt "unprotected wildlife." See how important it is to include all pests and varmints in the definition of "unprotected wildlife?"

(5) A person under the age of 12 years is not permitted to hunt for protected wildlife except as provided by rules of the Wildlife Board.

U.C.A. 23-20-29. Interference with hunting prohibited -- Action to recover damages -- Exceptions.

"Plain Talk"

Militant "Vegans," violent animal-"rights" activists, and other psychologically-unbalanced people who interfere with a hunt, are guilty of a class B misdemeanor.[54] Fortunately, this code section also permits hunters to sue these crazy people for civil damages. I wonder what a Panguitch jury would award an elk hunter who missed bagging a 6 X 7 trophy bull, a once-in-a-life-time opportunity, because one of these demented souls intentionally interfered with his or her hunt? Hopefully they would render a damage award large enough to bankrupt the radical organizations they belong to that advocate this kind of nonsense.

ACTUAL TEXT

(1) A person is guilty of a class B misdemeanor who intentionally interferes with the right of a person licensed and legally hunting under Title 23, Chapter 19, to take wildlife by driving, harassing, or intentionally disturbing any species of wildlife for the purpose of disrupting a legal hunt, trapping, or predator control.

(2) Any directly affected person or the state may bring an action to recover civil damages resulting from a violation of Subsection (1) or a restraining order to prevent a potential violation of Subsection (1).

(3) This section does not apply to incidental interference with a hunt caused by lawful activities including, but not limited to, ranching, mining, and recreation.

---

[54] Like that's any disincentive - hell, it should be a felony! When you mess up a person's hunt, you violate his right to get in touch with his inner self! Some sportsmen exhaust an entire year's vacation for a hunt. Hunting can provide an unsurpassed bonding experience between a father and his sons. Permit me to stop here before my blood pressure hits "point break."

R657-3-7. Nuisance Birds -- Nuisance Porcupine, Striped Skunk, and Squirrel.

"Plain Talk"

To hunt some species of "non-game" animals (like certain types of prairie dogs), hunters must have a "certificate of registration" from the state and/or a "federal permit" from the federal government. Neither the state nor the federal government requires such permits to hunt magpies, crows, porcupine, striped skunk or squirrel when their numbers create a nuisance or health hazard, or when they threaten certain plants and animals. The key words are, "when concentrated in such numbers and manner as to constitute a health hazard or other nuisance." These terms are not defined or explained in either Utah or corresponding federal regulations (Sections 50 C.F.R. 21.42 and 21.43). The precautions in the regulation for disposing of feathers and carcasses provide a strong argument that these animals always create a health hazard and may, therefore, be hunted at any time. Although the regulation contains language suggesting that only property owners protecting crops or domestic animals may kill these varmints ("allow any federal warden or conservation officer unrestricted access over the premises" . . . "kill crows or magpies . . . only on or over the threatened area"), the regulation plainly refers to "a person" rather than "a property owner or livestock owner" ("<u>A person</u> is not required to obtain a certificate of registration" . . ."<u>A person</u> may kill crows or magpies" . . ."<u>A person</u> may capture"). Therefore, there is a strong argument that anyone who follows these rules can hunt these animals.

ACTUAL TEXT

(1) (a) A person is not required to obtain a certificate of registration or a federal permit to take crows or magpies when found committing, or about to commit, depredations upon ornamental or shade trees, agricultural crops, livestock, or wildlife, or when concentrated in such numbers and manner as to constitute a health hazard or other nuisance, provided:

(i) none of the birds killed pursuant to this section, nor their plumage, are sold or offered for sale; and

(ii) any person taking crows or magpies shall:

(A) allow any federal warden or conservation officer unrestricted access over the premises where crows or magpies are taken; and

(B) furnish any information concerning the control operations to the division or federal official upon request.

(b) A person may kill crows or magpies only using a shotgun not larger than No. 10 gauge fired from the shoulder, and only on or over the threatened area.

(c) Crows and magpies killed pursuant to this section shall be collected immediately and must be disposed of at a landfill that accepts wildlife carcasses or must be buried or incinerated.

(d) This subsection incorporates Section 50 CFR 21.42 and 21.43, 1994 ed., by reference.

(2) (a) A person may capture, transport, and kill or release a nuisance porcupine, striped skunk, or squirrel without obtaining a certificate of registration.

(b) A nuisance porcupine, striped skunk, or squirrel may be released only as follows:

(i) within 48 hours of capture;

(ii) within the county in which it was captured; and

(iii) in a location where it does not pose a risk to human health or safety, or create other conflict with humans, agriculture, or other animals.

R657-3-7

Commentary

What?! Can you believe this? The state and federal government both allow Utahns to hunt magpies and crows? You won't find this in the hunting proclamation! But what does "depredating a shade tree" mean? This phrase is not defined either in the state or federal regulations or codes. The law is vague, so happy hunting! This regulation and the corresponding federal regulation should be amended to permit varmint hunters to shoot magpies and crows on the ground with varmint rifles. Because this Utah regulation parrots the corresponding federal regulation, it will take literally "an Act of Congress" to make the following changes:

(1) (a) A person is not required to obtain a certificate of registration or a federal permit to take crows or magpies ~~when found committing, or about to commit, depredations upon ornamental or shade trees, agricultural crops, livestock, or wildlife, or when concentrated in such numbers and manner as to constitute a health hazard or other nuisance,~~ provided:

. . .

(b) A person may kill crows or magpies ~~only using a shotgun not larger than No. 10 gauge fired from the shoulder, and only on or over the threatened area.~~ using any legal weapon. . . .

Did you know that Virginia has a "crow" season?

R657-5-4. Age Requirements and Restrictions.

> **"Plain Talk"**
>
> This regulation restates code section U.C.A. 23-20-20 discussed above. However, it goes a step further and permits a person 13 years of age to hunt big game if he turns 14 during the year of the hunt.

ACTUAL TEXT

(1) Any resident or nonresident 14 years of age or older may purchase a wildlife habitat authorization, and permit and tag to hunt big game. A person 13 years of age may purchase a wildlife habitat authorization, and permit and tag to hunt big game if that person's 14th birthday falls within the calendar year for which the wildlife habitat authorization, permit and tag are issued. A person must purchase a wildlife habitat authorization prior to obtaining a permit and tag to hunt big game.

(2)(a) A person 15 years of age or younger must be accompanied by his parent or legal guardian, or other responsible person 21 years of age or older and approved by his parent or guardian, while hunting big game with any weapon.

(b) As used in this section, "accompanied" means at a distance within which visual and verbal communication are maintained for the purposes of advising and assisting.

R657-5-9. Temporary Game Preserves [weapons restrictions].

> **"Plain Talk"**
>
> Unless you have a big game permit to hunt in special areas where trophy animals are found, wildlife officers do not want you to tempt yourself by possessing a gun or bow. Exceptions are upland game hunters carrying a shotgun loaded with birdshot, peace officers carrying service weapons and livestock owners protecting their herds.

ACTUAL TEXT

(1)(a) A person who does not have a valid permit to hunt on a temporary game preserve may not carry a firearm or archery equipment on any temporary game preserve while the respective hunts are in progress.

(b) "Carry" means having a firearm on your person while hunting in the field.

(2) As used in this section, "temporary game preserve" means all bull elk, buck pronghorn, moose, bison, bighorn sheep, Rocky Mountain goat, limited entry buck deer areas and cooperative wildlife management units, excluding incorporated areas, cities, towns and municipalities.

(3) Weapon restrictions on temporary game preserves do not apply to:

(a) a person licensed to hunt upland game or waterfowl provided the person complies with Rules R657-6 and R657-9 and the Upland Game

Proclamation and Waterfowl Proclamation, respectively, and possessing only legal weapons to take upland game and waterfowl;
   (b) livestock owners protecting their livestock; or
   (c) peace officers in the performance of their duties.

R657-5-10. Prohibited Weapons [for taking Big Game].

> **"Plain Talk"**
>
> Ya cain't use machine guns, night vision or laser sights to hunt big game. Unlike years past, there is no longer a limit on the number of bullets in a rifle magazine. Go ahead, use a fifty-shot clip, if you're that lousy of a shot!

ACTUAL TEXT
(1) A person may not use any weapon or device to take big game other than those expressly permitted in this rule.
(2) A person may not use:
   (a) a firearm capable of being fired fully automatic; or
   (b) any light enhancement device or aiming device that casts a beam of light.

R657-5-11. Rifles and Shotguns [Big Game].

> **"Plain Talk"**
>
> Hunters can harvest big game with rifles larger than a .22 rimfire firing expanding bullets and shotguns, 20 gauge and larger, shooting slugs[55] or number 4 buckshot.

ACTUAL TEXT
(1) The following rifles and shotguns may be used to take big game:
   (a) any rifle firing center-fire cartridges and expanding bullets; and
   (b) a shotgun, 20 gauge or larger, firing only number 4 buckshot or slug ammunition.

---

[55] For Jeopardy contestants, "What type of ammo generates sufficient recoil to give shooters a concussion?"

R657-5-12.　Handguns [Big Game].

> ### "Plain Talk"
> If you use a handgun to hunt big game, it has to be a "MAN'S GUN, not a little sissy gun."[56] Surprisingly, the Division of Wildlife Resources (DWR) considers any caliber less than .24 a "sissy gun," including a Thompson Contender shooting a .223 expanding bullet.

ACTUAL TEXT

(1) A handgun may be used to take deer and pronghorn, provided the handgun is a minimum of .24 caliber, fires a center-fire cartridge with an expanding bullet, has a barrel length of 6 inches or longer, and develops 500 foot-pounds of energy at the muzzle.

(2) A handgun may be used to take elk, moose, bison, bighorn sheep, and Rocky Mountain goat provided the handgun is a minimum of .24 caliber, fires a center-fire cartridge with an expanding bullet, has a barrel length of 6 inches or longer, and develops 500 foot-pounds of energy at 100 yards. **[Go ahead, make my day! Trade me your .454 Casull, for my .44 Magnum.]**

R657-5-13.　Muzzle Loaders [Big Game].

> ### "Plain Talk"
> You can hunt big game with a muzzle loader with some restrictions on the size of the lead slug. You can't take your muzzle loader on an archery hunt, and you can't possess modern firearms during a muzzle loader hunt. However, if you have an upland game permit, you can take a modern shotgun on the muzzle loader hunt (see R657-6-8). Ranchers on a muzzle loader hunt can use modern weapons to protect their livestock from predators. (new for 2001)

ACTUAL TEXT

(1) A muzzle loader may be used during any big game hunt, except an archery hunt, provided the muzzle loader:

    (a) can be loaded only from the muzzle;

    (b) has <u>open</u> sights, <u>peep sights</u>, or a fixed <u>non-magnifying</u> 1x scope;

    (c) has a single barrel;

    (d) has a minimum barrel length of 2~~1~~ <u>18</u> inches; and

    (e) is capable of being fired only once without reloading.

    <u>(f) powder and bullet, or powder, sabot and bullet are not bonded together as one unit for loading;</u>

---

[56] To quote El Secundo in the movie, *The Three Amigos.*

(g) is loaded with black powder or black powder substitute, which must not contain nitrocellulose based somkeless powder.

(2)   (a) A lead or expanding bullet or projectile of at least 40 caliber must be used to hunt big game.

(b) A 170 grain or ~~larger~~ heavier bullet, including sabots must be used for taking deer and pronghorn.

(c) A 210 grain or ~~larger~~ heavier bullet must be used for taking elk, moose, bison, bighorn sheep, and Rocky Mountain goat, except sabot bullets used for taking these species must be a minimum of 240 grains.

(3)   (a) A person who has obtained a muzzle loader permit may not possess or be in control of any firearm other than a muzzle loading rifle or have a firearm other than a muzzle loading rifle in his camp or motor vehicle during a muzzle loader hunt.

(b) The provisions of Subsection (a) do not apply to:

(i) a person licensed to hunt upland game or waterfowl provided the person complies with Rules R657-6 and R657-9 and the Upland Game Proclamation and Waterfowl Proclamation, respectively, and possessing only legal weapons to take upland game or waterfowl;

(ii) a person licensed to hunt big game species during hunts that coincide with the muzzleloader hunt; or

(iii) livestock owners protecting their livestock.

Commentary

So livestock owners can protect their cattle with modern weapons during a muzzle loader hunt, but fathers can't protect their children? Pancho don't theeenk that so good.

R657-5-14. Archery Equipment [Big Game - firearms restrictions only]

"Plain Talk"

This is a gun law (not bow law) book. . .so we covered only firearms restrictions and left the Robin Hood stuff out.

ACTUAL TEXT

(1) Archery equipment may be used during any big game hunt, except a muzzleloader hunt, provided:

. . .

(4)(a) A person who has obtained an archery permit may not possess or be in control of a **firearm** or have a **firearm** in his camp or motor vehicle during an archery hunt.

(b) The provisions of Subsection (a) do not apply to:

(i) a person licensed to hunt upland game or waterfowl provided the person complies with Rules R657-6 and R657-9 and the Upland Game

Proclamation and Waterfowl Proclamation, respectively, and possessing only legal weapons to take upland game or waterfowl;

(ii) a person licensed to hunt big game species during hunts that coincide with the archery hunt; or

(iii) livestock owners protecting their livestock. [but not dads protecting their kids]

R657-6-9. Firearms . . .[Upland Game]

"Plain Talk"

Upland game means game birds and game rabbits (not including jack rabbits). You can shoot upland game with a shotgun, a handgun (shooting BBs, not bullets) or a bow, but not a crossbow or a rifle. However, you cannot shoot migratory birds with a handgun (see R657-9-9). If you are hunting waterfowl, you must "plug" your shotgun so that it can only hold three shells. You can shoot game rabbits (cotton tails and snowshoe hares) with any firearm except a machine gun. You cannot spotlight or use laser sights to hunt upland game. [archery regs omitted]

ACTUAL TEXT

(1) A person may not use any weapon or device to take upland game except as provided in this section.

(2)(a) Upland game may be taken with . . .a shotgun no larger than 10 gauge, or a handgun. Loads for shotguns and handguns must be one-half ounce or more of shot size between no. 2 and no. 8, except:

(i) migratory game birds may not be taken with a shotgun capable of holding more than three shells, unless it is plugged with a one-piece filler, incapable of removal without disassembling the gun, so its total capacity does not exceed three shells;

(ii) wild turkey may be taken only with a . . . a shotgun no larger than 10 gauge and no smaller than 20 gauge, firing shot sizes between BB and no. 6;

(iii) cottontail rabbit and snowshoe hare may be taken with any firearm not capable of being fired fully automatic;   between BB and no. 6;

(iii) cottontail rabbit and snowshoe hare may be taken with any firearm not capable of being fired fully automatic;

. . .

(iv) only shotguns, firing shot sizes no. 4 or smaller, may be used on temporary game preserves as specified in the Big Game Proclamation.

. . .

(3) A person may not use:

(a) a firearm capable of being fired fully automatic; or

(b) any light enhancement device or aiming device that casts a beam of light.

R657-6-11. Firearms . . . in State Wildlife Management Areas.

> **"Plain Talk"**
> You can't pack a gun in these areas except during hunting season.

ACTUAL TEXT

A person may not possess a firearm . . .except during the specified hunting seasons or as authorized by the Division on the following wildlife management areas: Bear River Bottoms, Bud Phelps, Castle Dale, Huntington, Cedar, Goshen Warm Springs, James Walter Fitzgerald, Logan, Mallard Springs, Manti Meadows, Milford, Montez Creek, Nephi, Pahvant, Redmond Marsh, Richfield, Roosevelt, Scott M. Matheson Wetland Preserve, Vernal, and Willard Bay.

R657-6-12. Firearms . . . State Waterfowl Management Areas.

> **"Plain Talk"**
> You can't take a gun in these areas except during hunting season unless the Division of Wildlife Resources tells you otherwise. During hunting season you can carry a shotgun, but no other type of weapon.

ACTUAL TEXT

(1) A person may not possess a firearm . . . except during the specified waterfowl hunting seasons or as authorized by the Division on the following waterfowl management areas: Bicknell Bottoms, Brown's Park, Clear Lake, Desert Lake, Farmington Bay, Harold S. Crane, Howard Slough, Locomotive Springs, Mills Meadows, Ogden Bay, Powell Slough, Public Shooting Grounds, Salt Creek, Stewart Lake, and Timpie Springs.

(2) During the waterfowl hunting seasons, a shotgun is the only firearm that may be held in possession.

R657-6-13. Shooting Hours.

> **"Plain Talk"**
> No, this law does not refer to recycling old alarm clocks at the pistol range. Hunting hours generally begin one-half hour before sunrise until one hour after sunset with few exceptions.

ACTUAL TEXT

(1)(a) Except as provided in Subsection (b), shooting hours for upland game are as follows:

(i) Mourning dove, band-tailed pigeon and sandhill crane may be taken only between one-half hour before official sunrise through official sunset.

(ii) Sage grouse, ruffed grouse, blue grouse, sharp-tailed grouse, white-tailed ptarmigan, chukar partridge, Hungarian partridge, pheasant, quail, wild turkey, cottontail rabbit, and snowshoe hare may be taken only between one-half hour before official sunrise through one-half hour after official sunset.

(b) A person must add to or subtract from the official sunrise and sunset depending on the geographic location of the state. Specific times are provided in a time zone map in the proclamation of the Wildlife Board for taking upland game.

(2) Pheasant and quail may not be taken prior to 8 a.m. on the opening day of the pheasant and quail seasons.

(3) A person may not discharge a firearm on state owned lands adjacent to the Great Salt Lake, state waterfowl management areas or on federal refuges between official sunset through one-half hour before official sunrise.

R657-9-9. Firearms [Ducks and Other Migratory Birds].

"Plain Talk"
You can kill ducks and other migratory birds with a shotgun or a bow, but not a host of other exotic weapons.

ACTUAL TEXT

(1) Migratory game birds may be taken with a shotgun or archery tackle.

(2) Migratory game birds may not be taken with a . . . rifle, pistol, swivel gun, shotgun larger than 10 gauge, punt gun, battery gun, machine gun, . . . **[What? Did they spot a couple of dudes in a "Rat Patrol" jeep with a swiveling .50 machine gun hunting ducks with tracers?]**

(3) Migratory game birds may not be taken with a shotgun of any description capable of holding more than three shells, unless it is plugged with a one-piece filler, incapable of removal without disassembling the gun, so its total capacity does not exceed three shells.

R657-9-11. Use of Firearms on State Waterfowl Management Areas.

"Plain Talk"
You can never possess any firearm other than a shotgun in these waterfowl areas and if it ain't duck season ya can't even tote yer shotgun.

ACTUAL TEXT

(1) A person may not possess a firearm on the following waterfowl management areas any time of the year except during the specified waterfowl hunting seasons or as authorized by the division:

    (a) Box Elder County - Harold S. Crane, Locomotive Springs, Public Shooting Grounds, and Salt Creek;

    (b) Daggett County - Brown's Park;

    (c) Davis County - Farmington Bay, Howard Slough, and Ogden Bay;

    (d) Emery County - Desert Lake;

    (e) Millard County - Clear Lake;

    (f) Tooele County - Timpie Springs;

    (g) Uintah County - Stewart Lake;

    (h) Utah County - Powell Slough;

    (i) Wayne County - Bicknell Bottom; and

    (j) Weber County - Ogden Bay and Harold S. Crane.

(2) During the waterfowl hunting seasons, a shotgun is the only firearm that may be in possession.

R657-10-7. Firearms [Cougar Hunt].

"Plain Talk"

Cougar hunters can hunt the big cats with anything (including a .22 ; compare restrictions on bears below) but a machine gun. **[Isn't full auto a little tough on the pelt anyway?]**

ACTUAL TEXT

    A person may use the following to take cougar:

    (1) any firearm not capable of being fired fully automatic;

. . .

R657-10-26. Cougar Pursuit.

"Plain Talk"

Pursuit means "chase." Leave your guns home so you won't be tempted to shoot the kitty when you become the "chasee!"

ACTUAL TEXT

    (1) Cougar may be pursued only by persons who have obtained an annual cougar pursuit permit. The cougar pursuit permit does not allow a person to kill a cougar.

    (2) A person may not:

. . .

    (c) possess a firearm or any device that could be used to kill a cougar while pursuing cougar.

. . .

Commentary

> A similar regulation relating to pursuit of bear, R657-33-27, also prohibits possession of a firearm. Both of these are regs are probably preempted by state statutes giving a person a right to possess a firearm to protect himself and others. These regs should not prohibit possession of a firearm. Rather, they should prevent the injuring of a bear or cougar except in legitimate self defense (unless DWR considers bear and cougar more valuable than humans. Has DWR turned vegan?)

R657-12-4. Obtaining Authorization to Hunt from a Vehicle.

> ### "Plain Talk"
> Only those permanently confined to a wheelchair or crutches and amputees missing one or both legs may hunt from a vehicle. They have to be accompanied by a licensed hunter who is physically capable of helping them retrieve the animals they have shot. They cannot load their guns until they are ready to fire at game animals and they can't shoot on or across a road.

ACTUAL TEXT

(1) A person may receive a certificate of registration to take wildlife from a vehicle who is paraplegic, or otherwise permanently disabled so as to be permanently confined to a wheelchair or the use of crutches, or who has lost either or both lower extremities.

(2)(a) Applicants for the certificate of registration must appear in person at a division office and provide proof of disability as provided in Subsections R657-12-3(3)(a), (b), or (d).

(b) Certificates of registration may be renewed annually.

(3) Wildlife may be taken from a vehicle under the following conditions:

(a) Only those persons with a certificate of registration in possession allowing them to hunt from a vehicle may discharge a firearm or bow from, within, or upon any motorized terrestrial vehicle;

(b) Shooting from a vehicle on or across any established roadway is prohibited;

(c)(i) Firearms must be carried in an unloaded condition, and a round may not be placed in the firearm until the act of firing begins; and

(ii) Arrows must remain in the quiver until the act of shooting begins; and

(d) Certificate of registration holders must be accompanied by, and hunt with, a licensed hunter who is physically capable of assisting the certificate of registration holder in recovering wildlife.

(4) Certificate holders must comply with all other laws and rules pertaining to hunting wildlife.

R657-13-11. Restrictions on Taking Fish and Crayfish.

> **"Plain Talk"**
> In case you hadn't noticed, Jaws doesn't live here in Utah, so you can't shoot fish with guns.

ACTUAL TEXT

. .
(2) A person may not . . . use a . . . firearm, pellet gun . . . to take fish or crayfish.
. . .

R657-19-6. Utah Prairie Dog Provisions.

> **"Plain Talk"**
> You can hunt a certain species of prairie dog with a firearm as permitted in a "certificate of registration" obtained from DWR.

ACTUAL TEXT

(1)(a) A person may not take a Utah Prairie dog, Cynomys parvidens, without first obtaining a certificate of registration.

(2)(a) A person may take Utah prairie dogs with a firearm during daylight hours or by trapping as specified on the certificate of registration.
. . .

R657-20-39. Firearms [on Raptor Hunts].

> **"Plain Talk"**
> When you're hunting with your falcon, leave your gun at home (even if it shoots Black Talons).

ACTUAL TEXT

A person may not possess a firearm while pursuing any quarry with a raptor.

R657-22-18. Age Restrictions [on Commercial or Private Hunting Preserves].

> **"Plain Talk"**
> Your child must be at least 12 to hunt at the pheasant farm (or any other private hunting preserve for that matter). For children under 14, either a parent or guardian or someone 21 years or older, approved by a parent or guardian has to accompany the child. For

kids 14 or 15 years old, the parents don't have to accompany the child, but someone 21 or older does. "Accompany" means to be close enough to communicate with. Remember, these are hunting regulations. If the child simply possesses a dangerous weapon and is not hunting, there is more leeway as to who needs to accompany him. Rules pertaining to kids and guns are spread all over the code and regs, so don't forget to study Appendix F where we put it all together.

ACTUAL TEXT

(1) A person must be 12 years of age or older to hunt on commercial hunting areas.

(2)(a) A person 13 years of age or younger must be accompanied by his parent or legal guardian, or other responsible person 21 years of age or older and approved by his parent or guardian, while hunting with any weapon.

(b) A person 14 or 15 years of age must be accompanied by a person 21 years of age or older while hunting with any weapon.

(3) As used in this section, "accompanied" means at a distance within which visual and verbal communication is maintained for the purposes of advising and assisting.

R657-33-6. Firearms [Bear Hunt]

> **"Plain Talk"**
> You can use any gun to kill a bear, except a machine gun or a .22(including .22 Magnum).

ACTUAL TEXT
(1) A person may use the following to take bear:
(a) any firearm not capable of being fired fully automatic, except a firearm using a rimfire cartridge; . . .

R657-33-14. Use of Bait.

> **"Plain Talk"**
> If you have an archery permit to bait bear, you can't have a gun (leave your .44 Mag. under your pillow) in your possession. If you do and you are on federal land, you run the risk of being charged with a federal offense. (Doesn't this make you "high risk" for life insurance?)

ACTUAL TEXT
(1)(a) A person who has obtained a limited entry bear archery permit may use archery tackle only, even when hunting bear away from the bait station.

. . .

(c) Bear lured to a bait station may not be taken with any firearm or the use of dogs.

. . .

(6) Violations of this rule and the proclamation of the Wildlife Board for taking and pursuing bear concerning baiting on federal lands may be a violation of federal regulations and prosecuted under federal law.

R657-33-23. Livestock Depredation.

> **"Plain Talk"**
> Ranchers can kill a bear that is threatening or killing livestock with any firearm authorized to take bear [anything larger than .22 rimfire except a machine gun - see R657-33-6 above].

ACTUAL TEXT
(1) If a bear is harassing, chasing, disturbing, harming, attacking or killing livestock, or has committed such an act within the past 72 hours:
(a) in depredation cases, the livestock owner, an immediate family member or an employee of the owner on a regular payroll, and not hired specifically to take bear, may kill the bear;

. . .

(3) A depredating bear may be taken with any weapon authorized for taking bear.

. . .

R657-33-27. Bear Pursuit.

> **Plain Talk"**
> This hunt is for fun, so it's illegal to have a gun in your possession.[57]

ACTUAL TEXT

(1) Bear may be pursued only by persons who have obtained a bear pursuit permit. The bear pursuit permit does not allow a person to kill a bear.

. . .

(3) A person may not:

. . .

(c) possess a **firearm** or any device that could be used to kill a bear while pursuing bear.

. . .

R657-46-5. Use of Pen-Reared Game Birds for Dog Training.

> **"Plain Talk"**
> You can train a bird dog using pen-raised game birds, but you cannot

ACTUAL TEXT

(1) A person may train a dog using legally acquired pen-reared game birds provided:

(b) no live ammunition is in possession of the person or persons engaged in training the dogs.

(6) A person or group of persons may not use more than three firearms at any time, except four firearms may be used when training retrievers using the American Kennel Club quad flyer test.

R657-46-6. Use of Wild Game Birds for Dog Training.

> **"Plain Talk"**
> You can train your dog using wild game birds, but your firearm is restricted to a pistol loaded with blanks.

ACTUAL TEXT

(1) A person may train a dog on wild game birds provided:

(i) must not possess a firearm, except a pistol firing blank cartridges;

(ii) must comply with city and county ordinances pertaining to the discharge of any firearm;

. . .

R651-614-5. Hunting with Firearms [near State Park Facilities]

> **"Plain Talk"**
> You can't hunt with rifles or handguns within 1 mile of a state park "facility." This means buildings, camps, picnic sites, overlook, golf courses, boat ramps and developed beaches. You can't hunt with shotguns and archery equipment within a quarter mile of those types of areas.

ACTUAL TEXT
Hunting with rifles and handguns on park areas designated open is prohibited within one mile of all park area facilities including but not limited to buildings, camp/picnic sites, overlooks, golf courses, boat ramps, and developed beaches. Shotguns and archery equipment are prohibited within one-quarter mile of above stated areas.

> R651-614-5
> **Commentary**
> This section is too broad. It prohibits HUNTING, whereas, it should only prohibit the DISCHARGE OF A WEAPON. If you are legally hunting in a state park, you may have to walk within a mile or quarter mile of a park facility. If you do not discharge a weapon, the law should not punish you. By passing through the mile perimeter, you are technically still hunting, but you are no danger to anyone unless you discharge your weapon. Therefore, the regulation should be amended to say:
>
> Hunting with The discharge of rifles and handguns on park areas designated open is prohibited within one mile of all park area facilities including but not limited to buildings, camp/picnic sites, overlooks, golf courses, boat ramps, and developed beaches. The discharge of S shotguns and archery equipment are is prohibited within one-quarter mile of above stated areas.

R651-612-1. Weapons Prohibited [in State Park].

> **"Plain Talk"**
> You can't possess a loaded gun in a state park unless you are on a legal hunt or are a concealed weapon permit holder. Although this law was changed to conform to the concealed weapon statutes, the regulation still conflicts with the state law that preserves a person's right to protect his camp with a loaded firearm.

ACTUAL TEXT

Possession or use of firearms, including air and gas powered types, traps and all other devices capable of launching a projectile which could immobilize, injure, or kill any person or animal or damage property are prohibited in the park system unless:

(1) The weapon or device is unloaded and cased or otherwise packed away to prevent its use in the park area.

(2) The weapon or device is being used for the legal pursuit of wildlife, see R651-614, or in accordance with UCA 53-5-701 Concealed Weapons Act.

(3) The weapon or device is being used by authorized enforcement officers in the performance of their official duties.

R651-612-1

Commentary

This regulation was recently amended to conform to the Concealed Weapons Act. Nevertheless, it still conflicts with the code section that permits persons who are not concealed weapon permit holders to keep loaded weapons to protect their camps. This regulation should be further amended so that it doesn't violate the uniformity statute, U.C.A. 76-10-501, discussed in Chapter VII above. Only the Legislature has the power to regulate the use of firearms, NOT the Director of State Parks. A paragraph (4)should be added to read:

(4) This section shall also not apply to persons protecting their temporary residences and camps with a loaded firearm as permitted under U.C.A. 76-10-511.

Pancho's Wisdom

Bureaucrats "promulgating" regulations outside the authority given to them by Congress or a Legislature is kinda like conceiving children out of wedlock. The regulations drafted are bastards and those who promulgate them should have to pay "child support" to those who are illegally arrested for violating them.

Proposition 5

"Plain Talk"

Proposition 5, a constitutional amendment passed by Utah voters on November 3, 1998, makes it more difficult to change Utah's hunting laws through a process known as a "statewide initiative." A statewide initiative allows the "people," as opposed to the "Legislature," to initiate changes in the law. Before a statewide initiative can be placed upon the ballot during a general election, its proponents have to collect enough signatures to total 10% of the number of people who voted for governor in the last general election in at least 20 of Utah's 29 counties (U.C.A. 20A-7-201). Once the signatures are obtained, the proposed changes in the law can be placed on the ballot for vote of the people. This process completely bypasses the Legislature. The technique has been used in the past by various anti-hunting organizations who, through a media blitz and incomplete information, have persuaded voters to make drastic changes in the hunting laws of other states. Proposition 5 does not prevent either the Legislature or the Division of Wildlife Resources from changing Utah hunting laws. It prevents sweeping changes in the hunting laws as a result of a statewide voter initiative, unless the initiative passes by 66 2/3% of the vote rather than by a simple majority. In short, it makes it a lot harder for anti-hunters to stampede voters into passing anti-hunting laws. Because Proposition 5 was a constitutional amendment, two-thirds of each house of the Utah Legislature had to vote for it before it could be placed on the 1998 ballot. This suggests a strong, philosophical foundation in our Legislature favoring wholesome ideals such as hunting, the individual right to bear arms in self defense, and trusting law-abiding citizens with concealed weapons. Our current legislators didn't get elected in a vacuum. Their beliefs reflect those of their constituents. Utahns and their elected representatives know that the answer to violent crime is to make criminals, not law-abiding citizens, accountable. This is why, despite repeated verbal attacks by First-Amendment-loving-Second-Amendment-hating news editors, the Legislature refuses to place further restrictions on concealed weapon permit holders. This shows great wisdom and commitment to virtuous ideals in the face of unrelenting pressure from a misguided press.

ACTUAL TEXT

ARTICLE VI, SECTION 1
Be it resolved by the Legislature of the state of Utah, two-thirds of all members elected to each of the two houses voting in favor thereof:

Section 1. It is proposed to amend Utah Constitution **Article VI, Section 1,** to read:
Article VI, Section 1. [Power vested in Senate, House and People.]
The Legislative power of the State shall be vested:
1. In a Senate and House of Representatives which shall be designated the Legislature of the State of Utah.
2. In the people of the State of Utah, as hereinafter stated:

The legal voters or such fractional part thereof, of the State of Utah as may be provided by law, under such conditions and in such manner and within such time as may be provided by law, may initiate any desired legislation and cause the same to be submitted to a vote of the people for approval or rejection, or may require any law passed by the Legislature (except those laws passed by a two-thirds vote of the members elected to each house of the Legislature) to be submitted to the voters of the State before such law shall take effect. *Legislation initiated to allow, limit, or prohibit the taking of wildlife or the season for or method of taking wildlife shall be adopted upon approval of two-thirds of those voting.*

The legal voters or such fractional part thereof as may be provided by law, of any legal subdivision of the State, under such conditions and is such manner and within such time as may be provided by law, may initiate any desired legislation and cause the same to be submitted to a vote of the people of said legal subdivision for approval or rejection, or may require any law or ordinance passed by the law making body of said legal subdivision to be submitted to the voters thereof before such law or ordinance shall take effect.

(Note: This amendment took effect on January 1, 1999)

CHAPTER X:
CIVIL LIABILITY ARISING FROM USE OF FIREARMS

Pancho's Wisdom
A person should have a gun for every occasion. . . sometimes you feel like a Glock and sometimes you don't!

Civil liability makes people ACCOUNTABLE for their actions. ACCOUNTABILITY provides a disincentive to those who carelessly or intentionally misuse firearms to injure or kill others. This in turn, reduces the number of injuries and deaths. In contrast, gun control laws do nothing more than deprive law-abiding citizens of weapons, making them more vulnerable to criminal attack. If criminal and civil laws hold violent felons ACCOUNTABLE for their actions, we DON'T NEED gun control.

Up to this chapter, we have been talking about criminal penalties under Utah's gun laws. If you break a criminal law, you go to jail or pay a fine. Civil liability is different. If you negligently (carelessly) hurt someone, you become liable to that person for money damages. Because neither the law nor the wrongdoer can restore an injured person's health, the law imposes an award of money damages in an attempt to restore an injured person to his or her pre-injury life style. For example, if an injured person earned $30,000 a year before an injury, but can only earn $15,000 because of an accident, the defendant ("tortfeasor") is required to make up the difference. If the injured person is thirty years from retirement at the time of injury, it could be expensive for the defendant. Civil law (also called "tort law") also requires the defendant to reimburse the injured person for all out-of-pocket expenses such as medical bills, rehabilitation expenses, and property damage.

Because of an intense propaganda campaign by the insurance industry, the idea of civil liability offends many people. They think there are too many lawsuits. Although it's true that some people take advantage of the system, civil liability is GOOD because it makes wrongdoers ACCOUNTABLE for their actions. This beats taking gun rights away from innocent, law-abiding citizens in an attempt to reduce "gun violence." Think about it, which is the greater deterrent -- getting sued for a $100,000 for negligently injuring someone or getting fined $1,000 for committing a misdemeanor (two pizzas or one pizza)?

The concept of accountability is best illustrated by the criminal and civil trials involving O.J. Simpson. If O.J. actually killed Nicole Simpson and Ron Goldman, one might say that he "got away with murder." But he didn't really, because the victims' families won enormous civil verdicts against Simpson. The civil justice system held Simpson accountable for his actions, even though the criminal justice system failed (assuming Simpson is guilty - duh). Likewise, if a person intentionally or negligently injures someone with a firearm, the victim should not have to bear the burden of the injury; the aggressor should.

A. Negligence in General

Liability for negligence arises from the notion that everyone has a duty to use "reasonable care" to avoid injuring others. Utah Courts use the following jury instruction to explain to juries what negligence means:

> A person has a duty to use reasonable care to avoid injuring other people or property. "Negligence" simply means the failure to use reasonable care. Reasonable care does not require extraordinary caution or exceptional skill. Reasonable care is what an ordinary, prudent person uses in similar situation. **[You don't have to be an "A" student, just a "C" student.]**
>
> The amount of care that is considered "reasonable" depends on the situation. You must decide what a prudent person with similar knowledge would do in a similar situation. Negligence may arise in acting **[like shooting wildly into the bushes]** or in failing to act **[like failing to lock your guns away when your child's hyperactive-teenage-mutant-ninja- neighbor friend comes to your house for pizza and video games].**
>
> A party whose injuries or damages are caused by another party's negligent conduct may recover compensation from the negligent party for those injuries or damages. **[Comments in bold and brackets are mine.]**

The weapons laws we discussed in Chapter VII create civil, as well as criminal, liability. For example, it is a misdemeanor to carry a loaded firearm in a vehicle (unless you have a concealed weapon permit). If the loaded gun you leave in your car accidentally discharges injuring a passenger, a jury could find you negligent for violating the law prohibiting loaded firearms in a vehicle.

In a civil case, the fact finder, whether a jury or a judge, also decides if the injured person was negligent. In the example above, if the injured passenger knew the guns were loaded and did nothing about it, a jury would have to decide if this was negligent, and if so, how much of the fault to allocate to the injured passenger. The jury instruction generally given states:

> If you find that the defendant was negligent, you must decide if the plaintiff **[the injured person]** was also negligent. If the plaintiff was negligent and the plaintiff's negligence was a proximate cause of the plaintiff's own injuries, the plaintiff's negligence must be compared to the negligence of the defendant.
>
> A plaintiff whose negligence is less than 50 percent of the total negligence causing the plaintiff's injuries may still recover compensation, but the amount will be reduced by the percentage of the plaintiff's negligence. If the plaintiff's negligence is equal to or greater than [the negligence of the defendant] [the total negligence of all defendants], then the plaintiff may recover nothing. For example, if you find the plaintiff's negligence was 30 percent of all negligence causing the injuries, then the plaintiff's recovery will be reduced by 30 percent. On the other hand, if you find the plaintiff's negligence is 50 percent or greater, then the plaintiff will recover nothing.

You can see how the civil law reflected in these two jury instructions holds all wrongdoers, including those injured, accountable for their own actions. In Utah, if the fault of the injured person is equal to or greater than the fault of the person who injured him, the injured person loses the case and collects nothing.

B. Negligence Specifically Related to the Use of Firearms

It would be impossible to try to describe or predict every possible scenario in which gun owners could be held liable for negligence. As explained above, any act of carelessness causing injury could subject a person to liability. The question of whether or not a person's actions rise to the level of negligence or carelessness depends upon the circumstances of each case. Just because an injury occurs does not mean someone was negligent.

For example, suppose a deer hunter on a mountain sees a deer below him in a box canyon. Looking through binoculars, he sees no hunters near the deer. Because he will be shooting downhill into the canyon, he believes his bullets will drill into the ground if he misses. He shoots having no reason to believe his bullet will injure another hunter. The bullet misses the deer and unexpectedly hits a large flat rock submerged ½ inch below the dirt. It ricochets out of the ravine and hits a fellow deer hunter in an adjoining canyon. Is the shooter negligent? Probably not. He is only required to act reasonably, not perfectly. The law does not require him to foresee the unforeseeable.

Let's change the facts slightly. Suppose this same hunter takes an "over the hill" shot, discouraged by most safety instructors, and hits another person. Is he liable? He probably is, depending upon how foreseeable it is for someone to be in harm's way. If the shooter is hunting 420 miles from nowhere, a jury would be less likely to find him negligent than if a freeway were located just over the hill from where he took the shot.

Another hunting example illustrates the concept of "comparative negligence." Section (6) of the Utah archery regulations, section R657-5-41, requires bow hunters to wear hunter orange if a rifle hunt is in progress during a bow hunt:

> (5) Hunter orange fluorescent material must be worn if a centerfire rifle hunt is also in progress in the same area. Archers are cautioned to study rifle hunt tables and identify these areas described in the . . .[hunting] proclamation . . .

Suppose a bow hunter, who is not wearing flourescent orange, hides himself in a thicket during a rifle hunt. During the hunt, a rifle hunter, who doesn't see the bow hunter, shoots him. A jury will have to decide (1) whether the rifle hunter was negligent for failing to see the bow hunter, (2) whether the bow hunter was negligent for failing to wear hunter orange as required by the hunting regulations, (3) whether the negligence of either of the parties caused the injury, (4) what percentage of fault each hunter should be assessed and finally, (5) what the injured bow hunter's damages are.

Several factors could influence how a jury might decide these issues. If, for example, the bow hunter had been so well hidden that no one would have seen him, a jury would probably conclude the rifle hunter was not negligent. That would end the case; the injured bow hunter would lose and the rifle hunter would win. Suppose, however, four other hunters saw the bow hunter and they testified they didn't know how the rifle hunter could have failed to see him. Under these circumstances a jury would probably find the rifle hunter negligent for failing to notice the bow hunter.

After such a finding, the jury would then be required to decide whether the bow hunter was negligent. Anyone who has ever been on a general Utah deer hunt knows that wearing hunter orange is vital; a hunter takes his life into his own hands without it. If, during a rifle hunt, a bow hunter wears camouflage rather than fluorescent orange, he does so at his own peril. Under these circumstances, a jury would probably conclude the bow hunter was negligent. If the jurors believed the rifle hunter would have seen the bow hunter had he been wearing fluorescent orange, then they must conclude that the failure to wear orange caused the accident. At this point the jury would have to compare the fault between the hunters. If they decided the rifle hunter's fault was less than or equal to that of the bow hunter, the bow hunter would recover nothing. If, however, the jury decided the rifle hunter was at least 51% at fault, the bow hunter would recover the percentage of his damages assessed against the rifle hunter. For example, if the rifle hunter were found 75% at fault and the damages were $200,000, the verdict would be $150,000, a reduction by 25% because of the bow hunter's own negligence.

The following two cases involved my own clients. The first case occurred in Birmingham, Alabama. My client kept a .38 caliber revolver in his glove compartment because he worked in the bad part of town. One weekend, several friends came over to my client's home and began working on their cars. Coincidentally, one of the friends had a blank gun that looked REMARKABLY like my client's real gun. The young men, all in their late teens, passed the blank gun back and forth, "shooting" each other with blanks. Sometime later, my client, who owned the real gun, pulled it out of the glove compartment and showed it to his friend who owned the blank gun. He said something like, "I'll bet this gun looks real." The friend thought he said, "this gun really looks real." The friend grabbed the real gun out of my client's hands, thinking it was his own blank gun. Before my client could exclaim that the gun was his own real gun, the blank gun's owner shot him in the stomach with it. The round-nose lead bullet pierced the right side of the abdomen, missed most vital organs including the right kidney and exited out of the right lower part of the back, just above the waist. His doctors, worried about internal bleeding, performed exploratory surgery carving a nasty incision from his diaphragm to his navel. His recovery was extremely painful(the incision hurt more than the bullet).

My client filed a claim against his friend's homeowners insurance alleging the friend had been negligent for grabbing the real gun out of his hands and shooting him with it. The friend's insurance adjuster argued, on the other hand, that my client had been contributorily negligent for pulling the real gun out of his glove box without telling the others about it. In Alabama, unlike Utah, if the plaintiff (injured person) is found to be even 1% at fault he loses the case. Because we believed there was a substantial risk that a jury would find the client partially responsible for his own injury, we settled out of court for a sum substantially below the friend's homeowners insurance policy limits. As a result of the negotiations, the civil justice system held both boys accountable for their actions. The defendant, through his insurance company, had to pay part of my client's medical bills, but my client had to accept far less than his injury was worth because of his own carelessness.

In the second case, my client, who was in his early teens, was visiting a friend of the same age. During the visit and while my client was waiting in his friend's bedroom, the friend took a .12 gauge shotgun out of his father's closet. My client did not know his friend was playing with his dad's guns. Assuming it wasn't loaded, the defendant walked into his room where my client was playing with a model airplane, pointed the shotgun at close range and pulled the trigger. Luckily, the gun was pointed at my client's shoulder rather than his face or chest. The blast blew a 1 inch round hole in his left shoulder, destroying 1/3 of his clavicle. Although there was little disability, the scarring was unsightly and the boy will have lead pellets in his shoulder for the rest of his life. I notified the friend's father's homeowners insurance company of the claim. We had two theories of negligence (1) the father had been negligent for leaving a loaded shotgun accessible to children and (2) the son was negligent, indeed reckless, for pointing a gun at my client and pulling the trigger. The insurance adjuster agreed my client was probably not negligent, because he didn't know his friend would be getting into his dad's guns. The only real issue was the value of my client's injuries.

After the adjuster and I researched the range of verdicts and settlements involving similar injuries, we settled the case amicably without taking the case to trial. The settlement was several times greater than medical bills, because my client was not responsible for the injury. Furthermore, the injuries were serious and permanent. Because my client was a minor, the settlement required court approval. After the judge was satisfied that the best interests of the child would be met by the settlement, he approved it and we set up a trust fund for the boy. Again, the civil justice system held the wrongdoers accountable for their actions and helped to compensate an injured person for injuries suffered through no fault of his own.

It is important to note here that the homeowners insurance in both cases would not have been contractually obligated to pay a verdict or settlement if the shootings had been intentional rather than accidental. It is against public policy for people to avoid accountability for their intentional acts of violence through insurance coverage.

Both cases depict how the civil law makes people accountable for their actions whether they cause an injury to others or to themselves. And certainly, both cases show the wisdom of having homeowner's insurance. Homeowners insurance spreads the risk of household injury among thousands of insureds, rather than requiring a negligent person to bear the entire burden of an injury himself.

C. Negligent Storage of Firearms
(Accessibility to Children)

The following case shows how a jury allocated fault and awarded damages to a child injured because an adult left a loaded gun in an unlocked drawer. Think about how a gun safe or trigger lock might have prevented this boy's injury.

12 year-old Gohl (his first name was not given in the report),[58] visited his friend, Raymond Morales, who lived with his grandfather, Raymon Morales. While playing in the house alone, Gohl and Raymond discovered a semiautomatic pistol and a clip of bullets in an unlocked drawer. The pistol had been left in the drawer by the grandfather's brother, Dolphin. When Dolphin finished visiting his brother, he forgot to take his pistol with him.

Gohl and Raymond took the pistol to a nearby ditch to shoot. Gohl put the clip into the pistol. Raymond, who was apparently unfamiliar with the gun, accidentally pointed the gun at Gohl while trying to figure out how to work the safety. The gun fired unexpectedly, hitting Gohl in the right nostril.

The bullet pierced the front of his skull, shoving bone fragments into his brain. Neurosurgeons had to remove almost 25% of the right temporal lobe of his brain. Gohl now suffers from brain damage and a seizure disorder. His medical expenses were approximately $70,000.

Gohl sued the grandfather's brother, Dolphin, for negligently storing his gun in an unlocked drawer. He sued the grandfather, Raymon, who, he claimed, should have reminded his brother to take the pistol with him after his visit. He sued Raymond, his friend, for negligently pointing the gun at him while trying to secure the safety. The defendants in turn, alleged that Gohl, the injured boy, should not have placed the clip in the pistol.

Apparently Raymon and Raymond were insured by a homeowner's insurance policy with a $100,000 limit. Their insurance company paid the limit rather than subject Raymon and Raymond to even greater liability in a jury trial. The jury awarded $480,000 in damages, and allocated 55% of the fault to Dolphin for leaving the unloaded gun in an unlocked drawer. The jury held Raymond 18%

---

[58] The injured boy's attorney reported this case in the Journal of the Association of Trial Lawyers of America.

responsible for pointing the gun at Gohl and Gohl 17% responsible for loading the gun (Gohl's verdict was reduced by 17% making him partially accountable for his own stupidity). Although the case did not report it, there must have been an additional 10% awarded against the grandfather (the percentages of fault must always total 100%), Raymon, who didn't have to pay the verdict because his insurance had already paid. (The homeowner's insurance paid $100,000 on behalf of Raymon and Raymond. Their total fault was 28%, 10% for Raymon and 18% for Raymond. 28% of the verdict is $134,400. Raymon, Raymond and their insurance company saved $34,400 plus court costs by settling out of court. Their insurance adjuster was a hero for advising them to settle.) Thus, Dolphin became responsible for $264,000 (55%) of the $480,000 judgment plus interest, for negligently leaving a firearm in a place where he should have known it would be accessible to children.

Commentary

Although we have a right to bear arms, we also have a responsibility to conduct ourselves safely. If our carelessness injures another, we are responsible to that person for the damage we cause. It makes more sense to hold careless people accountable for their actions, than to take guns away from law-abiding citizens. Therefore, clear thinking gun owners should welcome the idea of civil liability related to gun use. The following safety rules would have prevented this accident:

a.   Storing ammunition and firearm in different locations,

b.   Keeping all firearms in the house in a locked gun safe or locked closet when not in use,

c.   Teaching children never to touch or handle a firearm without the supervision of an adult (This is exactly what the NRA's "Eddie Eagle" program teaches),

d.   Never point a gun at anything or anyone you don't intent to shoot, and

e.   Never rely on the gun's safety to prevent the gun from firing,

f.   Never put your finger on the trigger until you are ready to shoot intentionally at a target.

CHAPTER XI:
THE LAW OF SELF-DEFENSE
(Criminal and Civil)

Pancho's Wisdom
"I'd rather be tried by twelve
than carried by six!"
Gary Travis, Armed Response Institute

In Utah, a man's home is STILL his castle and you can shoot intruders breaking or sneaking into your home without worrying about being charged with a crime or sued for money damages.

A. SELF DEFENSE - CRIMINAL LAW

U.C.A. 76-2-402. Force in defense of person -- Forcible felony defined.

"Plain Talk"

This law defines exactly how much force a person can use in defending himself and others from violent criminals. Basically, a person can use whatever force is necessary to stop aggression, but cannot use so much force that he, in turn, becomes the aggressor. A person may only use as much non-deadly force as is necessary to stop the use of non-deadly force against him. Example, a slap for a slap. Deadly force can be repelled with deadly force. Example, bullets for bullets. A person cannot claim self defense if he:

      a.   starts a fight,

      b.   attempts to commit, is committing, or running away after committing a felony, or

      c.   agrees to a fight or duel unless he changes his mind and makes it very clear to the other person that he doesn't want to fight or duel.

In some states a person has to retreat before he uses force to defend himself. This is NOT true in Utah, if he is in a place where he has a lawful right to be (like a public street, supermarket, his house or someone else's house as a guest) unless he is there because of an agreement to fight ("meet me behind the gym") or duel ("meet me outside the saloon at high noon"). If someone is using deadly force against you or a third person (like a gun or a knife), you can defend yourself or another using deadly force . You can also use deadly force to prevent a "forcible felony" which includes the following crimes:

a. aggravated assault (intentionally causing serious bodily injury or using a dangerous weapon likely to cause death or serious bodily injury),

b. mayhem (cutting off or disabling a member of the body or slitting someone's nose, ear or lip),

c. aggravated murder (killing another person under a host of aggravating circumstances defined in U.C.A. 76-5-202 including sexual assault of a child, killing for money, killing while kidnaping, poisoning, torturing, etc.),

d. manslaughter (recklessly but not intentionally killing another),

e. kidnaping,

f. aggravated kidnaping (kidnaping while using a deadly weapon, holding someone for ransom, etc., see U.C.A. 76-5-302),

g. a continuing list of unspeakable crimes which are listed in (4) below, including sexual abuse of children, and

h. arson, robbery, burglary (caution: not burglary of a vehicle - you can't shoot someone who is trying to break into your car, unless you are in the car).

The word "imminent" means "about to happen." If a bad guy aims his pistol at you, the danger is "imminent." However, if he is ten miles away at home, loading his pistol and you think he is coming after you, this is not imminent and you cannot legally **DRIVE BY** his home with guns ablaze. Sections (5)(d), and (e) of this code section allow juries to look at patterns of abuse and previous violent acts committed by the victim to determine if the deadly force used against him was justified. If your spouse has nearly beaten you or your children to death in the past several months, and you think he is going to wake up in an hour and do it again, you may be justified (but not necessarily) in planting a bullet in his brain stem. Utah juries have to apply the rules stated in this code section every time the accused claims he or she killed in self defense or in defense of another. Included in the "Commentary" below are a series of short case summaries illustrating the principles we have just discussed.

ACTUAL TEXT

(1) A person is justified in threatening or using force against another when and to the extent that he or she reasonably believes that force is necessary to defend himself or a third person against such other's imminent use of unlawful force. However, that person is justified in using force intended or

likely to cause death or serious bodily injury only if he or she reasonably believes that force is necessary to prevent death or serious bodily injury to himself or a third person as a result of the other's imminent use of unlawful force, or to prevent the commission of a forcible felony.

(2) A person is not justified in using force under the circumstances specified in Subsection (1) if he or she:

(a) initially provokes the use of force against himself with the intent to use force as an excuse to inflict bodily harm upon the assailant;

(b) is attempting to commit, committing, or fleeing after the commission or attempted commission of a felony; or

(c)   (i) was the aggressor or was engaged in a combat by agreement, unless he withdraws from the encounter and effectively communicates to the other person his intent to do so and, notwithstanding, the other person continues or threatens to continue the use of unlawful force; and

(ii) for purposes of Subsection (i) the following do not, by themselves, constitute "combat by agreement":

(A) voluntarily entering into or remaining in an ongoing relationship; or

(B) entering or remaining in a place where one has a legal right to be.

(3) A person does not have a duty to retreat from the force or threatened force described in Subsection (1) in a place where that person has lawfully entered or remained, except as provided in Subsection (2)(c).

(4) For purposes of this section, a forcible felony includes aggravated assault, mayhem, aggravated murder, murder, manslaughter, kidnaping, and aggravated kidnaping, rape, forcible sodomy, rape of a child, object rape, object rape of a child, sexual abuse of a child, aggravated sexual abuse of a child, and aggravated sexual assault as defined in Title 76, Chapter 5, and arson, robbery, and burglary as defined in Title 76, Chapter 6. Any other felony offense which involves the use of force or violence against a person so as to create a substantial danger of death or serious bodily injury also constitutes a forcible felony. Burglary of a vehicle, defined in Section 76-6-204, does not constitute a forcible felony except when the vehicle is occupied at the time unlawful entry is made or attempted.

(5) In determining imminence or reasonableness under Subsection (1), the trier of fact may consider, but is not limited to, any of the following factors:

(a) the nature of the danger;

(b) the immediacy of the danger;

(c) the probability that the unlawful force would result in death or serious bodily injury;

(d) the other's prior violent acts or violent propensities; and

(e) any patterns of abuse or violence in the parties' relationship.

U.C.A. 76-2-402
Commentary

The following summaries come from actual Utah appellate court opinions discussing the law of self defense. Most district court libraries have law books containing these cases. For example, you can find the first case entitled *State v. Knoll*, 712 P.2d 211 (Utah 1985) in volume 712 of the Pacific Reporter at page 211. The Pacific Reporter has cases from Utah and thirteen of our neighbor states including Nevada, Colorado, California, Arizona, Alaska, Idaho, and Wyoming.

This first case illustrates the limits of the use of "REASONABLE FORCE" in defending oneself.[59] The defendant and the victim were two unemployed people sharing a bottle of wine.[60] There were no witnesses to the killing, but the defendant claims the victim starting punching him in the face and the head. They wrestled to the ground and the defendant struck his head. During the fight, the victim grabbed the defendant's knife and stabbed him in the back of the leg.[61] The defendant grabbed the knife leaving the victim on the ground WITHOUT A WEAPON. The defendant alleged the victim pulled his head down so he couldn't see the victim. Claiming that he was afraid the victim would try to kill him, the defendant started slashing and stabbing with the knife. The victim died of multiple stab wounds which penetrated his heart and liver. Rejecting his claim of self defense, the jury found the defendant guilty of manslaughter. The Appeals Court agreed with the verdict. It said the serious stab wounds could lead a reasonable jury to conclude that the defendant used MORE FORCE THAN WAS NECESSARY, especially against a person with no weapon. Although defendant had a right to defend himself, he should not have killed the victim after disarming him. See *State v. Knoll*, 712 P.2d

---

[59]   Although the defendant in this case did not use a firearm, the case illustrates well the principles of self defense and excessive force.

[60]   Alcohol and drugs often play a major role in violent crimes. Any surprise?

[61]   Most of these cases involve conflicting facts and unanswered questions. People generally resolve doubts in their own favor, and it's up to a jury or judge to decide what the truth is. Those who have served on juries will tell you it is often very difficult.

211 (Utah 1985).

The following case illustrates how THE DIFFERENCE IN SIZE AND STRENGTH can make a difference in justifying the use of deadly force in self defense. In this case a small, frail woman who had previously undergone several back surgeries was charged with 2nd degree murder for killing her large, powerful husband. They had both been drinking[62] and had been seen arguing at the husband's workplace. The defendant went home first and her husband arrived later, threatening, "I'm going to kill you, you bitch. You don't deserve to live." There were no witnesses. She claimed she tried to leave, but he slammed the door shut. When she ran upstairs, he grabbed her by the leg and dragged her down the stairs on her back. A medical doctor, who had examined her after the incident, testified that she had a herniated disk in her neck and carpet burns on her back consistent with her story. After she kicked him away, he retreated into the kitchen to pour another drink.

Meanwhile, the defendant ran back upstairs, grabbed a loaded .357 Magnum and returned to the top of the stairs. Her husband started up the stairs shouting threats and obscenities. She pled with him to give her a couple of days to pack her belongings and promised to leave. He kept coming up the stairs threatening to kill her. She finally shot him in the face, killing him instantly.

A trial judge, who heard the case without a jury, concluded that the wife was guilty of manslaughter. He said SHE HAD OTHER OPTIONS when her husband retreated into the kitchen after she kicked him. He had no weapon in his hands as he climbed the stairs toward her. The trial judge held that the danger was not "imminent," she could have called the police, escaped through a window or hit him with a piece of furniture, rather than shooting him in the face with a .357 Magnum. Two of the three judges on the Appeals Court overturned the trial judge's manslaughter conviction and cut the defendant loose. Their decision focused on the fact that the husband was LARGE AND STRONG that the defendant was SMALL AND FRAIL, having had four previous back surgeries. This was a close, two-to-one decision in the Appeals Court. The dissenting judge agreed with the trial judge that the defendant was guilty of manslaughter. He focused on her threat, "as soon as she

---

[62] And you wonder why the state passed, U.C.A. 76-10-528, making it illegal to be under the influence of alcohol and possess a firearm.

got her hands on a gun, he was a dead S.O.B." This case illustrates how different judges can focus on different facts when trying to decide between a guilty verdict and an acquittal on the grounds of self defense. *State v. Stribe*, 790 P.2d 98 (Utah Ct. App. 1990).

This next case shows how important it is NOT TO BE CONSIDERED THE AGGRESSOR if you are going to plead self defense. The defendant was a juvenile who had driven his father to a liquor store. After buying booze, the defendant's father headed for the car where his son was waiting. As he approached the car, two men followed him asking for money. At that point, the defendant's father fell against the car, either because he had been struck or because he was drunk. As the two men started to leave the scene, the defendant jumped out of the car and called them back. One of the men, Warlie, hit him with a nunchuck (ala Bruce Lee)[63] and the other struck him with his fist. The defendant pulled a gun and shot Warlie. Warlie laid his hands on the top of defendant's car, and defendant shot him again. He fell to the ground and later died. The other victim ran across the street with the defendant shooting at him. One shot grazed his head and the other lodged in his belt buckle. The defendant's father had gotten into the car before his son fired any of the shots at Warlie.

The Juvenile Court convicted the defendant of manslaughter. Upholding the conviction, the Utah Supreme Court pointed out that defendant's father had gotten into the car before any of the shots were fired. The Court said the defendant did not need to use deadly force to protect his father, who was safe inside the car when Warlie and his friend began walking away. When the defendant got out of the car and called them back, HE BECAME THE AGGRESSOR. Before that, neither he nor his father was in imminent danger, as required by the self-defense statute. *(State v Ex rel. Gonzales*, 545 P.2d 187 (Utah 1975).

Pancho's Wisdom
When women BEAR ARMS, sexual predators will keep HANDS OFF!

---

[63] Ouch! A nunchuck consists of two hardwood sticks dangling from both ends of a piece of leather lace or a chain.

U.C.A. 76-2-405. Force in defense of habitation.

"Plain Talk"

In Utah, a "man's (woman's) home is his (her) castle,"[64] and he can defend it with deadly force against those who break in, sneak in or who enter with the intent to commit a felony. It's his castle whether he is buying, renting or staying temporarily at someone else's place. If a stranger breaks into your home at night, has dark-colored clothing, a hood over his head and a knife or a gun in his hand, you can shoot him dead. What if the intruder is a vacuum-cleaner salesman, dressed in a business suit, "armed" with the latest model Hoover? If, in broad daylight, you shoot him full of holes when he sticks his foot in your door as you attempt to slam it in his face, you're in big trouble! These rules apply to both criminal and civil cases.

This statute says you will not be convicted of murder or manslaughter for killing a person who sneaks or breaks into your home, nor will his heirs win a suit for money damages against you. But if you blow away the vacuum salesman, his heirs could end up owning and living in your house while you're doing time in the "Big House."

ACTUAL TEXT

(1) A person is justified in using force against another when and to the extent that he reasonably believes that the force is necessary to prevent or terminate the other's unlawful entry into or attack upon his habitation; however, he is justified in the use of force which is intended or likely to cause death or serious bodily injury only if:

(a) the entry is made or attempted in a violent and tumultuous manner, surreptitiously, or by stealth, and he reasonably believes that the entry is attempted or made for the purpose of assaulting or offering personal violence to any person, dwelling, or being in the habitation and he reasonably believes that the force is necessary to prevent the assault or offer of personal violence; or

(b) he reasonably believes that the entry is made or attempted for the purpose of committing a felony in the habitation and that the force is necessary to prevent the commission of the felony.

(2) The person using force or deadly force in defense of habitation is presumed for the purpose of both civil and criminal cases to have acted reasonably and had a reasonable fear of imminent peril of death or serious bodily injury if the entry or attempted entry is unlawful and is made or attempted by use of force, or in a violent and tumultuous manner, or surreptitiously or by stealth, or for the purpose of committing a felony.

---

[64] See *State v. Mitcheson*, 560 P.2d 1120 (Utah 1977).

B. SELF DEFENSE - CIVIL LAW

The difference between self defense under criminal law as opposed to self defense under civil law was recently dramatically illustrated by the criminal and civil cases involving subway passenger Bernard Goetz. Four members of a black street gang approached Goetz on the New York subway. One of them brandished a screw driver and asked for five dollars. Goetz, who was illegally concealing a revolver, drew it and shot at all four, hitting two of them in the back. After the initial shooting Goetz found one of the gangsters, Darryl Cabey, lying wounded on a subway bench and reportedly said, "You seem to be all right, here's another"[65] and shot him again. The wounds left Cabey permanently brain damaged and paralyzed from the waste down. New York prosecutors charged Goetz with attempted murder. The jury in the criminal case acquitted Goetz of the attempted murder charge, convicting him only on the misdemeanor charge of possessing an illegal weapon (Goetz had no concealed carry permit). The jury was predominantly white.

Cabey later sued Goetz for damages and his lawyer filed the case in a jurisdiction consisting of mostly ethnic jurors. During the trial, Cabey's lawyer apparently convinced the jury of several facts terribly damaging to Goetz's case, who had since acquired the nickname of "subway vigilante." Cabey's attorney convinced the jury that Goetz calmly drew his pistol from his belt[66] and "methodically"[67] shot the young men as they tried to escape in the crowd.[68] The evidence implied that Goetz's "intention was to murder them, . . .to

---

[65] You Have To Think In A Cold Blooded Way, *N.Y. Times*, Apr. 30, 1987, at B6. [The footnotes referring to articles in the New York Times about Goetz and corresponding facts were taken from an article by D. Marvin Jones , Professor of Law, University of Miami School of Law in a 1998 article in the Contemporary Law Journal entitled "We're All Stuck Here For A While": Law and the Social Construction of the Black Male, 24 J. Contemp. L. 35.]

[66] Goetz Checked, Then Fired Another Round, *N.Y. Times*, Mar. 3, 1985, Section 4, at 6.

[67] See David E. Sanger, Callers Support Subway Gunman, *N.Y. Times*, Dec. 25, 1984, at A1.

[68] You Have To Think In A Cold Blooded Way, *N.Y. Times*, Apr. 30, 1987, at B6.

make them suffer as much as possible."[69] After hearing this, the jury returned a verdict against Goetz for 43 million dollars, most of which consisted of punitive damages intended to punish Goetz for EXCEEDING THE BOUNDS OF SELF DEFENSE AND ASSUMING THE ROLE OF AGGRESSOR. This shows that a criminal defendant found "not guilty" of a crime on the theory of self defense, can still be held civilly liable for BIG BUCKS!

In Utah, U.C.A. 76-2-402(1) states "a person is JUSTIFIED in threatening or using force against another when and to the extent that he or she reasonably believes that force is necessary to defend himself or a third person against such other's imminent use of unlawful force" (emphasis added). The key word is "JUSTIFIED." You are relieved of legal responsibility, if you do not use excessive force. In addition, under U.C.A. 76-2-402(4) you can shoot a person who is in the process of committing a "forcible felony" against you or another. Forcible felonies include assault with a deadly weapon, kidnaping, attempted rape and sexual abuse of a child. If you shoot and kill a person attempting to commit one of these heinous crimes against you or a family member, and his heirs sue you for money damages, you win!

Your home is your castle under the civil law as well as the criminal law. U.C.A. 76-2-405 entitled "Force in defense of habitation" states:

> (2) The person using force or deadly force in defense of habitation is PRESUMED for the purpose of both CIVIL and criminal cases to have acted reasonably and had a reasonable fear of imminent peril of death or serious bodily injury if the entry or attempted entry is unlawful and is made or attempted by use of force, or in a violent and tumultuous manner, or surreptitiously or by stealth, or for the purpose of committing a felony. (emphasis added)

KEEP IN MIND, HOWEVER, THAT A "PRESUMPTION" CAN BE REBUTTED! Suppose a person breaks into your home and you disarm him. You hold him while your relatives watch. Later you decide to execute him because he broke into your home. If your relatives testify against you and the jury believes them, the presumption that you "had a reasonable fear of imminent peril" is

---

[69] Kirk Johnson, Goetz Account of Shooting 4 Given On Tape, *N.Y. Times*, Apr. 30, 1987, at B1.

rebutted. You would be convicted of murder and held liable in a civil case.

The following several cases involving civil lawsuits illustrate the rules of law we have just discussed. They show how important it is to limit actions to DEFENSE rather than REVENGE. This is particularly true in cases where innocent bystanders are unintentionally injured during a shooting or attempted escape.

Our law firm subscribes to a computer service that allows lawyers to search combinations of words in millions of cases in a matter of seconds. To satisfy my curiosity about civil suits involving negligent self defense, I asked the computer to find all cases containing the words "gun or handgun or pistol or rifle or firearm" in the same paragraph as "negligence or negligent" in the same paragraph as "self defense" excluding criminal cases. "Negligent self defense" means using more force than is necessary to protect oneself from an attacker. I was shocked that there were only 27 cases reported. These cases dated back to the late 1940s. Of the 27 cases, some were criminal cases, although I tried to exclude them from my search. Others dealt entirely with insurance issues, and one or two dealt with the liability of business owners who failed to protect their patrons from criminal attacks. These issues are outside the scope of this chapter. The following five case summaries illustrate the breadth and depth of the civil law of self defense. I wasn't able to find any Utah cases involving a criminal who had been injured by his intended victim and had sued the victim for money damages.[70]

A. Attractive Teacher Shoots to Frighten Mouthy Teenager, Reaps Lawsuit.

As Estep, an attractive school teacher was driving her car in the country, she came up behind a slow-moving tractor driven by Williams, a teenager. When Estep pulled along side to pass, Williams, stirred by her resplendence, howled like a lovesick coyote. Not impressed, Estep backed up and furiously chastised him. Hurt and offended, the teenager asked Estep if she wanted her neck broken. He then drove away on his tractor. Apparently fed up with mouthy teenagers, she pulled a .410 shotgun out of her trunk and chased the impertinent youngster. Overtaking Williams, she forced him to the ground at gun point. Confronted with the unfriendly end of a scattergun, Williams dropped to his knees pleading forgiveness. Screaming you "no good S.O.B.," she motioned him to crawl away on

---

[70] Good news, eh?

his knees. Aiming near his legs, she fired and reloaded twice claiming, with 20 years of shooting experience, that she only intended to scare him. After the shooting, Williams' doctors were not able to remove all of the pellets from the boy's legs and they testified he would be permanently affected by his body's reactions to the lead. Estep's defense was that Williams had provoked her. She had earlier been convicted of an unspecified crime related to the incident and had come before the federal district court asking permission to settle the case for $10,000.[71] The court refused to approve the settlement stating a jury would probably find the shooting unjustified and award damages for far more than what she was offering to pay.

Commentary

It's not funny anymore when a teenage boy threatens to break a woman's neck. But such a comment does not justify what happened here. Estep was not in imminent (immediate) danger from Williams. Her actions quickly transformed her from victim to aggressor. She should have simply driven away and reported the incident to the police. The result would have been the same had this incident occurred in Utah.

B.   Bubba Shoots Jukebox Ninja, Verdict Exceeds Homeowner's Insurance Limits.

Harris and Pineset ["Bubba"] got into an argument over who had put quarters into a jukebox at a bar. Harris invited Pineset to "step outside" and Pineset accommodated. While confronting each other in the parking lot, Pineset drew a pistol. Harris tried to grab the gun, but it fired, striking him in the stomach. Surgeons had to remove part of his large bowel. The court held Pineset liable and awarded $203,728 in damages including $38,728 in medical expenses. Unfortunately Pineset only had $100,000 of homeowner's insurance coverage. Pineset appealed claiming he was JUSTIFIED in defending himself with a pistol, because Harris threatened to use KARATE on

---

[71] Most states require a court to approve the settlement of a minor. A minor does not have the mental capacity to enter into a contract (ask any parent who has teenagers). Therefore, the laws of most states require the courts to oversee such settlements to make sure that the best interests of the minor are met by the settlement. In this case, the court felt that the child deserved more than $10,000 for the shooting and that a jury would give him more if the case were tried. The case apparently settled for a confidential amount after that, because we were unable to find out what the ultimate settlement was.

him. The court disagreed that he was justified in using a firearm (deadly force) but it reduced the verdict by 10% because of Harris' contributory negligence in consenting to the fight in the first place. Pineset still ended up having to pay $83,000 out of his personal assets to satisfy the verdict. The court explained its reasoning:

> Resort to the use of a dangerous weapon to repel an attack is not justifiable except in exceptional cases where the actor's fear of the danger is not only genuine, but is founded upon facts which would be likely to produce similar emotions in men of reasonable prudence. . .

Harris v. Pineset, 499 So. 2d 499 at 503 (La. App. 2d Cir. 1986).

Commentary

A reasonable person might believe a person who threatens to use karate is threatening deadly force. If, before the fight, Harris had put on a "pre-fight" karate demonstration like on T.V., had broken two-by-fours with his bare hands and cinder blocks with his bald head, Pineset may have been justified in using deadly force.[72] He couldn't have been too worried Harris' hands were deadly weapons. He voluntarily agreed to fight Harris. If he was sincerely convinced Harris could kill him with his bare hands, Pineset should have gathered his guests, left the bar and refused to fight. Then, had Harris pursued him, Pineset might have been justified in protecting himself with a pistol. Instead, Pineset lost the case because he agreed to fight. The same result would occur under Utah law. U.C.A. 76-2-402(2) states:

> (2) A person is NOT JUSTIFIED IN USING FORCE under the circumstances specified in Subsection (1) if he or she:
>
> . . .
>
> (c)(i) was the aggressor or WAS ENGAGED IN A COMBAT BY AGREEMENT, unless he withdraws from the encounter and effectively communicates to the other person his intent to do so and, notwithstanding, the other person continues or threatens to continue the use of unlawful force: (emphasis added)

---

[72] How about dipping his hands into gooey syrup and then thrusting them into a bowl of "Gummy Bears?"

C.   Cause and Effect: Gas Station Attendant Shoots Fleeing Robber, Robber Runs into Innocent Motorist, Gas Station gets Sued.

Bender, a night manager at a Cleveland, Ohio gas station, lugged a .45 revolver in his overalls while on duty. Three men in an Oldsmobile pulled up, wielded a shotgun and demanded cash. Fearing for his life, Bender handed over $400. The robbers told Bender not to move as they slowly drove away. Before the thugs could get off the premises, Bender drew his handgun and blasted through the back window of the car. The slug penetrated the front seat and plunged deep into the driver's back, perforating his spleen, stomach and heart. Mortally wounded, the driver's legs stiffened, propelling the gas pedal to the floor. The Olds screeched into the street accelerating rapidly. A block and a half east of the station, it crashed head on into a Cadillac driven by an innocent motorist, Strother, who suffered serious injuries.[73] As usual, the criminals had no money or insurance so Strother sued Bender and his employer under the theory of negligent self defense.

Strother's attorney argued that Bender didn't need to shoot to protect himself, the criminals were almost out of the driveway when Bender began shooting. His actions, he alleged, created an unnecessary and unreasonable risk of harm to others. Despite his eloquent presentation, the trial court concluded Bender was not liable to Strother. The appeals court agreed with the trial court, pointing out that the getaway car was still in the gas station parking lot when Bender fired. It held Bender could not have foreseen the Olds would have lunged out of the parking lot to strike an oncoming car. As explained in Chapter X, a person is not liable if he cannot foresee that his actions will cause injury.

Commentary

The most difficult cases for courts to decide involve disputes such as this between two innocent people. Let's face it: Bender and Strother were both victims of a criminal act. Unfortunately most criminals don't have much money, so their victims are often forced to look elsewhere for fair compensation.

This was a close case. Strother's attorney made a strong argument that Bender was not privileged to shoot because the danger had already passed. After all, the car was pulling away as shown by the fact that Bender shot through the back window. Unless there was

---

[73] Welcome to earth, third rock from the sun!

evidence to show Bender was still in danger, his shots may not have been justified.

The Court had to stretch to hold an injury was not foreseeable to Bender. I agree that it was probably not foreseeable to Bender that his bullet would hit the driver in the back, the driver would stiffen up, pressing on the gas causing him to drive down the street at a high rate of speed, presumably already dead. Nevertheless, I think it is foreseeable that when you are shooting at somebody pulling away in a car, he might panic, "stomp on it" to get away, and cause an accident. This is the very reason many police departments forbid their officers to engage in dangerous, high-speed chases. Certainly Bender could have foreseen some injury, although not the manner or extent of the injury. His bullet could have missed and struck an innocent bystander (see the following case). In Utah, as in most states, if a person can foresee some harm, he is responsible for any injury even though he cannot foresee exactly how the injury will occur. If Bender believed the danger had passed, he should not have shot.

Despite these arguments, Bender and his employer would have had another defense in Utah. Utah law permits a person to use deadly force to prevent the commission of a forcible felony. U.C.A. 76-2-402 above defines robbery as a forcible felony and the robbery statute, U.C.A. 76-6-301, makes it clear that flight after a robbery falls within the definition of the "commission" of a robbery:

> (1) A person **COMMITS** robbery if:
>
> . . .
>
> (b) the person intentionally or knowingly uses force or fear of immediate force against another **IN THE COURSE OF COMMITTING A THEFT**.
>
> (2) An act shall be considered **"IN THE COURSE OF COMMITTING A THEFT"** if it occurs in an attempt to commit theft, commission of theft, or **IN THE IMMEDIATE FLIGHT AFTER** the attempt or commission. **(emphasis added)**

Because the bad guys were fleeing after committing a felony, Bender would have been justified in using deadly force in Utah. The jury would be instructed to consider the self defense statute, but would not be bound by it. If the jury felt that Bender's force created an unreasonable risk of harm to third persons, he could still be held liable (see the "Restatement" rule discussed in the next case).

If Bender had been sued and found liable by a Utah court, he still would not have to bear the entire burden of the verdict. Utah law states that no defendant is required to pay more than his proportional share of the fault. As discussed above, the fault of all culpable (guilty) parties is compared. Recently, the Utah Supreme Court held that if the identity of a criminal is known, his fault must be compared by the jury. In this case, if a jury found Bender to be 10% at fault and the criminals to be 90% at fault, Strother would collect only 10% of the verdict from Bender, even if the criminals had no assets. Given this example, if a jury awarded $500,000, Strother would only collect $50,000 (10% of $500,000) from Bender and his employer, unless he could collect something from the imprisoned criminals and the estate of their dead accomplice. If there was nothing to collect, Strother would be deprived of 90% of his damages. Unfortunately, this law places the risk of not being able to collect a verdict on an injured person, rather than a guilty co-defendant. In other states that apply the law of "joint and several" liability, the guilty co-defendant (in this case, Bender, assuming he had been found liable) would be required to pay the entire verdict, and then he, not Strother, would bear the burden of collecting the 90% from the criminals (turnips).[74]

D.   Shots into the Night at Peeping Tom Kill Innocent Bystander.

Another tragic case involving an alleged negligent self defense occurred in Nashville, Tennessee. Late one night in 1956, sixty-eight year old Norman Goodrich was walking home from work through a dark, heavily populated residential area. Meanwhile, a woman named Morgan heard a window rattling and thought it could be a prowler. She grabbed her pistol and went outside to sit on her front porch swing. She spotted a man enter her yard, crouch down on the ground and "peep" through a basement window at a woman undressing. Infuriated, Morgan pointed the handgun and cut loose with several shots. As bullets whizzed by, the intruder fled into the street and disappeared into the darkness, undoubtedly having experienced an immense adrenaline rush! Morgan heard someone call out "I've been shot." The bullet struck Mr. Goodrich in the chest ultimately killing him.

Mrs. Goodrich, wife of the deceased, sued Ms. Morgan for negligence but the trial court dismissed the case. The appeals court, however, sent the case back for a new trial, criticizing Morgan for literally "shooting into the dark" without knowing where her bullets would strike. The neighborhood was densely populated, the sidewalk

---

[74] They're hard to squeeze blood out of!

was obscured by thick shrubbery and the area was poorly lit. The rule of law that the court applied to the case was that "a person using a firearm or other weapon in the exercise of his self defense is not liable for any injury unintentionally inflicted upon a bystander unless he is guilty of some negligence or folly in the use of the weapon." The Court held that there was a question of fact whether Morgan had acted negligently and that a jury should decide that issue and not the trial court judge.

Commentary

There is no question that a person can use deadly force to protect others from deadly force. Here, had the "peeping" intruder confronted the woman in the basement with a deadly weapon, Morgan would have been justified in using deadly force to protect her. Under those circumstances, if the bullet had gone astray and hit Goodrich, Morgan would not have been liable. The Restatement of Torts, which most courts including Utah's, rely heavily upon, explains the rule of law with the following example:

> A points a pistol at B, threatening to shoot him. B attempts to shoot A, but his bullet goes astray and strikes C, an innocent bystander. B is NOT liable to C unless, taking into account the exigency [emergency] which A's act placed B, B fired his self-defensive shot in a manner UNNECESSARILY DANGEROUS to C (emphasis added).

Unfortunately for Morgan, there was no evidence to show that the intruder was armed. He ran away after the first shot. The shots into the street were not intended to defend as much as they were intended to frighten, punish or stop the criminal. The "Peeping Tom" was, at most, guilty of criminal trespass, a misdemeanor. Under these circumstances, a person is not privileged to use deadly force and may be liable for injuring innocent bystanders.

E.   Bartender Who Fails to Warn Drunken Patron to "Dance" held Liable for Shooting Patron in Foot.

The facts giving rise to this case occurred in 1948 in Wisconsin. Oshogay, a reservation Indian, had started a fight in the defendant's tavern a couple of weeks earlier. When he revisited the bar, Shultz, the bar owner, refused to serve him alcohol. He asked Oshogay to leave, but Oshogay refused. Finally, Shultz pulled a pistol from behind the bar and aimed near Oshogay's feet intending only to frighten him.[75] The bullet struck Oshogay in the foot. A jury awarded damages in the sum of $1,223.70, a sizeable verdict in 1950. The appeals court upheld the verdict, putting particular emphasis on the fact that the bar owner had not tried to get anyone to help remove the belligerent patron, nor had he summoned the police. *Oshogay v. Schultz*, 257 Wis. 323; 43 N.W.2d 485, Supreme Court of Wisconsin, June 30, 1950.

Commentary

Oshogay had not threatened anyone with deadly force. He was not armed with a gun or a knife. The bartender was not justified in using deadly force (a firearm), and was rightfully held liable for his actions.

F. CONCLUSION - CIVIL LIABILITY

Do not panic because our civil law holds people accountable for their actions. There is a very slim chance you will ever need to defend yourself with a firearm and if you do, an even slimmer chance you will be sued. If you ever have to defend yourself or your family with a firearm, the following suggestions should help you avoid civil liability.

a. Never threaten or use deadly force unless you reasonably believe you are being threatened with deadly force.

b. Stop shooting when your attacker no longer poses a threat.

c. Carry homeowners or renters insurance with a large umbrella policy just in case a jury does not agree with the way you approached the situation. You can buy a $1 million dollar "umbrella" liability policy for about $30 a month.

d. Retreat, if you can do so safely, though Utah law does not require it.

e. Make sure you legally possess and conceal the firearm you use for self defense.

f. If you are involved in an incident involving self defense, always consult with a lawyer before agreeing to give any statements. Have someone else call the police or the ambulance if possible, so that your recorded comments to the dispatcher cannot be used against you in a criminal case or civil suit.

---

[75] You just wanted to see him dance, right?

Pancho: An Army of One

CHAPTER XII:
MISCELLANEOUS GUN LAWS

Pancho's Wisdom
Pancho sleeps with two guns under his pillow;
one gives him a STIFF NECK!

A. INTRODUCTION

We found some of Utah's gun laws in the darnedest places. They appear in code sections dealing with motor vehicles, public education, state lands etc. We threw all these "maverick" gun laws altogether in this chapter.

U.C.A. 53-3-220. Offenses requiring mandatory revocation, denial, suspension, or disqualification of license.

"Plain Talk"

We discussed this one earlier, but just in case you didn't get it - if you shoot your gun out your car window or out of the back of your pickup and get caught, your drivers license must be immediately revoked. This makes sense for in the city limits, but not when you are out in the middle of nowhere. See our "Commentary" in Chapter VII for U.C.A. 76-10-508(2).

ACTUAL TEXT

(1)(a) The division shall immediately revoke or, when this chapter or Title
41, Chapter 6, Traffic Rules and Regulations, specifically provides for denial, suspension, or disqualification, the division shall deny, suspend, or disqualify the license of a person upon receiving a record of his conviction for any of the following offenses:

. . .

        (xi) discharging or allowing the discharge of a firearm from a vehicle in violation of Subsection 76-10-508(2);

. . .

        (b) The division shall immediately revoke the license of a person upon receiving a record of an adjudication under Title 78, Chapter 3a, Juvenile Courts, for any of the following offenses:
        (i) discharging or allowing the discharge of a firearm from a vehicle in violation of Subsection 76-10-508(2);

U.C.A. 53A-11-904. Grounds for Suspension or Expulsion from a Public School.

> ### "Plain Talk"
> If your kid takes a real or play gun to school, he gets expelled for at least a year unless the school district superintendent gives him a break.

ACTUAL TEXT

. . .

(2)(a) A student shall be suspended or expelled from a public school for any of the following reasons:

     (i) . . . the possession, control, or actual or threatened use of a real, look alike, or pretend weapon . . .under Section 53A-3-502.

  (b) A student who commits a violation of Subsection (a) involving a real, look alike, or pretend firearm, explosive, or flammable material shall be expelled from school for a period of not less than one year, unless the district superintendent determines, on a case-by-case basis, that a lesser penalty would be more appropriate.

> ### Commentary
> Uh, so how do you take your gun to school to put on a skit or participate in hunter's safety? Notice the reference to 53A-3-502. 502 allows a person to get permission from the responsible school administrator to participate in legal activities involving firearms, U.C.A. 53A-3-502(2)(a). See discussion in Chapter VII in the commentary under U.C.A. 76-10-505.5.

U.C.A. 58-37-8. Prohibited acts — Penalties.

> ### "Plain Talk"
> Under this code subsection a court can add 1-5 years to a jail sentence of a convicted drug dealer to run "consecutively" [after] rather than "concurrently" [at the same time] with any other penalty.

ACTUAL TEXT

. . .

(c) Any person who has been convicted of a violation of Subsection (1)(a)(ii) or (iii) **[sell drugs or possess drugs with intent to sell]** may be sentenced to imprisonment for an indeterminate term as provided by law, but if the trier of fact finds a firearm as defined in Section 76-10-501 was used, carried, or possessed on his person or in his immediate possession during the commission or in furtherance of the offense, the court shall additionally sentence the person convicted for a terms of one year to run consecutively and not concurrently; and the court may additionally sentence the person convicted for an indeterminate term not to exceed five years to run consecutively and not concurrently.

U.C.A. 65A-3-2. Prohibited acts on state lands.[Shooting tracer bullets]

> **"Plain Talk"**
>
> You can't shoot tracer bullets on state lands. The excuse for passing this law seems to be the potential fire danger. There is a similar federal law that prohibits firing tracers on National Forest property (36 C.F.R .261.5, the relevant section follows U.C.A. 65A-3-2 below). Notice that these laws don't claim to regulate firearms, but rather fire hazards; therefore, individual counties may have similar ordinances. If you are not on private land, you better check with the governments who claim jurisdiction before you amuse yourself with tracer bullets. The Utah Bureau of Criminal identification takes the position that this prohibits shooting tracers anywhere in the state except military installations, but the title of this code section seems to confine the prohibition to "state lands." You MIGHT be able to get away with shooting tracers on private land. This statute is confusing at best.

ACTUAL TEXT
(1) A person is guilty of a class B misdemeanor who:

. . .

(d) fires any tracer or incendiary ammunition anywhere except within the confines of established military reservations.

36 C.F.R. 261.5 Fire. [Shooting Tracer Bullets]
The following are prohibited:

. . .

(b) Firing any tracer bullet or incendiary ammunition.

U.C.A. 76-5-102.8. Disarming a peace officer.

> **"Plain Talk"**
>
> Have you ever been tempted to see if you could "quick draw" a peace officer's pistol before he can? Forget it! It is a first degree felony under newly enacted (new in 1999) code section UCA 76-5-102.8.

ACTUAL TEXT
A person is guilty of a first degree felony who intentionally takes or removes, or attempts to take or remove, a firearm from the person or immediate presence of a person he knows is a peace officer:
(1) without the consent of the peace officer; and

(2) while the peace officer is acting within the scope of his authority as a peace officer.

U.C.A. 76-5-104. Consensual altercation no defense to homicide or assault if dangerous weapon used or participants are engaged in an ultimate fighting match.

> ### "Plain Talk"
> "It was a fair fight officer: he agreed to meet me in front of Blimpie's at high noon, both of us totin' single action 'hog legs.'" Sorry Stud, consent to a duel or gun fight is no defense to the charge of murder or assault, not even if the victim drew first. [This sure puts the dampers on making a living as a gunslinger!]

ACTUAL TEXT

In any prosecution for criminal homicide under Part 2 of this chapter or assault, it is no defense to the prosecution that the defendant was a party to any duel, mutual combat, or other consensual altercation if during the course of the duel, combat, or altercation any dangerous weapon as defined in Section 76-1-601 was used or if the defendant was engaged in an ultimate fighting match as defined in Section 76-9-705.

U.C.A. 77-18-10. Petition -- Expungement of records of arrest, investigation, and detention -- Eligibility conditions -- No filing fee.

> ### "Plain Talk"
> If you have had the misfortune of being convicted of a felony or other serious criminal offense, the following several sections explain how you MIGHT be able to have your criminal record wiped clean so your civil rights, including the right to bear arms, can be restored. In short, if you have been "straight" for a long time and your crimes were not too serious, a court might agree to restore your rights.
> "Expungement" rightfully incorporates the concepts of repentance and forgiveness into the law. The process is described in detail in sections U.C.A. 77-18-10 through 17. If you have been convicted of a capital felony, first degree felony, second degree forcible felony or any sexual act against a minor, you can forget about expungement.

ACTUAL TEXT

(1) A person who has been arrested with or without a warrant may petition the court in which the proceeding occurred or, if there were no court proceedings, any court in the jurisdiction where the arrest occurred, for an order expunging any and all records of arrest, investigation, and detention which may have been made in the case, subject to the following conditions:

(a) at least 30 days have passed since the arrest for which expungement is sought;

(b) there have been no intervening arrests; and

(c) one of the following occurred:

(i) the person was released without the filing of formal charges;

(ii) proceedings against the person were dismissed;

(iii) the person was discharged without a conviction and no charges were refiled within 30 days;

(iv) the person was acquitted at trial; or

(v) the record of any proceedings against the person has been sealed.

(2)　　(a) A person seeking expungement under Subsection (1) may petition the court for expungement before the expiration of the 30 days required by Subsection (1)(a) if he believes extraordinary circumstances exist and the court orders the division to proceed with the eligibility process.

(b) A court may, with the receipt of a certificate of eligibility, order expungement if the court finds that the petitioner is eligible for relief under this subsection and in the interest of justice the order should be issued prior to the expiration of the 30-day period required by Subsection (1)(a).

(3) As provided in Subsection 21-1-5(1)(i), there is no fee for a petition filed under Subsection (2).

(4) The petitioner shall file a certificate of eligibility issued by the division to be reviewed by the prosecuting attorney and the court prior to issuing an order granting the expungement.

(5) If the court finds that the petitioner is eligible for relief under this section, it shall issue an order granting the expungement.

(6) No filing fees or other administrative charges shall be assessed against a successful petitioner under this section.

(7) A person who has received expungement of an arrest under this section may respond to any inquiry as though the arrest did not occur, unless otherwise provided by law.

U.C.A. 77-18-11. Petition -- Expungement of conviction -- Certificate of eligibility -- Notice -- Written evaluation -- Objections -- Hearing.

"Plain Talk"

The victim of a crime, or in the case of death, the victim's family must be notified that a convicted criminal is petitioning the court for an expungement or cleansing of his record. The prosecuting attorney is also notified. This gives these people a chance to object to the expungement if they want to. If objections are received, the court sets up a hearing date. If no objections are received, the court can grant the expungement without a hearing. People who have been convicted of a capital felony, first degree felony, second degree forcible felony or sexual act against a minor may not have their records expunged. Of course, the person petitioning the court for expungement must show that he has completed all the requirements of sentencing, probation or parole.

ACTUAL TEXT

(1) A person convicted of a crime may petition the convicting court for an expungement of the record of conviction.

(2) (a)The court shall require receipt of a certificate of eligibility issued by the division under Section 77-18-12.

(b) The fee for each certificate of eligibility is $25. This fee remains in effect until changed by the division through the process under Section 63-38-3.2.

(c) Funds generated under Subsection (2)(b) shall be deposited in the General Fund as a dedicated credit by the department to cover the costs incurred in providing the information.

(3) The petition and certificate of eligibility shall be filed with the court and served upon the prosecuting attorney and the Department of Corrections.

(4) A victim shall receive notice of a petition for expungement if, prior to the entry of an expungement order, the victim or, in the case of a minor or a person who is incapacitated or deceased, the victim's next of kin or authorized representative, submits a written and signed request for notice to the office of the Department of Corrections in the judicial district in which the crime occurred or judgment was entered.

(5) The Department of Corrections shall serve notice of the expungement request by first-class mail to the victim at the most recent address of record on file with the department. The notice shall include a copy of the petition, certificate of eligibility, and statutes and rules applicable to the petition.

(6) The court in its discretion may request a written evaluation by Adult Parole and Probation of the Department of Corrections.

(a) The evaluation shall include a recommendation concerning the petition for expungement.

(b) If expungement is recommended, the evaluation shall include certification that the petitioner has completed all requirements of sentencing and probation or parole and state any rationale that would support or refute consideration for expungement.

(c) The conclusions and recommendations contained in the evaluation shall be provided to the petitioner and the prosecuting attorney.

(7) If the prosecuting attorney or a victim submits a written objection to the court concerning the petition within 30 days after service of the notice, or if the petitioner objects to the conclusions and recommendations in the evaluation within 15 days after receipt of the conclusions and recommendations, the court shall set a date for a hearing and notify the prosecuting attorney for the jurisdiction, the petitioner, and the victim of the date set for the hearing.

(8) Any person who has relevant information about the petitioner may testify at the hearing.

(9) The prosecuting attorney may respond to the court with a recommendation or objection within 30 days.

(10) If an objection is not received under Subsection (7), the expungement may be granted without a hearing.

(11) A court may not expunge a conviction of a:

    (a) capital felony:

    (b) first degree felony:

    (c) second degree forcible felony: or

    (d) any sexual act against a minor.

U.C.A. 77-18-12. Grounds for denial of certificate of eligibility -- Effect of prior convictions.

"Plain Talk"

Several combinations of convictions can result in a denial of a petition for expungement. Before an expungement is granted, the following time periods MUST lapse from the time the convict satisfies all conditions of incarceration, parole, probation and fines:

    a.   seven years in the case of a felony,

    b.   six years for an alcohol related traffic offense,

    c.   five years for a class A misdemeanor,

    d.   three years for any other type of misdemeanor or infraction, and

    e.   fifteen years in a case of multiple class B or class C misdemeanors.

ACTUAL TEXT

(1) The division shall issue a certificate of eligibility to a petitioner seeking to obtain expungement for a criminal record unless prior to issuing a certificate of eligibility the division finds, through records of a governmental agency, including national criminal data bases that:

    (a) the conviction for which expungement is sought is a capital felony, first degree felony, second degree forcible felony, a conviction involving a sexual act against a minor, any registerable sex offense as defined in Section 77-27-21.5(1)(c) (d), or an attempt, solicitation, or conspiracy to commit any offense listed in that subsection:

    (b) the petitioner's record includes two or more convictions for any type of offense which would be classified as a felony under Utah law, not arising out of a single criminal episode, regardless of the jurisdiction in which the convictions occurred:

    (c) the petitioner has previously obtained expungement in any jurisdiction of a crime which would be classified as a felony in Utah:

    (d) the petitioner has previously obtained expungement in any jurisdiction of two or more convictions which would be classified as misdemeanors in Utah unless the convictions would be classified as class B or class C misdemeanors in Utah and 15 years have passed since these misdemeanor convictions:

(e) the petitioner was convicted in any jurisdiction, subsequent to the conviction for which expungement is sought and within the time periods as provided in Subsection (2), of a crime which would be classified in Utah as a felony, misdemeanor, or infraction;

(f) the person has a combination of three or more convictions not arising out of a single criminal episode including any conviction for an offense which would be classified under Utah law as a class B or class A misdemeanor or as a felony, including any misdemeanor and felony convictions previously expunged, regardless of the jurisdiction in which the conviction or expungement occurred; or

(g) a proceeding involving a crime is pending or being instituted in any jurisdiction against the petitioner.

(2) A conviction may not be included for purposes of Subsection (1)(e), and a conviction may not be considered for expungement until, after the petitioner's release from incarceration, parole, or probation, whichever occurs last and all fines ordered by the court have been satisfied, at least the following period of time has elapsed:

(a) seven years in the case of a felony;

(b) six years in the case of an alcohol-related traffic offense under Title 41, *Motor Vehicles*;

(c) five years in the case of a class A misdemeanor;

(d) three years in the case of any other misdemeanor or infraction under Title 76, *Utah Criminal Code*; or

(e) 15 years in the case of multiple class B or class C misdemeanors.

(3) A petitioner who would not be eligible to receive a certificate of eligibility under Subsection (1)(d) or (f) may receive a certificate of eligibility for one additional expungement if at least 15 years have elapsed since the last of any of the following:

(a) release from incarceration, parole, or probation relating to the most recent conviction; and

(b) any other conviction which would have prevented issuance of a certificate of eligibility under Subsection (1)(e).

(4) If, after reasonable research, a disposition for an arrest on the criminal history file is unobtainable, the division may issue a special certificate giving discretion of eligibility to the court.

Commentary

Because this is a book about gun law, not expungement, sections U.C.A. 77-18-13 through 17 have been omitted from this edition. You may contact a lawyer or the Bureau of Criminal Identification (BCI) for more information about the process of expungement.

U.C.A. 78-27-64. Regulation of firearms reserved to state -- Lawsuits prohibited.

> **"Plain Talk"**
>
> This law, passed in 2000, prevents Utah cities and counties from bringing lawsuits against gun manufacturers like those brought by Chicago and New Orleans. Such cities have caused their own crime problems by taking guns away from the law-abiding and by encouraging generations of welfare. Rather than accept responsibility for the problems this "social engineering" has caused, the mayors of these cities are suing innocent gun manufacturers with the intent to bankrupt. Fortunately, many of these lawsuits have been dismissed (the dismissal of New Orleans' lawsuit was just upheld by the Louisiana Supreme Court). Rep. Matt Throckmorton, R-Springville, you win the Pancho Vilos Infamous Revolutionary Pistolero Freedom Award for sponsoring this law. May you live forever!

ACTUAL TEXT

(1) As prescribed by Section 76-10-500 , all authority to regulate firearms is reserved to the state through the Legislature.

(2) A person who lawfully designs, manufactures, markets, advertises, transports, or sells firearms or ammunition to the public may not be sued by the state or any of its political subdivisions for the subsequent use, whether lawfully or unlawfully, of the firearm or ammunition, unless the suit is based on the breach of a contract or warranty for a firearm or ammunition purchased by the state or political subdivision.

R28-2-2. Surplus Firearms -- Definitions.

> **"Plain Talk"**
>
> The term "firearms" refers to all confiscated firearms. This includes guns seized during an arrest, and surplus guns that are no longer used by local police departments and other agencies which allow their employees to carry guns. The Utah state agency that deals with surplus firearms is referred to as "USASP." You will see that handguns are treated differently than rifles and shotguns. Wouldn't it be nice to buy confiscated and surplus guns from the state at a discount price? Forget it, they only sell to licensed dealers.

ACTUAL TEXT

"Firearms" means all state owned firearms, including any confiscated or seized firearms (that the state has authority to sell) and any firearms declared surplus by local subdivisions.

"USASP" means Utah State Agency for Surplus Property.

"Handgun" means pistols and revolvers.

"Hunting and sporting rifles" means long barreled shotguns and rifles manufactured for hunting or sporting purposes.

"Nonlicensee" means an individual or organization not licensed by the Federal Bureau of Alcohol, Tobacco and Firearms to buy or sell firearms.

R28-2-2

Commentary

As explained below, the State has targeted handguns. Once confiscated, they destroy them. Do you get the feeling that the State is falling for the anti-self-defense philosophy that "it's the guns that are bad, not the people?"

R28-2-3. Surplus Firearms -- Procedures.

"Plain Talk"

The Utah State Agency for Surplus Property cannot sell surplus guns directly to the general public, they have to sell them to gun dealers. This applies only to rifles and shotguns. Handguns are either sold to law enforcement agencies, sent to the crime lab or destroyed. If your gun was used in a crime you didn't commit, and you can prove it's your gun, you will probably get it back. However, if you used the gun to commit a crime, Hasta la Vista, Baby! It will either be sold to a police agency, kept by the crime lab to prosecute you or reappear on store shelves as a frying pan! Retiring police officers can buy their service pistols at ½ of their current replacement cost (not fair market value).

ACTUAL TEXT

A.   All state owned firearms shall be disposed of under the procedures of Rule R28-1.

1.   As an exception to the purchase priority listed in Section R28-1-4, the sale of firearms directly to the general public by the USASP is prohibited.

2.   Hunting and sporting rifles meeting Federal Firearms regulations may be sold only to firearms dealers licensed by the Federal Bureau of Alcohol, Tobacco and Firearms in accordance with the purchase priority listed in Section R28-1-4.

a.   The sale of handguns directly to firearms dealers licensed by the Federal Bureau of Alcohol Tobacco and Firearms by the USASP is prohibited.

3.   Handguns not purchased by legally constituted state law enforcement agencies and all firearms not meeting Federal Firearms regulations will either be transferred to the Utah State Public Safety Crime Lab for use or be destroyed.

B.   A peace officer retiring from state service and desiring to retain his service firearm, may purchase his assigned firearm at one-half of its current replacement cost.

1. Proof of intent to retire shall be sent to the USASP along with a completed standard form SP-1 and shall be signed by an authorized agent of the owning agency.

2. The replacement cost shall be determined by the most recent state purchase order or other documentation for the specified firearm(s) and a copy shall accompany the completed standard form SP-1.

3. All retentions must be in accordance with Federal Firearms regulations pursuant to Sections 921(a)(19) and 922(s) of Title 18, United States Code.

a. Written certification that surplus firearms meet federal firearms regulations shall be provided by the owning agency or a qualified armorer.

4. All retentions shall be subject to good working condition of the firearm.

a. Written certification specifying the condition of surplus firearms shall be provided by the owning agency or a qualified armorer.

5. A five day waiting period is required for handgun sales to a nonlicensee.

a. An exception to the five day waiting period will be made when the retiring officer presents a written statement from the Department or Division Head or authorized agent verifying that possession of the handgun by the purchaser would not violate the law.

C. The USASP Director or designee may make exceptions to the firearms rule for good cause. A good cause exception requires a weighing of:

1. The cost to the state;
2. The potential liability to the state;
3. The overall best interest of the state.

ADDITIONAL REGULATIONS "PROMULGATED" BY BUREAUCRATS ATTEMPTING TO REGULATE FIREARMS

The Utah Constitution gives only the Legislature the authority to regulate the use of firearms (see Chapter VI). Unless the Legislature delegates this authority by statute to another governmental entity, including the executive branch (the governor), that entity has no authority to regulate the possession or use of firearms. Unfortunately, a host of bureaucrats have promulgated regulations claiming to regulate firearms. We don't have room to put the full text of all of these regulations in at this point. To the extent that they conflict with the Utah code sections contained in Chapters VII and VIII these regulations are unenforceable. No "Plain Talk" summaries are needed, but they certainly invite critical commentary. These offensive regulations are listed in numerical order as follows:

R65-7-11. General Conduct [Horse Racing]

. . .

6. **Firearms.** No person shall possess any firearm within the enclosure [racing facility and parking lot] unless he is a fully qualified peace officer as defined in the laws of the State of Utah.

. . .

R65-7-11

Commentary

As stated in the Utah Constitution and Utah code, only the Legislature has the authority to regulate firearms unless it specifically delegates that authority to an administrative agency. We find no code sections giving the Utah Horse Racing Commission specific authority to regulate firearms. Therefore, this regulation is not enforceable. It's just another example of how bureaucrats tend to encroach on individual freedoms whenever given the chance. Pancho suggests any bureaucrats caught "promulgating" away individual freedoms without legislative authority should have their stripes and buttons torn off and their retirement benefits forfeited.

R430-100-14. Safety [Child Care Centers]

. . .

(5) There shall be no firearms or other weapons accessible to children. Firearms and other weapons shall be stored separately from ammunition and all shall be in a locked cabinet or area.

R430-100-14

Commentary

The first sentence is consistent with Utah code sections keeping children from having unauthorized possession of firearms and weapons. However, if the second sentence is interpreted and used to keep concealed weapon holders from carrying concealed firearms at child care centers, it is illegal and unenforceable.

R477-9-1. Standards of [Employee] Conduct. [State Human Resource Management]

. . .

(5) Employees shall not carry firearms in any facility owned or operated by the state, or in any state vehicle, or at any time or any place while on state business.

(a) This rule shall not apply to sworn officers as defined by Section 53-13-103, or employees whose assigned duties require them to use a firearm.

(b) Employees who violate this rule shall be subject to disciplinary action pursuant to R477-11.

AUTHORITY:

Utah Code Section 67-19-6

R477-9-1

Commentary

This is the regulation that prohibits state employees, whose job duties do not require them to have a firearm, from having a firearm. This is being enforced illegally, in my opinion, against concealed weapon permit holders. Notice at the bottom of the regulation, it cites U.C.A. 67-19-6 as the authority from the Legislature giving the personnel department the power to disarm innocent concealed weapon permit holders. Let's look at 67-19-6 and see if there is anything in it authorizing the regulation of firearms.

U.C.A. 67-19-6. Responsibilities of director

(1) The director shall:

(a) develop, implement, and administer a statewide program of personnel management for state employees that will:

(i) aid in the efficient execution of public policy;

(ii) foster careers in public service for qualified employees; and

(iii) render assistance to state agencies in performing their missions;

(b) perform those functions necessary to implement this chapter unless otherwise assigned or prohibited;

(c) perform duties assigned by the governor or statute;

(d) adopt rules for personnel management according to the procedures of Title 63, Chapter 46a, Utah Administrative Rulemaking Act;

(e) establish and maintain a management information system that will furnish the governor, the Legislature, and agencies with current information on authorized positions, payroll, and related matters concerning state personnel;

(f) in cooperation with other agencies, conduct research and planning activities to:

(i) determine and prepare for future state personnel needs;

(ii) develop methods for improving public personnel management; and

(iii) propose needed policy changes to the governor;

(g) study the character, causes, and extent of discrimination in state employment and develop plans for its elimination through programs consistent with federal and state laws governing equal employment opportunity and affirmative action in employment;

(h) when requested by counties, municipalities, and other political subdivisions of the state, provide technical service and advice on personnel management at a charge determined by the director;

(i) establish compensation policies and procedures for early voluntary retirement;

(j) confer with the heads of other agencies about human resource policies and procedures;

(k) submit an annual report to the governor and the Legislature; and

(l) (i) identify all employee positions in each agency that have been vacant for more than 90 days as of August 1 of each year; and

(ii) by no later than September 1, of each year, provide a report of all employee positions in each agency identified in Subsection (1)(l)(i) to:

(A) the Governor's Office of Planning and Budget; and

(B) the Office of the Legislative Fiscal Analyst.

(2) (a) After consultation with the governor and the heads of other agencies, the director shall establish and coordinate statewide training programs.

(b) The programs developed under this Subsection (2) shall have application to more than one agency.

(c) The department may not establish training programs that train employees to perform highly specialized or technical jobs and tasks.

(3) (a) (i) The department may collect fees for training as authorized by this Subsection (3).

(ii) Training funded from General Fund appropriations shall be treated as a separate program within the department budget.

(iii) All money received from fees under this section will be accounted for by the department as a separate user driven training program.

(iv) The user training program includes the costs of developing, procuring, and presenting training and development programs, and other associated costs for these programs.

(b) (i) Funds remaining at the end of the fiscal year in the user training program are nonlapsing.

(ii) Each year, as part of the appropriations process, the Legislature shall review the amount of nonlapsing funds remaining at the end of the fiscal year and may, by statute, require the department to lapse a portion of the funds.

Did you see anything about regulating firearms in this code section? I didn't. See bureaucrats just stretch their authority as far as they can before someone complains. But the employees are afraid to complain because the personnel managers have the authority to fire them. Of course if an employee-concealed-weapon-permit-holder doesn't have a firearm to protect himself from an armed attack and is killed, let's blame the guns. After all we have POLICIES preventing guns from being brought to work.

Pancho hopes you personnel managers can live with yourselves when your employees are killed or injured because of your cowardly and foolish "no weapons policies." You employees need to band together and let your employees know how you feel about this. Also, take your employers and managers to the shooting range (as participants, not targets, of course!). When people become comfortable around firearms, they can better understand the advantage of "grabbing a 9mm" rather than "dialing 911." For an authoritative opinion, ask the father and son team managing a Salt Lake City pawn shop who were wearing guns when robbers burst into their store with guns ablaze in the Spring of 2001. The pawn shop employees sent the would be killers packing with a bullet lodged in one of them. They were caught after the wounded attacker sought medical help in Pocatello, Idaho. These employees told newsmen that they would have been killed had they not been armed. Why can't state personnel managers be wise enough to encourage concealed weapon permit holders to help protect their co-employees?

R501-12-8. Safety.

. . .

E. Foster parents maintaining firearms in the home shall assure that the firearms are inaccessible to children at all times. Firearms and ammunition shall be securely locked. Firearms kept in the home or on the premises will be rendered inoperable when possible.

F. No firearms shall be allowed in foster homes that contract with DYC.

R501-12-8

Commentary

The first sentence is consistent with Utah code sections keeping children from having unauthorized possession of firearms and weapons. However, if the second sentence is interpreted and used to keep concealed weapon holders from carrying concealed firearms in foster homes, it is illegal and unenforceable. Did it ever occur to these bureaucrats that responsible foster parents protect their own children and could also protect foster children with a gun kept in the home? After all, Utahns have an absolute right to protect their homes with a firearm (see Chapter VII, U.C.A. 76-10-511). But these bureaucrats don't care about the rights and liberties of the good guys; they are setting up a defense to a lawsuit. If a foster child somehow got ahold of a foster parents gun and was injured, the child's parents would sue the state. The state would respond, "we have a policy against having guns in the home. Therefore, we can't be liable." So I guess it comes down to this, "The rights of insurance underwriters to decide whether the people can keep and bear arms, shall not be infringed."

Actually, prohibiting foster parents from allowing the foster child to have access to a firearm without the express written consent of the child's parent or guardian is sufficient to protect the state from liability. But state officials don't just want a shield, they want a bunker, even if it means eroding important civil rights.

R539-6-8. Code of Conduct.

f. No firearms are allowed in residential or day training facilities. Specialized foster homes, Professional Parents, and Respite providers must follow the licensing standards for Foster Care in regard to storage of firearms. (R501-12-9)

R539-6-8

Commentary

More of the same. Overkill. Just say they have to keep the guns out of the kid's hands unless the guardian consents to letting the child shoot a gun with adult supervision. What's the matter with that? Afraid the kid might like it and begin to appreciate the benefit of owning a firearm? Come on. Pancho knows there are bureaucrats that understand the importance of an armed citizenry. Have the courage to stand up for what is right. Pretty soon your employers and personnel managers will respect your courage and begin doing the right thing themselves. Be brave patriots; not non-assertive puppets whose consciences are fettered by the fear of speaking out and losing your state pension benefits.

R614-4-15. Slurry, Water Gel and Emulsions.

3. No person shall be allowed to smoke, carry matches or any flame-producing devices, or carry any firearms while in or about bulk vehicles effecting the mixing, transfer, or down-the-hole loading of slurry, water gels, and emulsions, at or near the blasting site.

R614-4-15

Commentary

Okay, Pancho understands the need to keep construction workers from shooting their guns in the air around highly explosive materials. "Hey, you tanker truck guys. Watch me shoot the cap right off your tanker spout . . ." Baaaalllllooooooooooouuuuuuiiiiiieeee!!!!! But why not just prohibit them from SHOOTING their guns instead of POSSESSING them? You can't keep concealed weapon permit holders from possessing guns anyway. This regulation is preempted by the concealed weapon statutes.

R728-404-5. Special Regulations.

. . .

D. Firearms.

1. Any firearm brought into the Academy by a resident student must be surrendered for storage in the weapons vault. Unload all such weapons prior to entering the building. No weapons are allowed in student dormitory rooms under any condition.

2. The firearm may be retrieved at the conclusion of the course or prior to departure on the weekends. Routinely checking the weapon out at the end of each training day will not be possible.

3. Weapons may be checked out for use on the range, for weekends, or as directed by the training staff.

4. Any discharge of a weapon on the Academy property, unless a part of the training experience, will result in immediate suspension from the Academy pending an investigation.

. . .

R728-404-5

Commentary

Okay, this one involves Police Academy attendees. Isn't it comforting to know that the State doesn't think it's officers are mature enough to possess a firearm in their dormitories (temporary residences), see Chapter VII, U.C.A. 76-10-511, the state statute that probably preempts this regulation. A similar regulation (R728-505-6) applies the same rule to canine officer trainees.

CHAPTER XIII: THE BRADY LAW AND OTHER FEDERAL STATUTES

Pancho's Wisdom
Buying a gun is not a purchase, it's a celebration; Shooting is not a sport; it's a jubilee!

INTRODUCTION

The purpose of this chapter is to give the reader an overview of a few of the most important federal gun laws that affect Utahns. There is no way we could include a discussion of all federal firearms laws. We didn't feel like sticking a 500-page chapter on federal gun law, into the middle of a 300-page book about Utah gun law. We focus on laws that affect all Utah gun owners and hunters rather than laws that affect people with more specialized interests such as gun dealers, security guards and the few people who own machine guns. People involved in such enterprises generally know the rules because of their unique interests. If you have the overwhelming desire to read every federal code section relating to firearms, get Alan Korwin's book, *Gun Laws of America*, referred to in the footnote below.[76] Comprised of just over 350 pages, *Gun Laws* contains all of the firearms laws found in the United States Code. Even Korwin's book didn't have room for the thousands of additional pages of gun laws contained in the Code of Federal Regulations and the Federal Register.

We find the most notorious federal gun laws in the Gun Control Act of 1968, passed largely as a result of the assassinations of President John F. Kennedy and Senator Robert Kennedy. In the federal code it extends from 18 U.S.C.§ 921 to 930.[77] There is not enough space in this book permitting commentary on the whole act,

---

[76] *Gun Laws of America*, by Alan Korwin with Attorney Michael P. Anthony. The book can be ordered through Bloomfield Press, 12629 N. Tatum #440, Phoenix, AZ, 85032, or call (602) 996-4020 or (800) 707-4020, and also through Dillon Distributors, the reloading company that publishes "The Blue Press," Dillon Precision Products, Inc., 8009 E. Dillon's Way, Scottsdale, AZ 85260-9865, (800) 762-3845.

[77] U.S.C. is an abbreviation for United States Code. Title 18 deals with crime and criminal procedure. Section 922 describes what is unlawful. Section 923 applies to the licensing of gun dealers. The penalties for violating section 922 are in section 924.

but we have included the sections most relevant to Utahns. These include the Brady Act, the Lautenberg Amendment, the Assault Weapon Ban and the Gun Free School Zone Act.

Each "Plain Talk" section begins with a phrase introducing the main topic of that particular subsection, for example, "GUN DEALERS - 18 U.S.C. § 922 (a)(1)," "BUYING GUNS ACROSS STATE LINES - 18 U.S.C. § 922(a)(3)," "GUN FREE SCHOOL ZONE ACT - 18 U.S.C. § 922(q)," " THE BRADY ACT - 18 U.S.C. § 922(s),(t)," etc. These are also listed in the Table of Contents for quick reference. Also included in this edition are federal laws relating to restoring one's right to bear arms ("Relief from Disabilities") 18 U.S.C. § 925, remedies against the state and federal government for improper denial of the right to buy a gun under the Brady Act (including an award of attorney fees) 18 U.S.C. § 925A, how to transport your guns when traveling out of state, even in states that don't permit certain types of firearms, 18 U.S.C. § 926A, the effect federal law has on state law, 18 U.S.C. § 927, possession of firearms in federal facilities (including post offices), 18 U.S.C. § 930.

Congress claims it had the authority under the "Commerce Clause" to pass the Gun Control Act of 1968.   But the Commerce Clause, Section 8, paragraph (3) wasn't enacted to give Congress the authority to regulate firearms. It simply states, that Congress has the authority "To regulate commerce with foreign nations, and among the several states, and with the Indian tribes." Obviously it was written to regulate TRADE between the U.S. and foreign nations, the Indian tribes and among the several states i.e. to keep these government bodies from treating each other unfairly in business deals. Neither the terms "firearms" nor "weapons" appear anywhere in the text of the clause. In fact, as late as the 1920's Congress hadn't ever regulated firearms or weapons by means of the Commerce Clause. When it tried to figure out a way to keep bootleggers from machine-gunning each other, it turned to Congress' taxing power to enact the National Firearms Act. That was pretty awkward, because the purpose of Congress' power to tax was to raise money, not to lock bootleggers up.

Hopefully, the "constitutionalists" on the Supreme Court, Justices Scalia and Thomas (Pancho prays for them nightly), will lead the charge to keep Congress from continuing to infringe on the right of American citizens to bear arms.   The Supreme Court's recent decisions striking down the Gun Free School Zone Act (section 922(q) of the Gun Control Act of 1968) and the Violence Against Women Act as exceeding Congress' Commerce powers, suggest that these courageous and intellectually honest Supreme Court Justices have already begun to have a positive influence on the rest of the Court.

18 U.S.C. § 922 Unlawful acts.

> ### GUN DEALERS - 18 U.S.C. § 922 (a)(1)
> #### "Plain Talk"
> If you don't have a federal firearms license (FFL), i.e. if you're not a gun dealer, you CAN'T RUN A BUSINESS importing, manufacturing, SELLING or shipping FIREARMS[78] in interstate or foreign commerce. If you are buying and selling guns for a profit and don't have your dealer's license, you could be charged with a federal offense.
>
> Many people with clean criminal records, who could buy a gun from a dealer, prefer instead to buy from a private citizen so the gun doesn't have to be registered in their name. They are afraid that the logical result of federal gun registration will be the eventual confiscation of all firearms by the federal government. It is a legitimate concern for people living in a society that considers owning a gun to be politically incorrect.

ACTUAL TEXT
(a) It shall be unlawful--
    (1) for any person--
        (A) except a licensed importer, licensed manufacturer, or licensed dealer, to engage in the business of importing, manufacturing, or dealing in firearms, or in the course of such business to ship, transport, or receive any firearm in interstate or foreign commerce; or
        (B) except a licensed importer or licensed manufacturer, to engage in the business of importing or manufacturing ammunition, or in the course of such business, to ship, transport, or receive any ammunition in interstate or foreign commerce;

> ### GUN DEALERS - 18 U.S.C. § 922 (a)(1)
> #### Commentary
> Unfortunately, many laws enacted to stop "gun runners," go too far and restrict law-abiding citizens from selling or giving guns to other law-abiding citizens. These laws are "over kill" and should be repealed. There has been an enormous increase in the number of

---

[78] The term "firearm" as used in this code section does not include most black powder and muzzleloader rifles and pistols unless they were designed to use modern ammunition, 18 U.S.C. § 921(3)(16). That is why you can still order these guns out of a catalog from out-of-state stores.

federal gun laws since 1968. They have done little to keep illegal weapons out of the hands of criminals (kinda like drug laws don't keep dopers from buying meth); but they have created substantial obstacles for law-abiding citizens who want to protect themselves and their families. Read on and you'll see what I mean.

BUYING GUNS ACROSS STATE LINES - 18 U.S.C. § 922(a)(3)

"Plain Talk"

It's against the law to buy a gun, or receive one as a gift, from anyone living outside your state of residence. A grandpa can't gift a .22 rifle to his grandson who lives in a different state without jumping through the right hoops. The "Hoops" are:

☻ you can INHERIT a gun from an out-of-state relative[79] (18 U.S.C. § 922(a)(3)(A)).

☻ you can buy a RIFLE OR SHOTGUN from an out-of-state dealer (18 U.S.C. § 922(a)(3)(B)) if:

- the sale is not prohibited by the state where the dealer resides

- it's not illegal in the state where the purchaser resides, AND

- the purchaser meets in person with the dealer (18 USC § 922(b)(3)(A)).

☻ you can BORROW or RENT a gun temporarily for lawful sporting purposes, such as shooting at a target range or hunting on a game preserve (18 U.S.C. § 922(b)(3)(B)). A few years ago, I spiced up my summer vacation in Panama City, Florida by renting a Smith & Wesson 686 at a local shooting range.

☻ A DEALER can send firearms across state lines to other dealers (18 U.S.C. § 922(a)(2)). You can buy a gun from an out-of-state gun store, but you will have to get an in-state dealer to fill out the "Brady" paperwork. Generally, in-state dealers charge $25 to $35 for this service. If your Uncle Mike, who lives in Idaho, wants to give you his double-barreled coach shotgun you have always coveted for your cowboy action shooting matches, you or he will have to pay two

---

[79] Remember, "inherit" means the relative is DEAD! If he or she is alive, it's a gift and it's ILLEGAL, unless the gift passes through a gun dealer as explained here.

transfer fees, one to a gun dealer in Idaho and another to a gun dealer in Utah.

ACTUAL TEXT [It shall be unlawful–]

(3) for any person other than a licensed importer, licensed manufacturer, licensed dealer, or licensed collector to transport into or receive in the State where he resides (or if the person is a corporation or other business entity, the State where it maintains a place of business) any firearm purchased or otherwise obtained by such person outside that State, except that this paragraph

(A) shall not preclude any person who lawfully acquires a firearm by bequest or intestate succession in a State other than his State of residence from transporting the firearm into or receiving it in that State, if it is lawful for such person to purchase or possess such firearm in that State,

(B) shall not apply to the transportation or receipt of a firearm obtained in conformity with subsection (b)(3) of this section, and

(C) shall not apply to the transportation of any firearm acquired in any State prior to the effective date of this chapter [effective Dec. 16, 1968];

TRANSFERRING OUT OF STATE - 18 U.S.C. § 922(a)(5)
"Plain Talk"

This subsection is the flip side of the one above. That subsection made it unlawful to RECEIVE a firearm from out of state, this one makes it unlawful for you to GIVE OR SELL guns to someone in another state. The same exceptions apply to this subsection as the one above, inheritance, rifles and shotguns, etc. You can't legally give your Browning "Sweet 16" shotgun to your nephew who lives in Texas. But, you can transfer the weapon to a dealer here, who can, in turn, send it to a dealer in Texas. The Texas dealer will then fill out the paperwork and hand the shotgun over to your nephew (assuming he is 18 years of age or older and the transaction does not violate the laws in the State of Texas). Aren't you glad Congress makes grandpa pay to give guns to their grandchildren so we can keep guns out of the hands of violent criminals?

ACTUAL TEXT

(5) for any person (other than a licensed importer, licensed manufacturer, licensed dealer, or licensed collector) to transfer, sell, trade, give, transport, or deliver any firearm to any person (other than a licensed importer, licensed manufacturer, licensed dealer, or licensed collector) who the transferor knows or has reasonable cause to believe does not reside in (or if the person is a corporation or other business entity, does not maintain a

place of business in) the State in which the transferor resides; except that this paragraph shall not apply to

(A) the transfer, transportation, or delivery of a firearm made to carry out a bequest of a firearm to, or an acquisition by intestate succession of a firearm by, a person who is permitted to acquire or possess a firearm under the laws of the State of his residence, and

(B) the loan or rental of a firearm to any person for temporary use for lawful sporting purposes;

Commentary

This section and the one above create substantial restrictions on the rights of law-abiding citizens to buy, sell or give away firearms to other citizens without criminal records. Congress passed these laws under the guise of keeping guns out of the hands of criminals. Isn't it enough that the feds have imposed heavy penalties on those who knowingly sell guns to felons (10 years) and upon felons who possess firearms (10 years) or give false information to buy them (10 years)? Why penalize a kind, old grandfather who simply wants his grandson to have his trusty old .22 to remember him by if neither the grandpa nor the grandson are felons? This is NONSENSE and more of us hard-working taxpayers need to start making noise about it.

LYING TO BUY A GUN OR AMMO - 18 U.S.C. § 922(a)(6)
"Plain Talk"

If you lie to buy a gun or ammunition, you could be imprisoned for up to ten years (see 18 U.S.C. 924(2)). You then become ineligible to possess a firearm or ammunition under 18 U.S.C. § 922(g) (see discussion below).

ACTUAL TEXT

(6) for any person in connection with the acquisition or attempted acquisition of any firearm or ammunition from a licensed importer, licensed manufacturer, licensed dealer, or licensed collector, knowingly to make any false or fictitious oral or written statement or to furnish or exhibit any false, fictitious, or misrepresented identification, intended or likely to deceive such importer, manufacturer, dealer, or collector with respect to any fact material to the lawfulness of the sale or other disposition of such firearm or ammunition under the provisions of this chapter [18 U.S.C. 921 et seq.];

AGE RESTRICTIONS ON BUYING GUNS AND AMMO - 18 U.S.C. § 922(b)(1)

"Plain Talk"

This subsection of the federal Gun Control Act of 1968 prohibits gun dealers from selling handguns or handgun ammunition to persons under 21 years of age. Persons under 18 can't buy rifles, shotguns or ammunition for rifles and shotguns from gun dealers. It is interesting, however, that persons OTHER THAN GUN DEALERS may sell handguns to persons 18 or older, but younger than 21, if they are not simply acting as "middlemen" to help gun dealers get around this age restriction.

ACTUAL TEXT

(b) It shall be unlawful for any licensed importer, licensed manufacturer, licensed dealer, or licensed collector to sell or deliver--

(1) any firearm or ammunition to any individual who the licensee knows or has reasonable cause to believe is less than eighteen years of age, and, if the firearm, or ammunition is other than a shotgun or rifle, or ammunition for a shotgun or rifle, to any individual who the licensee knows or has reasonable cause to believe is less than twenty-one years of age;

18 U.S.C. § 922(b)(1)

Commentary

Young adults between the ages of 18 and 21 with CLEAN CRIMINAL RECORDS are not the ones creating a problem. It's the gangsters with histories of violent crimes. Both state and federal laws already provide severe penalties for convicted felons to possess any firearm. The laws should not prevent young adults with clean records from protecting themselves with handguns. The law-abiding majority should not be held accountable for the actions of the lawbreaking minority. State law prohibits anyone to sell any firearm to a minor outside the presence of his parent or guardian, U.C.A. 76-10-509.9, and this is sufficient to protect children. Unfortunately, state law could give gun dealers the impression that it is legal to sell a handgun to a minor as long as the child's parent is present. Federal law does not allow such a sale even if the parent is present. This law should be amended as follows:

(b) It shall be unlawful for any licensed importer, licensed manufacturer, licensed dealer, or licensed collector to sell or deliver--

(1) any firearm or ammunition to any individual who the licensee knows or has reasonable cause to believe is less

than eighteen years of age, ~~and, if the firearm, or ammunition is other than a shotgun or rifle, or ammunition for a shotgun or rifle, to any individual who the licensee knows or has reasonable cause to believe is less than twenty-one years of age~~ **unless authorized by state law.**

This amendment would empower the states to pass laws more lenient than federal law if they want to. Utah legislators have decided that a dealer should be able to sell to a minor if the minor's parents are present. This amendment would allow Utah legislators to make such a decision.

SELLING OR GIVING GUNS TO PEOPLE WHO CAN'T LEGALLY BUY FROM A GUN DEALER - 18 U.S.C. § 922(d)

"Plain Talk"

You, AS A NON-GUN DEALER, cannot SELL or GIVE a firearm to anyone that YOU KNOW has been convicted of a felony, or a federal offense punishable by a prison term exceeding one year. The same applies to unlawful users of controlled drugs, drug addicts, fugitives from justice, illegal aliens, people with mental defects, those who have been dishonorably discharged, people who renounced their citizenship to the United States, and those having a restraining order against them preventing them from threatening or attempting to injure an intimate partner or child (relating to spouse or child abuse). In other words, DO NOT agree to act as a MIDDLE MAN for someone who cannot legally buy a gun from a licensed gun dealer. If you do, you are subject to imprisonment up to ten years and will lose your rights to bear arms. (18 U.S.C. § 924(2)).

ACTUAL TEXT

(d) It shall be unlawful for any person to sell or otherwise dispose of any firearm or ammunition to any person knowing or having reasonable cause to believe that such person--

(1) is under indictment for, or has been convicted in any court of, a crime punishable by imprisonment for a term exceeding one year;

(2) is a fugitive from justice;

(3) is an unlawful user of or addicted to any controlled substance (as defined in section 102 of the Controlled Substances Act (21 U.S.C. 802));

(4) has been adjudicated as a mental defective or has been committed to any mental institution;

(5) who, being an alien, is illegally or unlawfully in the United States;

(6) who has been discharged from the Armed Forces under dishonorable conditions;

(7) who, having been a citizen of the United States, has renounced his citizenship;

(8) is subject to a court order that restrains such person from harassing, stalking, or threatening an intimate partner of such person or child of such intimate partner or person, or engaging in other conduct that would place an intimate partner in reasonable fear of bodily injury to the partner or child, except that this paragraph shall only apply to a court order that--

(A) was issued after a hearing of which such person received actual notice, and at which such person had the opportunity to participate; and

(B) (i) includes a finding that such person represents a credible threat to the physical safety of such intimate partner or child; or

(ii) by its terms explicitly prohibits the use, attempted use, or threatened use of physical force against such intimate partner or child that would reasonably be expected to cause bodily injury; or

(9) has been convicted in any court of a misdemeanor crime of domestic violence.

TAKING YOUR GUNS ON AIRPLANE TRIPS - 18 U.S.C. § 922(e)

"Plain Talk"

If you want to take your guns with you on an airplane, you must "declare" that you have them and turn them over to the airlines. You can't take a firearm or ammunition with you on a bus or any other interstate carrier. This section also prohibits the carrier from labeling your luggage or package on the outside telling the world (and potential thieves) that the package or luggage contains firearms or ammunition. If you are going to ship a firearm or ammunition, you have to give the carrier (such as UPS) written notice.

The law not only prohibits passengers from carrying weapons, it sets forth detailed procedures airlines must follow to keep firearms out of the passenger compartments of airliners. The Code of Federal Regulations, 14 C.F.R. 108.11, spells out these procedures. We only included the paragraphs relevant to commercial passengers. The airline must require:

a. that the passenger declares in writing or orally the weapon is unloaded, and

b. pistols must be locked in the luggage, and only the passenger can retain the key or combination.

> The airline has the discretion to decide what kind of container to store the firearm in during flight. Airlines that require more than this exceed the law.

ACTUAL TEXT

(e) It shall be unlawful for any person knowingly to deliver or cause to be delivered to any common or contract carrier for transportation or shipment in interstate or foreign commerce, to persons other than licensed importers, licensed manufacturers, licensed dealers, or licensed collectors, any package or other container in which there is any firearm or ammunition without written notice to the carrier that such firearm or ammunition is being transported or shipped; except that any passenger who owns or legally possesses a firearm or ammunition being transported aboard any common or contract carrier for movement with the passenger in interstate or foreign commerce may deliver said firearm or ammunition into the custody of the pilot, captain, conductor or operator of such common or contract carrier for the duration of the trip without violating any of the provisions of this chapter [18 U.S.C. § 921 et seq.]. No common or contract carrier shall require or cause any label, tag, or other written notice to be placed on the outside of any package, luggage, or other container that such package, luggage, or other container contains a firearm.

14 CFR 108.11 Carriage of weapons.
. . .

(d) No certificate holder **[airline or other interstate carrier]** may knowingly permit any person to transport, nor may any person transport or tender for transport, any unloaded firearm in checked baggage aboard an airplane unless--

　(1) The passenger declares to the certificate holder, either orally or in writing before checking the baggage, that any firearm carried in the baggage is unloaded;

　(2) The firearm is carried in a container the certificate holder considers appropriate for air transportation;

　(3) When the firearm is other than a shotgun, rifle, or other firearm normally fired from the shoulder position, the baggage in which it is carried is locked, and only the passenger checking the baggage retains the key or combination; and

. . .

18 U.S.C. § 922(e)

Commentary

　It's easier to take your guns with you on an airline (domestic flights only; not international) trip than you might think. It's part of my in-flight entertainment package to watch a busy ticket agent struggle to remember the protocol for checking a firearm ("Hmm, let's see, I remember seeing this in the instruction manual somewhere; is it procedure 649 or 496?"). Plan on checking your luggage at the ticket counter, though. You can't take your firearms into the passenger compartment of the plane, so carry-on luggage is out of the question. Sky caps at the Salt Lake Airport are not authorized to accept a Declaration of Firearms.

Let me share with you how a twisted member of the "Gun Culture" gets his jollies declaring a firearm. First, I always place my unloaded pistol or revolver in a hard gun case that fits inside my suit case. Most of the hard plastic cases have one or two small holes in the latches for placement of a luggage lock (I use the tiny cheap ones[80] that are no larger than a quarter -- You may want an extra one for the suitcase itself, just in case the agent interprets 14 C.F.R. 108.11(3) to mean that the suitcase must be locked). Because C.F.R. 108.11(2) gives airlines the discretion to decide what kind of case is suitable to carry a firearm, if you're not familiar with the requirements of a particular airline, you had better call in advance. This is particularly true if you are flying on more than one airline during the trip. You don't want to have an airline disapprove of your gun case when you are running late for a connecting flight and you have no one to leave your gun with.

I place my ammo, which is still in the original cardboard container, in a separate suitcase. I usually take my North American Arms mini revolver that holds five .22 Magnum rounds so that I can conceal easily in states that recognize my Utah permit. By calling the police departments in the cities in which I will be staying, I check the

---

[80] Unless I'm carrying a particularly valuable gun.

concealed carry laws.[81] Appendix E contains the phone number of the attorney general of each state.

I take clips (containing no ammunition of course) out of pistols and if possible, cylinders out of revolvers, to put airline agents at ease. It helps them to verify the guns are unloaded and safely stored. Some ask to see the guns, and others simply have me sign the bright orange tags declaring the guns to be unloaded. Federal law requires the tags be placed INSIDE suitcases, not OUTSIDE. If tags were attached to the outside of suitcases, they would be like miniature neon signs broadcasting to luggage handlers and fellow passengers, many of whom may be ineligible to buy guns, that you have a firearm in your suitcase.

When agents ask to see my gun, if I have my mini revolver, I tell them to brace themselves for the biggest, most repulsive looking revolver they have ever seen. When they, especially the lady ticket agents, see my tiny little "derringer," the usual response is a sigh of relief and something like, "Oh, how CUTE!" I then close and lock the gun case, zip the red Firearm Declaration Label INSIDE my suit case and hand it to the agent. To keep me from having to buy cartridges in a strange city, I pack them in their original container in a SEPARATE suitcase (some airlines have added this requirement). Consistent with my attitude of full disclosure, I tell the ticket agent about the bullets. If you follow these steps, you should have no trouble traveling by air with your guns.

PERSONS PROHIBITED FROM POSSESSING FIREARMS UNDER FEDERAL LAW - 18 U.S.C. § 922(g)

---

[81] I also ask officers what the laws are with respect to carrying a weapon in a rental car and keeping it loaded in my hotel room. Most policemen are very helpful and empathetic. When I tell them I have a Utah concealed weapon permit, several have invited me to conceal in their state, even though their state does not recognize Utah's concealed weapon permit. A peace officer in the Florida Panhandle once told me, "whose gonna know ya got it unless ya gotta use it?" He meant if I needed a gun to protect myself or my family, I would probably rather be charged with a misdemeanor, rather than be defenseless against an armed criminal. Hmm...(I'm not advising you to break the law, I'm simply telling you what I've been told.) But always remember to ask what the penalty is for concealing within a particular jurisdiction. Don't forget, concealing on a Utah bus or in a bus terminal without a permit is a felony (see discussion in Chapter VII above) and other states may have similar laws.

"Plain Talk"

If you have been convicted of a crime punishable by a prison term of more than one year, are a fugitive of justice, are an unlawful user of or are addicted to any controlled drugs, have been found by a court to be mentally defective or committed to a mental institution, are an illegal alien, a nonimmigrant status alien [like a tourist or here on a visa, not intending to immigrate] and don't meet certain exceptions [here for hunting or sporting purposes, on official diplomatic business etc.], have been dishonorably discharged, have renounced your citizenship, are subject to a court order preventing you from abusing your wife or child, or have been convicted of a misdemeanor of domestic violence, it is illegal to possess or transfer a firearm or ammunition "in interstate commerce." (I'm not sure how anyone possesses a firearm in interstate commerce, but that's what it prohibits.) Violators could be sentenced to 10 years in prison.

Section 922(g)(8) prohibits possession of firearms by anyone subject to a court order related to domestic violence if the order either (1) makes a finding that the person represents a threat or (2) prohibits the use of force against a family member. This section was the subject of a recent case in U.S. District Court in Salt Lake City. Because this case involved a Utah citizen, I thought it was important to include it in these materials and to inform Utah citizens of a similar Second Amendment case decided in another federal circuit, a case in which the judge sustains the plain meaning of the Second Amendment.

In December of 2000, Utah Federal District Judge Dale Kimball, a Clinton appointee, followed the line of cases holding that the Second Amendment is not an individual right, but rather a collective right somehow connected to a "state militia." See Judge Kimball's unpublished order in *U.S. v. Bayles*, available at http://www.nysd.uscourts.gov/courtweb/.

Like many judges, Kimball cited an old U.S. Supreme Court case, *United States v. Miller*, 307 U.S. 174, 83 L. Ed. 1206, 59 S. Ct. 816 (1939), for the idea that gun control legislation can be upheld on constitutional grounds. In *Miller*, a bootlegger was arrested under the National Firearms Act for carrying a sawed-off shotgun. The Federal District Court of Arkansas held the Act violated the Second Amendment of the United States Constitution by infringing on the right to bear arms, and let Miller go. By the time the case got to the Supreme Court, Miller had disappeared and wasn't represented by counsel.[82] The Supreme Court held that a sawed-off shotgun wasn't the kind of gun the militia would normally use, and reversed the District Court.

Ever since, many courts have held that the right to bear arms is a collective right associated with being in the militia.   But the Court's decision *Miller* focused on the TYPE of weapon (sawed-off shotgun v. guns normally used by a military organization), not the NATURE of the right (collective v. individual).   Despite the narrowness of *Miller's* holding, the later cases, including Judge Kimball's decision, somehow extrapolate from *Miller* that the Second Amendment's right to bear arms is collective, not individual. In this author's opinion (as well as the opinion of our new U.S. Attorney General, John Ashcroft), they are totally wrong. The fallacy of their reasoning is apparent when one reads the decision of U.S. District Court Judge Sam R. Cummings in *United States v. Emerson*, 46 F. Supp. 2d 598, 1999 WL 198865 (N.D. Tex. 1999). In that case Judge Cummins explained in detail why he concluded that the Second Amendment guarantees an individual right to bear arms. His analysis includes an exhaustive review of the Second Amendment on historical, textual and structural grounds. He concluded that evidence regarding the intent of the Framers as well as the positioning of the Second Amendment within the Bill of Rights (a collection of individual rights) mean that the Second Amendment is unequivocally an individual right. The full text of Judge Cummings' opinion is available at http://www.shadeslanding.com/firearms/USvsEmmerson.pdf.

If you are interested enough to pull these cases off the internet and compare them, I'm sure you will find that Judge Cummings' analysis of the Second Amendment in the *Emerson* case makes much more sense than Judge Kimball's decision.

Section (g)(9) of section 922 and section (33) of the definitions contained in 921[83] combine to form what is know as the "Lautenberg Amendment," named after its misguided author. This amendment, EX POST FACTO, made every person ever convicted (no matter how long ago, ten, twenty, fifty years) of a misdemeanor crime of domestic violence, a felon on the effective date of the act

---

[82] Kind of like the opposing team didn't show up for the ball game.

[83] The text of which appears just below that of section (g)(9).

(September 30, 1996) for not IMMEDIATELY getting rid of his or her guns. Anti-gun congressmen reportedly passed the law by inserting it into a gigantic budget bill (a common practice nowadays) and no one in the gun lobby noticed it. It is a very disturbing piece of legislation, because it is the first time that the conviction of a MISDEMEANOR has been used to deprive citizens of important civil rights. The courts should find this section of the Gun Control Act to be unconstitutional on several theories: (1) the law is being applied ex post facto (a penalty that did not exist when the crime was committed, is now being imposed), (2) it imposes double jeopardy (citizens who have paid their debt to society by successfully completing their sentences or probation are now being subjected to additional penalties), (3) it deprives people of the right to bear arms, an important civil right, for simply committing a misdemeanor, (4) it violates the Fifth and Fourteenth Amendments of the U.S. Constitution by depriving citizens of property without due process of law (people who have legally owned firearms for years, with values ranging from hundreds to thousands of dollars, are suddenly required to get rid of them without notice or a hearing). To repeal the "Lautenberg Amendment" Congress should strike out the following words in subsection (9) of 18 U.S.C. § 922(g) "~~or (9) who has been convicted in any court of a misdemeanor crime of domestic violence,~~" and of course it should delete all of 18 U.S.C. § 921(a)(33), the definition of "misdemeanor crime of domestic violence."

ACTUAL TEXT

(g) It shall be unlawful for any person–

(1) who has been convicted in any court of, a crime punishable by imprisonment for a term exceeding one year;

(2) who is a fugitive from justice;

(3) who is an unlawful user of or addicted to any controlled substance (as defined in section 102 of the Controlled Substances Act (21 U.S.C. 802));

(4) who has been adjudicated as a mental defective or who has been committed to a mental institution;

(5) who, being an alien–

(A) is illegally or unlawfully in the United States; or

(B) except as provided in subsection (y)(2), has been admitted to the United States under a nonimmigrant visa (as that term is defined in section 101(a)(26) of the Immigration and Nationality Act (8 U.S.C. 1101(a)(26)).[84]

(6) who has been discharged from the Armed Forces under dishonorable conditions;

(7) who, having been a citizen of the United States, has renounced his citizenship;

(8) who is subject to a court order that--

(A) was issued after a hearing of which such person received actual notice, and at which such person had an opportunity to participate;

(B) restrains such person from harassing, stalking, or threatening an intimate partner of such person or child of such intimate partner or person, or engaging in other conduct that would place an intimate partner in reasonable fear of bodily injury to the partner or child; and

(C) (i) includes a finding that such person represents a credible threat to the physical safety of such intimate partner or child; or

(ii) by its terms explicitly prohibits the use, attempted use, or threatened use of physical force against such intimate partner or child that would reasonably be expected to cause bodily injury; or

(9) who has been convicted in any court of a misdemeanor crime of domestic violence, to ship or transport in interstate or foreign commerce, or possess in or affecting commerce, any firearm or ammunition; or to receive any firearm or ammunition which has been shipped or transported in interstate or foreign commerce.

[Definition of domestic violence, 18 U.S.C. § 921(a)(33), as used in 18 U.S.C. § 922(g).]

(33) (A) Except as provided in subparagraph (C), the term "misdemeanor crime of domestic violence" means an offense that--

(i) is a misdemeanor under Federal or State law; and

(ii) has, as an element, the use or attempted use of physical force, or the threatened use of a deadly weapon, committed by a current or former spouse, parent, or guardian of the victim, by a person with whom the victim shares a child in common, by a person who is

---

84 There are exceptions which permit nonimmigrant status aliens to possess firearms. Aliens who are admitted for hunting or sporting purposes with a lawful permit or aliens who qualify as a "distinguished foreign visitor" [I've got friends in low places . . . ♫♪] may possess firearms. There are other exceptions described in 18 U.S.C. 922(y).

guardian, or by a person similarly situated to a spouse, parent, or guardian of the victim.

(B) (i) A person shall not be considered to have been convicted of such an offense for purposes of this chapter [18 U.S.C. § 921 et seq.], unless--

(I) the person was represented by counsel in the case, or knowingly and intelligently waived the right to counsel in the case; and

(II) in the case of a prosecution for an offense described in this paragraph for which a person was entitled to a jury trial in the jurisdiction in which the case was tried, either

(aa) the case was tried by a jury, or

(bb) the person knowingly and intelligently waived the right to have the case tried by a jury, by guilty plea or otherwise.

(ii) A person shall not be considered to have been convicted of such an offense for purposes of this chapter [18 U.S.C. § 921 et seq.] if the conviction has been expunged or set aside, or is an offense for which the person has been pardoned or has had civil rights restored (if the law of the applicable jurisdiction provides for the loss of civil rights under such an offense) unless the pardon, expungement, or restoration of civil rights expressly provides that the person may not ship, transport, possess, or receive firearms. (**As defined in 18 U.S.C. § 921.**)

---

18 U.S.C. § 922(g)

Commentary

The broad definition of domestic violence under Utah law, U.C.A.77-36-1 (2), makes this law subject to enormous abuse by a vindictive domestic partner or his or her aggressive divorce lawyer. The definition includes such vague offenses as the "threat of physical harm," "telephone harassment," and "offenses against property." If a mean-spirited person knows that owning a gun is extremely important to that person's spouse, an allegation of domestic violence could be used to gain unfair advantage in negotiating a divorce settlement. A conviction of domestic violence, used in combination with the Lautenberg Amendment, could permanently deprive a person of his or her right to bear arms.

Furthermore, if a temporary restraining order is granted against a person in a domestic dispute, this order will cause the person to be denied the right to purchase a firearm. (18 U.S.C. 922 (g)(8).

If Congress [at Pancho's request] doesn't repeal sections 922(g) (8) [protective orders] and 922(g)(9) [domestic violence], Utah lawmakers should impose severe penalties, including attorney fees, court costs and compensation, perhaps treble damages, for the temporary loss of the right to bear arms, in the event an allegation of domestic violence turns out to be untrue.

GUN FREE SCHOOL ZONE ACT - 18 U.S.C. § 922(q)

"Plain Talk"

This subsection prohibits carrying firearms within 1,000 feet of school property. There are several exceptions (thank goodness). If you live within the 1,000-foot zone, you can keep your weapons in your home and on your own property. You may drive through with your guns unloaded and in a locked case or gun rack. By virtue of Utah's concealed weapon law and 18 U.S.C. § 922(2)(B)(ii), those with a valid Utah concealed weapon permit, can possess a gun in a school zone. Hunters can cross these zones to get to their hunting area, if authorized by school personnel.[85] Of course, the act prohibits the discharge of a firearm in a school zone. There are three exceptions given: (1) discharging them on private property not part of the school grounds, (2) discharging them as part of a program approved by the school (like R.O.T.C. training) and (3) by law enforcement and private security officers performing their official duties.

ACTUAL TEXT

(q)   (1) The Congress finds and declares that--

(A) crime, particularly crime involving drugs and guns, is a pervasive, nationwide problem;

(B) crime at the local level is exacerbated by the interstate movement of drugs, guns, and criminal gangs;

(C) firearms and ammunition move easily in interstate commerce and have been found in increasing numbers in and around schools, as documented in numerous hearings in both the Committee on the Judiciary of the House of Representatives and the Committee on the Judiciary of the Senate;

(D) in fact, even before the sale of a firearm, the gun, its component parts, ammunition, and the raw materials from which they are made have considerably moved in interstate commerce;

---

[85] Does this mean school officials must authorize hunters to carry a weapon or simply to drive through the school zone? If simply to drive through, does a public right of way over a city street constitute authorization? This subsection is unclear about that.

(E) while criminals freely move from State to State, ordinary citizens and foreign visitors may fear to travel to or through certain parts of the country due to concern about violent crime and gun violence, and parents may decline to send their children to school for the same reason;

(F) the occurrence of violent crime in school zones has resulted in a decline in the quality of education in our country;

(G) this decline in the quality of education has an adverse impact on interstate commerce and the foreign commerce of the United States;

(H) States, localities, and school systems find it almost impossible to handle gun-related crime by themselves--even States, localities, and school systems that have made strong efforts to prevent, detect, and punish gun-related crime find their efforts unavailing due in part to the failure or inability of other States or localities to take strong measures; and

(I) the Congress has the power, under the interstate commerce clause and other provisions of the Constitution, to enact measures to ensure the integrity and safety of the Nation's schools by enactment of this subsection.

(2)   (A) It shall be unlawful for any individual knowingly to possess a firearm that has moved in or that otherwise affects interstate or foreign commerce at a place that the individual knows, or has reasonable cause to believe, is a school zone.

(B) Subparagraph (A) does not apply to the possession of a firearm--

(i) on private property not part of school grounds;

(ii) if the individual possessing the firearm is licensed to do so by the State in which the school zone is located or a political subdivision of the State, and the law of the State or political subdivision requires that, before an individual obtains such a license, the law enforcement authorities of the State or political subdivision verify that the individual is qualified under law to receive the license;

(iii) that is--

(I) not loaded; and

(II) in a locked container, or a locked firearms rack that is on a motor vehicle;

(iv) by an individual for use in a program approved by a school in the school zone;

(v) by an individual in accordance with a contract entered into between a school in the school zone and the individual or an employer of the individual;

(vi) by a law enforcement officer acting in his or her official capacity; or

(vii) that is unloaded and is possessed by an individual while traversing school premises for the purpose of gaining access to public or private lands open to hunting, if the entry on school premises is authorized by school authorities.

(3)   (A) Except as provided in subparagraph (B), it shall be unlawful for any person, knowingly or with reckless disregard for the safety of another, to discharge or attempt to discharge a firearm that has moved in or that otherwise affects interstate or foreign commerce at a place that the person knows is a school zone.

(B) Subparagraph (A) does not apply to the discharge of a firearm--

(i) on private property not part of school grounds;

(ii) as part of a program approved by a school in the school zone, by an individual who is participating in the program;

(iii) by an individual in accordance with a contract entered into between a school in a school zone and the individual or an employer of the individual; or

(iv) by a law enforcement officer acting in his or her official capacity.

(4) Nothing in this subsection shall be construed as preempting or preventing a State or local government from enacting a statute establishing gun free school zones as provided in this subsection.

. . .

[Definition of School Zone, 18 U.S.C. 921(a)(25), as used in 18 U.S.C. § 922(q).]

(25) The term "school zone" means--

(A) in, or on the grounds of, a public, parochial or private school; or

(B) within a distance of 1,000 feet from the grounds of a public, parochial or private school.

(26) The term "school" means a school which provides elementary or secondary education, as determined under State law. (**See 18 U.S.C. § 921. Definitions**)

18 U.S.C. § 922(q)

Commentary

Notice a "school zone" is defined as an area 1000 feet around a school property. Virtually all schools are adjacent to roads and highways. This means that anyone without a concealed weapon permit who drives through a school zone with a gun that is not locked in a case (e.g. hunters with UNLOADED guns in their UNLOCKED gun racks) are in violation of this law, a federal felony! In 922(q)(1) subparagraphs (A) through (I) above, Congress attempts to justify the "Gun Free School Zone Act" based on its power to regulate interstate commerce.[86] Apparently, however, Congress had not placed this introductory language in section 922 until AFTER the Fifth Circuit Court of Appeals overturned the conviction of a Texas high school boy named Lopez, who was prosecuted for carrying a concealed weapon to school. The Fifth Circuit held that the Commerce Clause does not give Congress the authority to control activities in local schools, that control over this activity is reserved to state and local governments. As this case moved through the appeal process headed for the United States Supreme Court, Congress went back to the drawing board and inserted the language now appearing in subparagraphs (A) through (I). When the *Lopez* case finally reached the Supreme Court, the government attorney prosecuting the case tried to convince the Court that it had to accept Congress' finding that guns in the schools affect commerce. The Supreme Court in a 5 to 4 decision refused to buy the argument. It held the Gun Free School Zone Act unconstitutional stating there was not a sufficient "nexus" (connection) between the purpose of the statute and its effect on commerce. See *United States v. Lopez*, 131 L.Ed 2d 626, 115 S.Ct 1624, 95 CDOS 3074, 8 FLW Fed S 752 (1995, US). Of course, the question remains whether the subsequent amendment by Congress explaining the connection between crime in schools and interstate

---

[86] Congress cannot just pass any ol' law. It has to pass them within the authority that the Constitution gives it. The "Commerce Clause" of the U.S. Constitution gives Congress the authority to "regulate commerce." Congress takes the position that everything that happens affects interstate commerce; therefore, it has the power to regulate everything (how about whether to fold or bunch toilet paper made out of trees in Georgia, shipped through Arkansas, and used in Milford, Utah)! Fortunately, the courts do not always agree.

commerce, cures the defect.[87] Based upon the language of the case, I don't think it does. As recently as May of 2000, the Supreme Court used the *Lopez* case as precedent to hold the federal Violence Against Women Act unconstitutional as exceeding the Commerce Clause. This sends a strong message that the Supreme Court is not going to continue to let Congress use the Commerce Clause as a ticket to control every activity in America. Some activities like regulating crime in our schools and violence against women are exclusively intrastate, as opposed to interstate, activities and Congress should keep its mits off! Utah doesn't need the federal act anyway. Utah law not only prohibits students from bringing real guns to school, it prohibits them from bringing play guns or even objects that look like guns (U.C.A. 53A-11-904, see discussion in Chapter XII). Congress should back off and let each state handle the problem as they see fit. This whole subsection should be repealed.

Pancho's Wisdom

When the Brady Act became law, ATF sent tons of paper "Brady Forms" to gun dealers. No tellin' how many trees Jim and Sarah Brady have killed. I know, let's repeal the Brady Act and save the Rain Forest!

---

[87] Lopez carried a gun to school BEFORE Congress added paragraphs (A) through (I) to the Gun Free School Zone Act. Therefore, the amendment was "ex post facto" as it related to him. The prosecutor argued that, because Congress already had the authority under the Commerce Clause to enact the law, the law is constitutional even though Congress didn't originally recite how guns in the schools affect commerce. The Court disagreed.

What happens if someone is arrested for carrying guns into school zones now, AFTER Congress added paragraphs (A) through (I)? I think the language of the case is broad enough to suggest the Supreme Court will again find the Gun Free School Zone Act to be unconstitutional. But, hey, it was a 5 to 4 decision, so don't bet your favorite horse on it.

THE BRADY ACT - 18 U.S.C. § 922(s),(t)

"Plain Talk"

Subsections (s) and (t) of section 922 are the "Brady Handgun Violence Prevention Act."[88] Subsection (s) describes the Brady rules for the first five years, from November 30, 1993 until November 30, 1998. Subsection (t) explains the National Criminal Instant Check System (NICS) that took effect on November 30, 1998. From correspondence I received as a licensed gun dealer, it appears federal and state officials had to really scramble to meet the November 30, 1998 deadline. Since NICS has been up and running the computer has crashed several times. Once in the Spring of 2000 the FBI computer was down four days and no one in the country could buy a gun during that time. If the feds had kept newspapers out of circulation for four days, the media would have tried to overthrow the government.

Under Brady, the states have had the option of conducting an instant background check rather than requiring a buyer to wait 3 days before he or she could buy a handgun. Utah has been using the instant-check option for handgun purchases for five years now. Before November 30, 1998, dealers didn't have to do background checks to sell rifles and shotguns; now they do. The current procedure is set forth in U.C.A. 76-10-526 (above in Chapter VII). Until the state raises the price, the background check costs the buyer $7.50. Utah concealed weapon permit holders are exempt from the instant-check search and fee, but the Bureau of Criminal Identification still requires dealers to call BCI before selling a gun. BCI checks its CWP database to ensure that the CWP is still valid.

---

[88] Anti-gun politicians are very clever choosing words to cover up their real intent, i.e., to eventually deprive all law-abiding citizens of their guns. The Brady Act was first "sold" to the public as a law that would reduce the number of "handguns" used to commit violent crimes. But this "handgun" law has now "spread and grown" to include rifles and shotguns. Is it any wonder why gun owners fear that these politicians won't stop until they take all the guns away? Can you see why sportsmen and hunters, represented by the NRA, refuse to budge an inch when new gun laws are proposed? They never regain ground once it is lost.

During the FBI computer Spring 2000 power outages, the Utah Bureau of Criminal Identification (BCI) was requiring NICS checks on CWPs although not charging the $7.50 fee. Input by the author on behalf of the Utah Gun Owner's Legal Defense Fund (U-Gold - see Chapter XVI below) helped convince BCI to stop this practice. Now, if the omniscient but mortal FBI computer convulses, Utah CWPs may purchase a gun from a dealer after a local background check to verify that the Utah CWP is still valid. Permit holders, please keep the mother board to Utah BCI's local computer in your nightly prayers!

As a gun dealer, I recently received information that is cause for concern. On November 24, 1998, I received a letter from the Bureau of Criminal Identification stating:

> You will receive one of three responses on a background check: Approved, denied or research. If you receive a research response it is unlawful for you to transfer the firearm until you receive an approval from the department. The Brady operator is required to tell you approximately how long the research period will take but there is not a mandatory time frame. *Again, it is unlawful for a dealer to transfer a firearm to a buyer unless they have received an approval from the department.* (Italics in original.)

In other words, if the computer is tied up for months, it could take you that long to get a gun! Even the Brady Act only makes buyers wait three days; if, by the end of the third day, the dealer hasn't received a response prohibiting the sale, he can sell the gun to the proposed buyer, 18 U.S.C. § 922(t)(1)(B)(ii). Brady, however, doesn't seem to prohibit states from imposing longer waiting periods, 18 U.S.C. § 922(t)(2). Again we see the good guys losing out. Criminals can get machine guns overnight from gun runners; good guys may have to wait indefinitely to buy a bolt-action rifle if FBI or BCI computers are overloaded or are "glitching."

Incidently, if the state or federal government improperly deny a purchase, citizens can sue and be awarded attorney fees (see discussion of 18 U.S.C. 935A below).

ACTUAL TEXT

(s) (1) Beginning on the date that is 90 days after the date of enactment of this subsection [enacted Nov. 30, 1993] and ending on the day before the date that is 60 months after such date of enactment, it shall be unlawful for any licensed importer, licensed manufacturer, or licensed dealer to sell, deliver, or transfer a handgun (other than the return of a handgun to the person from whom it was received) to an individual who is not licensed under section 923 unless–

(A) after the most recent proposal of such transfer by the transferee--

(i) the transferor has--

(I) received from the transferee a statement of the transferee containing the information described in paragraph (3);

(II) verified the identity of the transferee by examining the identification document presented;

(III) within 1 day after the transferee furnishes the statement, provided notice of the contents of the statement to the chief law enforcement officer of the place of residence of the transferee; and

(IV) within 1 day after the transferee furnishes the statement, transmitted a copy of the statement to the chief law enforcement officer of the place of residence of the transferee; and

(ii)(I) 5 business days (meaning days on which State offices are open) have elapsed from the date the transferor furnished notice of the contents of the statement to the chief law enforcement officer, during which period the transferor has not received information from the chief law enforcement officer that receipt or possession of the handgun by the transferee would be in violation of Federal, State, or local law; or

(II) the transferor has received notice from the chief law enforcement officer that the officer has no information indicating that receipt or possession of the handgun by the transferee would violate Federal, State, or local law;

(B) the transferee has presented to the transferor a written statement, issued by the chief law enforcement officer of the place of residence of the transferee during the 10-day period ending on the date of the most recent proposal of such transfer by the transferee, stating that the transferee requires access to a handgun because of a threat to the life of the transferee or of any member of the household of the transferee;

(C)(i) the transferee has presented to the transferor a permit that--

(I) allows the transferee to possess or acquire a handgun; and

(II) was issued not more than 5 years earlier by the State in which the transfer is to take place; and

(ii) the law of the State provides that such a permit is to be issued only after an authorized government official has verified that the information available to such official does not indicate that possession of a handgun by the transferee would be in violation of the law;

(D) the law of the State requires that, before any licensed importer, licensed manufacturer, or licensed dealer completes the transfer of a handgun to an individual who is not licensed under section 923, an authorized government official verify that the information available to such official does not indicate that possession of a handgun by the transferee would be in violation of law;

(E) the Secretary has approved the transfer under section 5812 of the Internal Revenue Code of 1986 [26 USCS § 5812]; or

(F) on application of the transferor, the Secretary has certified that compliance with subparagraph (A)(i)(III) is impracticable because--

(i) the ratio of the number of law enforcement officers of the State in which the transfer is to occur to the number of square miles of land area of the State does not exceed 0.0025;

(ii) the business premises of the transferor at which the transfer is to occur are extremely remote in relation to the chief law enforcement officer; and

(iii) there is an absence of telecommunications facilities in the geographical area in which the business premises are located.

(2) A chief law enforcement officer to whom a transferor has provided notice pursuant to paragraph (1)(A)(i)(III) shall make a reasonable effort to ascertain within 5 business days whether receipt or possession would be in violation of the law, including research in whatever State and local recordkeeping systems are available and in a national system designated by the Attorney General.

(3) The statement referred to in paragraph (1)(A)(i)(I) shall contain only--

(A) the name, address, and date of birth appearing on a valid identification document (as defined in section 1028(d)(1)) of the transferee containing a photograph of the transferee and a description of the identification used;

(B) a statement that the transferee--

(i) is not under indictment for, and has not been convicted in any court of, a crime punishable by imprisonment for a term exceeding 1 year, and has not been convicted in any court of a misdemeanor crime of domestic violence;

(ii) is not a fugitive from justice;

(iii) is not an unlawful user of or addicted to any controlled substance (as defined in section 102 of the Controlled Substances Act [21 USCS § 802]);

(iv) has not been adjudicated as a mental defective or been committed to a mental institution;

(v) is not an alien who is illegally or unlawfully in the United States;

(vi) has not been discharged from the Armed Forces under dishonorable conditions; and

(vii) is not a person who, having been a citizen of the United States, has renounced such citizenship;

(C) the date the statement is made; and

(D) notice that the transferee intends to obtain a handgun from the transferor.

(4) Any transferor of a handgun who, after such transfer, receives a report from a chief law enforcement officer containing information that receipt or possession of the handgun by the transferee violates Federal, State, or local law shall, within 1 business day after receipt of such request, communicate any information related to the transfer that the transferor has about the transfer and the transferee to--

(A) the chief law enforcement officer of the place of business of the transferor; and

(B) the chief law enforcement officer of the place of residence of the transferee.

(5) Any transferor who receives information, not otherwise available to the public, in a report under this subsection shall not disclose such information except to the transferee, to law enforcement authorities, or pursuant to the direction of a court of law.

(6)   (A) Any transferor who sells, delivers, or otherwise transfers a handgun to a transferee shall retain the copy of the statement of the transferee with respect to the handgun transaction, and shall retain evidence that the transferor has complied with subclauses (III) and (IV) of paragraph (1)(A)(i) with respect to the statement.

(B) Unless the chief law enforcement officer to whom a statement is transmitted under paragraph (1)(A)(i)(IV) determines that a transaction would violate Federal, State, or local law--

(i) the officer shall, within 20 business days after the date the transferee made the statement on the basis of which the notice was provided, destroy the statement, any record containing information derived from the statement, and any record created as a result of the notice required by paragraph (1)(A)(i)(III);

(ii) the information contained in the statement shall not be conveyed to any person except a person who has a need to know in order to carry out this subsection; and

(iii) the information contained in the statement shall not be used for any purpose other than to carry out this subsection.

(C) If a chief law enforcement officer determines that an individual is ineligible to receive a handgun and the individual requests the officer to provide the reason for such determination, the officer shall provide such reasons to the individual in writing within 20 business days after receipt of the request.

(7) A chief law enforcement officer or other person responsible for providing criminal history background information pursuant to this subsection shall not be liable in an action at law for damages--

(A) for failure to prevent the sale or transfer of a handgun to a person whose receipt or possession of the handgun is unlawful under this section; or

(B) for preventing such a sale or transfer to a person who may lawfully receive or possess a handgun.

(8) For purposes of this subsection, the term "chief law enforcement officer" means the chief of police, the sheriff, or an equivalent officer or the designee of any such individual.

(9) The Secretary shall take necessary actions to ensure that the provisions of this subsection are published and disseminated to licensed dealers, law enforcement officials, and the public.

(t)(1) Beginning on the date that is 30 days after the Attorney General notifies licensees under section 103(d) of the Brady Handgun Violence Prevention Act [note to this section] that the national instant criminal background check system is established, a licensed importer, licensed manufacturer, or licensed dealer shall not transfer a firearm to any other person who is not licensed under this chapter [18 U.S.C. § 921 et seq.], unless--

(A) before the completion of the transfer, the licensee contacts the national instant criminal background check system established under section 103 of that Act [note to this section];

(B)   (i) the system provides the licensee with a unique identification number; or

(ii) 3 business days (meaning a day on which State offices are open) have elapsed since the licensee contacted the system, and the system has not notified the licensee that the receipt of a firearm by such other person would violate subsection (g) or (n) of this section; and

(C) the transferor has verified the identity of the transferee by examining a valid identification document (as defined in section 1028(d)(1) of this title) of the transferee containing a photograph of the transferee.

(2) If receipt of a firearm would not violate section 922 (g) or (n) or State law, the system shall--

(A) assign a unique identification number to the transfer;

(B) provide the licensee with the number; and

(C) destroy all records of the system with respect to the call (other than the identifying number and the date the number was assigned) and all records of the system relating to the person or the transfer.

(3) Paragraph (1) shall not apply to a firearm transfer between a licensee and another person if--

(A)(i) such other person has presented to the licensee a permit that--

(I) allows such other person to possess or acquire a firearm; and

(II) was issued not more than 5 years earlier by the State in which the transfer is to take place; and

(ii) the law of the State provides that such a permit is to be issued only after an authorized government official has verified that the information available to such official does not indicate that possession of a firearm by such other person would be in violation of law;

(B) the Secretary has approved the transfer under section 5812 of the Internal Revenue Code of 1986 [26 USCS § 5812]; or

(C) on application of the transferor, the Secretary has certified that compliance with paragraph (1)(A) is impracticable because--

(i) the ratio of the number of law enforcement officers of the State in which the transfer is to occur to the number of square miles of land area of the State does not exceed 0.0025;

(ii) the business premises of the licensee at which the transfer is to occur are extremely remote in relation to the chief law enforcement officer (as defined in subsection (s)(8)); and

(iii) there is an absence of telecommunications facilities in the geographical area in which the business premises are located.

(4) If the national instant criminal background check system notifies the licensee that the information available to the system does not demonstrate that the receipt of a firearm by such other person would violate subsection (g) or (n) or State law, and the licensee transfers a firearm to such other person, the licensee shall include in the record of the transfer the unique identification number provided by the system with respect to the transfer.

(5) If the licensee knowingly transfers a firearm to such other person and knowingly fails to comply with paragraph (1) of this subsection with respect to the transfer and, at the time such other person most recently proposed the transfer, the national instant criminal background check system was operating and information was available to the system demonstrating that receipt of a firearm by such other person would violate subsection (g) or (n) of this section or State law, the Secretary may, after notice and opportunity for a hearing, suspend for not more than 6 months or revoke any license issued to the licensee under section 923, and may impose on the licensee a civil fine of not more than $.5,000.

(6) Neither a local government nor an employee of the Federal Government or of any State or local government, responsible for providing information to the national instant criminal background check system shall be liable in an action at law for damages--

(A) for failure to prevent the sale or transfer of a firearm to a person whose receipt or possession of the firearm is unlawful under this section; or

(B) for preventing such a sale or transfer to a person who may lawfully receive or possess a firearm.

---

18 U.S.C. § 922(s),(t)

Commentary

Printz v. United States, 138 L.Ed. 2d 914, 117 S.Ct. 2365 (1997), held, among other things, that the provision in Brady requiring the states to enforce a federal regulatory scheme at their expense, violated the sovereignty of the states, and, therefore, is UNCONSTITUTIONAL. Kind of makes you wonder why the other 48 states, including Utah, are still spending tons of money to enforce Brady, huh? Congress should repeal the Brady Act and federal prosecutors should begin enforcing existing laws providing enhanced penalties (including the death penalty) when felons use firearms to commit violent crimes.

Pancho's Wisdom

Take your sweetheart for frequent walks. The public needs to see you having a healthy relationship with an attractive light weapon (such as an AR-15 or AK-47). If you really want to turn their heads, let them see you cuddling your MP-5. If the idea makes you uncomfortable, are you succumbing to the "politically correct" notion that its bad for good people to protect themselves with the best tools available?

BAN OF ASSAULT WEAPONS AND LARGE CAPACITY AMMUNITION FEEDING DEVICES - 18 U.S.C. § 922(v),(w)

"Plain Talk"

ASSAULT WEAPONS BAN - Section 922(v)[89] is called the Assault Weapons Ban. The word "ban" doesn't really apply to the general public, who can still buy every weapon banned as long as it was manufactured on or before September 13, 1994. Only manufacturers were "banned," after the effective date of the bill (September 13, 1994), from manufacturing specifically named SEMIAUTOMATIC WEAPONS that "look mean" including such popular models as the Colt AR-15 (the semiautomatic version of the fully automatic M-16 used in Vietnam), the Uzi (an Israeli machine gun), the Steyr AUG (what the bad guys used in the movie "Harley Davidson and the Marlboro Man") and the "Street Sweeper" shotgun. Any such guns manufactured before September 13, 1994, are legal to possess, trade, sell and shoot (except the "Street Sweeper" which is considered a "Class III" weapon requiring the type of registration needed to own a machine gun). So if you have a "pre-ban" AR-15, with a threaded barrel, flash suppressor, and two thirty-round clips, it's not only legal, it's worth a heckava lot more now than it was worth before the ban -- so hang on to it!

To get around the ban, most gun manufacturers, including Colt, made a few slight modifications leaving off features like flash suppressors, threads on the barrel (for silencers and flash suppressors), bayonet holders, and grenade launchers. These "politically correct" versions come with magazines or clips holding 10 rounds or less, but most models will accept a "high capacity magazine" holding far more than 10 cartridges, typically 30 to 50.

Rifles and shotguns with bolt actions, lever actions and pump actions, are not considered semiautomatic assault weapons. 18 U.S.C. § 922 contains an "Appendix A" (not to be confused with our Appendix A), listing all of the rifles and shotguns not considered semiautomatic assault weapons. This was to assure gun manufacturers that their bolt action, lever action, and pump action guns, many of which have been manufactured for over a hundred years, would be excluded from the ban, no matter how the courts

---

[89] The definitions of "semiautomatic assault weapon" and "large capacity ammunition feeding device," sections (30) and (31) of 18 U.S.C. 921, are also included below.

interpret the term "assault weapon."[90]   We have not included this list (Brady's Appendix A), because it is several pages long. LARGE CAPACITY AMMUNITION FEEDING DEVICES - 18 U.S.C. § 922(w) -"Enlightened" members of Congress decided that clips and magazines for semiautomatic weapons holding over 10 bullets are "wicked" and should be "banned." Like the assault weapons ban, the public may still own the banned clips, but manufacturers are banned from making such magazines as of Sept. 13, 1994. Investors familiar with firearm-accessory prices wish they could have purchased millions of dollars worth of "large capacity ammunition feeding devices." As the clips and magazines begin to wear out, their prices will increase, making them attractive investments.

ACTUAL TEXT

(v)   (1) It shall be unlawful for a person to manufacture, transfer, or possess a semiautomatic assault weapon.

(2) Paragraph (1) shall not apply to the possession or transfer of any semiautomatic assault weapon otherwise lawfully possessed under Federal law on the date of the enactment of this subsection [enacted Sept. 13, 1994].

(3) Paragraph (1) shall not apply to--

(A) any of the firearms, or replicas or duplicates of the firearms, specified in Appendix A to this section, as such firearms were manufactured on October 1, 1993;

(B) any firearm that--

(i) is manually operated by bolt, pump, lever, or slide action;

(ii) has been rendered permanently inoperable; or

(iii) is an antique firearm;

(C) any semiautomatic rifle that cannot accept a detachable magazine that holds more than 5 rounds of ammunition; or

(D) any semiautomatic shotgun that cannot hold more than 5 rounds of ammunition in a fixed or detachable magazine. The fact that a firearm is not listed in Appendix A shall not be construed to mean that paragraph (1) applies to such firearm. No firearm exempted by this

---

[90]   If the courts can read "abortion" and "homosexuality" into the Bill of Rights, then gun manufacturers have reasonable cause to fear that they might also conclude that pump and lever action guns, many of which can fire up to 15 bullets quite rapidly, are "assault weapons."

subsection may be deleted from Appendix A so long as this subsection is in effect.

(4) Paragraph (1) shall not apply to--

(A) the manufacture for, transfer to, or possession by the United States or a department or agency of the United States or a State or a department, agency, or political subdivision of a State, or a transfer to or possession by a law enforcement officer employed by such an entity for purposes of law enforcement (whether on or off duty);

(B) the transfer to a licensee under title I of the Atomic Energy Act of 1954 [42 U.S.C.S. 2011 et seq.] for purposes of establishing and maintaining an on-site physical protection system and security organization required by Federal law, or possession by an employee or contractor of such licensee on-site for such purposes or off-site for purposes of licensee-authorized training or transportation of nuclear materials;

(C) the possession, by an individual who is retired from service with a law enforcement agency and is not otherwise prohibited from receiving a firearm, of a semiautomatic assault weapon transferred to the individual by the agency upon such retirement; or

(D) the manufacture, transfer, or possession of a semiautomatic assault weapon by a licensed manufacturer or licensed importer for the purposes of testing or experimentation authorized by the Secretary.

(w) (1) Except as provided in paragraph (2), it shall be unlawful for a person to transfer or possess a large capacity ammunition feeding device.

(2) Paragraph (1) shall not apply to the possession or transfer of any large capacity ammunition feeding device otherwise lawfully possessed on or before the date of the enactment of this subsection [enacted Sept. 13, 1994].

(3) This subsection shall not apply to--

(A) the manufacture for, transfer to, or possession by the United States or a department or agency of the United States or a State or a department, agency, or political subdivision of a State, or a transfer to or possession by a law enforcement officer employed by such an entity for purposes of law enforcement (whether on or off duty);

(B) the transfer to a licensee under title I of the Atomic Energy Act of 1954 [42 U.S.C.S. §§ 2011] for purposes of establishing and maintaining an on-site physical protection system and security organization required by Federal law, or possession by an employee or contractor of such licensee on-site for such purposes or off-site for purposes of licensee-authorized training or transportation of nuclear materials;

(C) the possession, by an individual who is retired from service with a law enforcement agency and is not otherwise prohibited from receiving ammunition, of a large capacity ammunition feeding device transferred to the individual by the agency upon such retirement; or

(D) the manufacture, transfer, or possession of any large capacity ammunition feeding device by a licensed manufacturer or licensed importer for the purposes of testing or experimentation authorized by the Secretary.

(4) If a person charged with violating paragraph (1) asserts that paragraph (1) does not apply to such person because of paragraph (2) or (3), the Government shall have the burden of proof to show that such paragraph (1) applies to such person. The lack of a serial number as described in section 923(i) of this title shall be a presumption that the large capacity ammunition feeding device is not subject to the prohibition of possession in paragraph (1).

Definitions of "semiautomatic assault weapon" and "large capacity ammunition feeding device" from 18 U.S.C. § 921, sections (30) and (31)

(30) The term "semiautomatic assault weapon" means--

(A) any of the firearms, or copies or duplicates of the firearms in any caliber, known as--

(i) Norinco, Mitchell, and Poly Technologies Avtomat Kalashnikovs (all models);

(ii) Action Arms Israeli Military Industries UZI and Galil;

(iii) Beretta Ar70 (SC-70);

(iv) Colt AR-15;

(v) Fabrique National FN/FAL, FN/LAR, and FNC;

(vi) SWD M-10, M-11, M-11/9, and M-12;

(vii) Steyr AUG;

(viii) INTRATEC TEC-9, TEC-DC9 and TEC-22; and

(ix) revolving cylinder shotguns, such as (or similar to) the Street Sweeper and Striker 12;

(B) a semiautomatic rifle that has an ability to accept a detachable magazine and has at least 2 of--

(i) a folding or telescoping stock;

(ii) a pistol grip that protrudes conspicuously beneath the action of the weapon;

(iii) a bayonet mount;

(iv) a flash suppressor or threaded barrel designed to accommodate a flash suppressor; and

(v) a grenade launcher;

(C) a semiautomatic pistol that has an ability to accept a detachable magazine and has at least 2 of--

(i) an ammunition magazine that attaches to the pistol outside of the pistol grip;

(ii) a threaded barrel capable of accepting a barrel extender, flash suppressor, forward handgrip, or silencer;

(iii) a shroud that is attached to, or partially or completely encircles, the barrel and that permits the shooter to hold the firearm with the nontrigger hand without being burned;

(iv) a manufactured weight of 50 ounces or more when the pistol is unloaded; and

(v) a semiautomatic version of an automatic firearm; and

(D) a semiautomatic shotgun that has at least 2 of--

(i) a folding or telescoping stock;

(ii) a pistol grip that protrudes conspicuously beneath the action of the weapon;

(iii) a fixed magazine capacity in excess of 5 rounds; and

(iv) an ability to accept a detachable magazine.

(31) The term "large capacity ammunition feeding device"--

(A) means a magazine, belt, drum, feed strip, or similar device manufactured after the date of enactment of the Violent Crime Control and Law Enforcement Act of 1994 [enacted Sept. 13, 1994] that has a capacity of, or that can be readily restored or converted to accept, more than 10 rounds of ammunition; but

(B) does not include an attached tubular device designed to accept, and capable of operating only with, .22 caliber rimfire ammunition. **(See 18 U.S.C. § 922)**

---

18 U.S.C. § 922(v),(w)

Commentary

The mere choice of words can make good things sound bad, and bad things sound good. The expression "assault weapons" creates a mental image of weapons designed to assail the innocent or mow down a platoon of soldiers. The truth is that most of these guns are used for righteous purposes like home protection, rifle competitions (especially the Colt AR-15), hunting and "plinking." Many respectable people have as fervent interest in plinking, as others have in golfing or reading. None of these activities are harmful when conducted lawfully by honorable people. These guns are simply semiautomatic weapons. The true "assault weapons" are the fully automatic weapons smuggled in by drug dealers and gun runners, the real villains. Keeping semiautomatic weapons from honest citizens does nothing to keep them out of the hands of criminals, who get them illegally. The only real effect of the assault weapon ban is that it shifts the balance of fire power from law-abiding citizens to criminals, terrorists and tyrants. If criminals and dictators have fully-automatic weapons and high capacity magazines, the law-abiding should have equal firepower. Countries like Switzerland and Israel routinely hand out fully automatic weapons to their citizens. In fact, every able-bodied man in Switzerland has a machine gun and a full can of ammo. This is undoubtedly one of the reasons Hitler chose not to attack Switzerland during World War II.[91] Hitler knew he could defeat the Swiss in a major battle, but he had to have known it would have been impossible for Germany to occupy Switzerland for any significant length of time, given its heavily armed citizenry. The United States with all its firepower, could not conquer the tiny nation of Vietnam. The Viet Cong had fully automatic "assault weapons." Similarly, if significant numbers of   U.S. citizens possessed

---

[91]   When I tell people this, they tell me the Swiss Alps stopped Hitler. If you look at a map of Europe, you'll see the Alps run through the southern part of Switzerland, and Germany is north of Switzerland. The only barrier that separates the two countries is the Rhine River, which did not pose a difficult obstacle for the Nazis.

reasonably modern hand-held weapons,[92] a conquering foreign power could not safely retain control for very long.

The most important reason to keep citizens well armed is the ever present threat of tyranny. The Founding Fathers of the United States Constitution recognized this and, indeed, it was one of the reasons behind the passage of the Second Amendment. Joseph Story, one of the great legal minds of the early 1800s stated:

> One of the ordinary modes by which TYRANTS accomplish their purposes without resistance is by DISARMING THE PEOPLE, and MAKING IT AN OFFENSE TO KEEP ARMS, and by SUBSTITUTING A REGULAR ARMY IN THE STEAD OF a resort to THE MILITIA. The friends of a free government can not be too watchful, to overcome the dangerous tendency of the public mind to sacrifice, for the sake of mere private convenience, this powerful check on the designs of ambitious men (emphasis added).[93]

---

[92] Every civil right has its limitations. Free speech does not guarantee the right to commit libel or slander or sell pornography. Freedom of religion does not give ministers the right to offer human sacrifice! Likewise, the right to bear arms is not absolute. It does not give a private citizen the right to possess a tank, a missile launcher or an atomic warhead. The written and historical context of the phrase "to bear arms," suggests the right is limited to hand-held weapons used by contemporary infantrymen. "Carry" and "shoulder" are synonyms for "bear," which implies that the phrase referred to weapons that could be carried and fired by one person. During the Revolutionary War, Colonial soldiers owned and carried rifles and pistols similar to those used by British soldiers. Thus, with no language in the Second Amendment to imply otherwise, the historical context hints that the Founding Fathers intended citizens to retain the right to possess weapons modern enough to repel an attack by enemy foot soldiers. Applying the concept to modern times, a reasonable interpretation should permit most citizens to possess semiautomatic weapons, and others, with reasonable experience and training, to possess fully automatic weapons, restricting hand grenades and bazookas (which are hand-held, but not necessary to repel an enemy infantry attack if a significant number of citizens possess fully automatic weapons) to members of the armed forces.

[93] Joseph Story, "A Familiar Exposition of the Constitution of the United States," §450 at 264 (1840). Mr. Story was an associate justice on the United States Supreme Court from 1811 - 1845 and taught law at

Depriving honest citizens of modern weapons is an outrageous act of tyranny (whether committed by the executive, legislative or judicial branch of government) that should never be tolerated by any free people! It's now too late for the British; the government has already confiscated nearly all of their guns. The Australians let their politicians take away all of their semi-automatic weapons including shotguns. If either of these countries is overrun by a foreign power, who do you think they will call to bail them out? "Come on over you 'Yank Cowboys.' Bring your guns and save us from our own stupidity." Pancho has a message Great Britain, Australia and Canada. "When Chinese troops are marching down your streets with AK-47s and your ~~citizens~~ subjects are powerless to do anything because you have disarmed them, don't call us, call Scotland Yard!" (Maybe a few carloads of British Bobby Cops with night sticks will scare 'em off!)

Pancho's Wisdom

Politicians who disarm the innocent, knowing gun control doesn't work, are tyrants; and those who vote for them, fully understanding the threat to freedom and liberty, are traitors.

JUVENILES AND HANDGUNS - 18 U.S.C. § 922(x)

"Plain Talk"

Juveniles (called "minors" under Utah law) cannot posses handguns or handgun ammunition except to participate in the activities specifically listed in 18 U.S.C. § 922(x)(3). These activities consist of farming and ranching, target practice, hunting (remember, Utahns can hunt deer with a pistol and persons as young as 14 may hunt deer), and instruction in the use of a handgun. When participating in these endeavors, a minor must transport the handgun in a locked container, unloaded, from the place where he receives possession of the handgun to the place where he uses it. It also requires the juvenile's parent or guardian to give WRITTEN CONSENT, which the juvenile must carry at all times during the activity. APPENDIX A contains a FORM parents can use to give their teenagers written consent to legally possess and shoot handguns. 18 U.S.C. § 922(x)(3)(A)(iii) requires the juvenile to have the consent form IN HAND, EVEN IF ACCOMPANIED BY THE PARENT OR GUARDIAN! So remember, anytime you take a person under 18, including your own child, to shoot pistols, make sure the person has the written consent form with him; otherwise both of you are violating 922(x), a federal crime punishable by up to one year in prison.

ACTUAL TEXT

(x)   (1) It shall be unlawful for a person to sell, deliver, or otherwise transfer to a person who the transferor knows or has reasonable cause to believe is a juvenile--

(A) a handgun; or

(B) ammunition that is suitable for use only in a handgun.

(2) It shall be unlawful for any person who is a juvenile to knowingly possess–

(A) a handgun; or

(B) ammunition that is suitable for use only in a handgun.

(3) This subsection does not apply to--

(A) a temporary transfer of a handgun or ammunition to a juvenile or to the possession or use of a handgun or ammunition by a juvenile if the handgun and ammunition are possessed and used by the juvenile--

(i) in the course of employment, in the course of ranching or farming related to activities at the residence of the juvenile (or on property used for ranching or farming at which the juvenile, with the permission of the property owner or lessee, is performing activities related to the operation of the farm or ranch), target practice, hunting, or a course of instruction in the safe and lawful use of a handgun;

(ii) with the prior written consent of the juvenile's parent or guardian who is not prohibited by Federal, State, or local law from possessing a firearm, except--

(I) during transportation by the juvenile of an unloaded handgun in a locked container directly from the place of transfer to a place at which an activity described in clause (i) is to take place and transportation by the juvenile of that handgun, unloaded and in a locked container, directly from the place at which such an activity took place to the transferor; or

(II) with respect to ranching or farming activities as described in clause (i), a juvenile may possess and use a handgun or ammunition with the prior written approval of the juvenile's parent or legal guardian and at the direction of an adult who is not prohibited by Federal, State or local law from possessing a firearm;

(iii) THE JUVENILE HAS THE PRIOR WRITTEN CONSENT IN THE JUVENILE'S POSSESSION AT ALL TIMES WHEN A HANDGUN IS IN THE POSSESSION OF THE JUVENILE **[see Appendix A containing a consent form parents may use]**; and

(iv) in accordance with State and local law;

(B) a juvenile who is a member of the Armed Forces of the United States or the National Guard who possesses or is armed with a handgun in the line of duty;

(C) a transfer by inheritance of title (but not possession) of a handgun or ammunition to a juvenile; or

(D) the possession of a handgun or ammunition by a juvenile taken in defense of the juvenile or other persons against an intruder into the residence of the juvenile or a residence in which the juvenile is an invited guest.

(4) A handgun or ammunition, the possession of which is transferred to a juvenile in circumstances in which the transferor is not in violation of this subsection shall not be subject to permanent confiscation by the Government if its possession by the juvenile subsequently becomes unlawful because of the conduct of the juvenile, but shall be returned to the lawful owner when such handgun or ammunition is no longer required by the Government for the purposes of investigation or prosecution.

(5) For purposes of this subsection, the term "juvenile" means a person who is less than 18 years of age.

(6)   (A) In a prosecution of a violation of this subsection, the court shall require the presence of a juvenile defendant's parent or legal guardian at all proceedings.

(B) The court may use the contempt power to enforce subparagraph (A).

(C) The court may excuse attendance of a parent or legal guardian of a juvenile defendant at a proceeding in a prosecution of a violation of this subsection for good cause shown **(emphasis added)**.

18 U.S.C. 925. Exceptions: Relief from disabilities

---

18 U.S.C. § 925

"Plain Talk"

I put this code subsection in to show you how Congress likes to treat gun owners. This section says if you commit a felony (which is extremely easy nowadays) you can petition the Secretary (ATF) for relief from the prohibition against possessing a firearm. When Brady was passed, some Congressmen probably expressed horror that a person convicted of a felony could be deprived of the right to protect himself or his family for the rest of his life (kinda like declawing a cat). Congressmen pushing Brady assured those concerned that they had a provision to permit those deprived of the right to get it back. Well guess what? ATF just informed all gun dealers that Congress hasn't funded the following "relief from disabilities" since 1996. So you commit a felony and you lose your right to protect yourself and your family FOR LIFE!

ACTUAL TEXT

. . .

(c) A person who is prohibited fro possessing, shipping, transporting or receiving firearms or ammunition may make application to the Secretary for relief from disabilities imposed by Federal laws with respect to the acquisition, receipt, transfer, shipment, transportation or possession of firearms, and the Secretary may grant such relief if it is established to his satisfaction that the circumstances regarding the disability, and the applicants's record and reputation, are such that the applicant will not be likely to act in a manner dangerous to public safety and that the granting of the relief would not be contrary to the public interest. Any person whose application for relief from disabilities is denied by the Secretary may file a petition with the United States district court for the district in which he resides for a judicial review of such denial. The court may in its discretion admit additional evidence where failure to do so would result in a miscarriage of justice.

18 U.S.C. 925A. Remedy for erroneous denial of firearm

Suing governments for improper denial under Brady Act- 18 U.S.C. § 925A

"Plain Talk"

Governments Beware! If you improperly deny us citizens the right to purchase a firearm under the Brady Act, we can sue your sovereign back sides! The courts can make the government -federal, state or local - pay our attorney's fees.

ACTUAL TEXT

Any person denied a firearm pursuant to subsection (s) or (t) of section 922--

(1) due to the provision of erroneous information relating to the person by any State or political subdivision thereof, or by the national instant criminal background check system established under section 103 of the Brady Handgun Violence Prevention Act [18 USC 922 note] or

(2) who was not prohibited from receipt of a firearm pursuant to subsection (g) or (n) of section 922, may bring an action against the State or political subdivision responsible for providing the erroneous information, or responsible for denying the transfer, or against the United States, as the case may be, for an order directing that the erroneous information be corrected or that the transfer be approved, as the case may be. In any action under this section, the court, in its discretion, may allow the prevailing party a reasonable attorney's fee as part of the costs.

18 U.S.C. 926A. Interstate transportation of firearms

"Plain Talk"

If you lock your unloaded gun and ammo in the trunk, or if you don't have a trunk, in a locked case (but not in the glove box or console) you can drive from anywhere where it's lawful to possess a firearm (e.g Utah) to anywhere else it's lawful (e.g. Vermont) even if you drive through Washington D.C. or Chicago where the gun laws are outrageously strict. This federal law preempts state and local laws that attempt to disarm you as you travel in interstate commerce.

Pancho's Los Pistolas Vacation - Of course, if you need your gun to protect your baby, it ain'ta gonna do ya a lotta good locked away. But the politician that passes such ridiculous laws doesn't care; he has armed body guards. Makes ya wanna spit some Beechnut in that dude's eye and holler FREEEEEEEEDOM!!!!!!!!!!!!!!!!!!!!!!!!!!!!!!!

ACTUAL TEXT

Notwithstanding any other provision of any law or any rule or regulation of a State or any political subdivision thereof, any person who is not otherwise prohibited by this chapter **[felons]** from transporting, shipping, or receiving a firearm shall be entitled to transport a firearm for any lawful purpose from any place where he may lawfully possess and carry such firearm to any other place where he may lawfully possess and carry such firearm if, during such transportation the firearm is unloaded, and neither the firearm nor any ammunition being transported is readily accessible or is directly accessible from the passenger compartment of such transporting vehicle: Provided, That in the case of a vehicle without a compartment separate from the driver's compartment the firearm or ammunition shall be contained in a locked container other than the glove compartment or console.

18 USC 930. Possession of firearms and dangerous weapons in Federal facilities (including post offices)

"Plain Talk"

You can't take a firearm or other dangerous weapon into a federal building (presumably including a post office). If you do it's a federal misdemeanor (punishable by imprisonment for less than one year) unless the weapon was used in commission of a crime (five year felony) or in a murder or attempted murder (obviously big time felonies). The feds want you to be disarmed when one of their employees gets sick of their bureaucratic B.S. and "goes postal."

This section requires federal facilities to post notice of the law in a conspicuous place or you can't be convicted unless you have actual knowledge of the law (if you read this before you get arrested, you're toast). If you carry a pocket knife with a teensy-weensy blade (less than 2 ½ inches), it's not considered a dangerous weapon.

This section gives the courts the power to make their own rules so they can be even more strict if they want to. For example, although pocket knives with blades less than 2 ½ inches are not dangerous weapons, the federal courts could exclude all pocket knives if they want to. Be sure to read the public notice before entering a court house, or ask the security guards.

EXCEPTIONS - Persons excepted from the general rule are described in subsection (d). Subsection (d) specifically permits federal and state police officers and employees, who carry weapons as part of their official duties, to carry a firearm. Paragraph (d)(3) is interesting because it allows carrying of firearms "incident to hunting or other lawful purposes." This leads us to a discussion of CWP holders.

CONCEALED WEAPON PERMIT HOLDERS - This section has no express exception for state concealed weapon holders (compare the federal "Gun Free School Zone Act"). Courts that have established "secured areas" are definitely off limits to CWP holders (see discussion of U.C. A. 76-10-523.5 and U.C.A. 78-7-6 in Chapter VII). With respect to courts with secured areas, federal law and state law are in harmony, they seem to prohibit everyone, including CWP holders from carrying weapons into these areas.

But what about federal buildings like post offices that have no metal detectors and are not posted? Unless you have a lot of money for attorney fees to prove a point, you probably don't want to pack your piece into a post office. A zealous U.S. prosecutor might feel inclined to prosecute you despite the language of (d)(3). I believe the language of (d)(3) together with the stated purpose of the Gun Control Act of 1968, section 18 U.S.C. 927, and the Utah Concealed Weapons Laws authorizes CWPs to take their weapons into federal facilities. For my rationale, see the Commentary following the "Actual Text" below.

ACTUAL TEXT

(a) Except as provided in subsection (d), whoever knowingly possesses or causes to be present a firearm or other dangerous weapon in a Federal facility (other than a Federal court facility), or attempts to do so, shall be fined under this title or imprisoned not more than 1 year, or both.

(b) Whoever, with intent that a firearm or other dangerous weapon be used in the commission of a crime, knowingly possesses or causes to be present such firearm or dangerous weapon in a Federal facility, or attempts to do so, shall be fined under this title or imprisoned not more than 5 years, or both.

(c) A person who kills or attempts to kill any person in the course of a violation of subsection (a) or (b), or in the course of an attack on a Federal facility involving the use of a firearm or other dangerous weapon, shall be punished as provided in sections 1111, 1112, and 1113.

(d) Subsection (a) shall not apply to--

(1) the lawful performance of official duties by an officer, agent, or employee of the United States, a State, or a political subdivision thereof, who is authorized by law to engage in or supervise the prevention, detection, investigation, or prosecution of any violation of law;

(2) the possession of a firearm or other dangerous weapon by a Federal official or a member of the Armed Forces if such possession is authorized by law; or

(3) the lawful carrying of firearms or other dangerous weapons in a Federal facility incident to hunting or other lawful purposes.

(e) (1) Except as provided in paragraph (2), whoever knowingly possesses or causes to be present a firearm in a Federal court facility, or attempts to do so, shall be fined under this title, imprisoned not more than 2 years, or both.

(2) Paragraph (1) shall not apply to conduct which is described in paragraph (1) or (2) of subsection (d).

(f) Nothing in this section limits the power of a court of the United States to punish for contempt or to promulgate rules or orders regulating, restricting, or prohibiting the possession of weapons within any building housing such court or any of its proceedings, or upon any grounds appurtenant to such building.

(g) As used in this section:

(1) The term "Federal facility" means a building or part thereof owned or leased by the Federal Government, where Federal employees are regularly present for the purpose of performing their official duties.

(2) The term "dangerous weapon" means a weapon, device, instrument, material, or substance, animate or inanimate, that is used for, or is readily capable of, causing death or serious bodily injury, except that such term does not include a pocket knife with a blade of less than 2 ½ inches in length.

(3) The term "Federal court facility" means the courtroom, judges' chambers, witness rooms, jury deliberation rooms, attorney conference rooms, prisoner holding cells, offices of the court clerks, the United States attorney, and the United States marshal, probation and parole offices, and adjoining corridors of any court of the United States.

(h) Notice of the provisions of subsections (a) and (b) shall be posted conspicuously at each public entrance to each Federal facility, and notice of subsection (e) shall be posted conspicuously at each public entrance to each Federal court facility, and no person shall be convicted of an offense under subsection (a) or (e) with respect to a Federal facility if such notice is not so posted at such facility, unless such person had actual notice of subsection (a) or (e), as the case may be.

18 USC 930 Federal Buildings

Commentary

The language in the federal statutes quoted below makes me believe Congress intended to leave it to the states to establish an exception to the rule prohibiting persons from taking weapons into federal facilities.

Article VI of the United States Constitution says the U.S. Constitution and federal laws constitutionally enacted are the "supreme Law of the Land." This means that federal law preempts (trumps, takes precedence over, rules over, has more power than, etc.) state law when they conflict. If there are any apparent conflicts between state and federal law the courts will look closely to see if they can be reconciled. Sometimes Congress expressly tells the courts that federal law does not preempt state law.

At first blush there appears to be a conflict between state law and federal law on the issue of concealed weapon permit holders taking weapons into federal facilities which have not established secured areas. The federal law contained in 18 U.S.C. 930 prohibits anyone from taking weapons into a federal facility. State concealed weapon holders are not expressly excepted. In apparently direct conflict with federal law, the state law allows CWPs to pack "throughout the state without restriction." The state law specifically prohibits CWPs to carry concealed in "secured areas" see Chapter VII. Can the federal law be reconciled with the state law pertaining to CWPs? I think it can.

Section 18 U.S.C. 927 says:

927. Effect on State law No provision of this chapter [18 USC 921 et seq.] shall be construed as indicating an intent on the part of the Congress to <u>occupy the field</u> in which such provision operates to the exclusion of the law of any State on the same subject matter, unless there is a <u>direct and positive conflict</u> between such provision and the law of the State so that <u>the two cannot be reconciled</u> or consistently stand together (emphasis added).

The relevant sections of the stated purpose of the Gun Control Act of 1968 say:

Sec. 101. The Congress hereby declares . . . it is not the purpose of this title to place any undue or unnecessary federal restrictions or burdens on law-abiding citizens with respect to the . . . possession, or use of firearms appropriate to the purpose of hunting . . . personal protection, or any other lawful activity (emphasis added).

Then in subsection (d)(3) of 18 U.S.C. 930 Congress allowed "the lawful carrying of firearms . . .in a federal facility incident to hunting or other lawful purposes." Hunting is obviously a state regulated activity, not federal. Congress, rather than listing all of the other lawful activities that may be regulated by state statute simply stated "other lawful purposes." Thus, Congress thus gave to each state the right to allow or disallow certain activities rather than trying to "occupy the field" or preempt the states from defining their own "lawful purposes." In the introduction to the act Congress recognized "personal protection" as a "lawful purpose." Licensed persons in Utah carry concealed weapons for personal protection. Utah took the initiative and gave its CWPs authority to carry concealed weapons throughout the state without restriction, except in the courts and in secured areas. Thus, Utah's concealed weapons law may be "reconciled" and "consistently stand" together with the federal government's exceptions to its general prohibition of weapons in federal facilities. If this wasn't Congress' intent, then the statute is "void for vagueness" (invalid as a law because it's so vague it can't be understood) because it even fooled me AND I'M AN ATTORNEY (so don't mess with me)!

36 CFR 2.2 and 2.4 [Firearm and Hunting Restrictions in National Parks]

"Plain Talk"

You are prohibited from possessing firearms or hunting in national parks unless you are specifically authorized under federal and state law. The term "national park" includes national monuments (see 36 C.F.R. § 8.1 (a)). 36 CFR 2.4(a)(3) says you can take your unloaded firearms through a national park in a vehicle or keep them in your tent or camper if they are in a case that prevents their "ready" use. Pancho, do you have an observation? "Hell, that'll do ya a lot of good when a camp invader or grizzly busts into your tent! But don't worry, just use your cell phone and call park rangers. They'll be there in less than four hours!"

Notice these prohibitions are REGULATIONS ("promulgated" by an appointed federal bureaucrat). They are NOT part of the United States Code (enacted by elected officials of Congress). It is one thing when Congressional leaders pass a law after they debate its virtues on the floor of the House or Senate; but it is another when they give government bureaucrats the authority to "promulgate regulations" which have the effect of law. This is why federal laws affecting the civil rights of citizens are so dangerous. Before you know it, you have a whole "truckload" of regulations that stomp on individual liberties. It's kind of like cancer cells migrating from a tumor. (For additional scathing criticism see "Commentary" below.)

ACTUAL TEXT

36 CFR 2.2 - NATIONAL PARKS

2.2 Wildlife protection.

(a) The following are prohibited:

(1) The taking of wildlife, except by authorized hunting and trapping activities conducted in accordance with paragraph (b) of this section.

(2) The feeding, touching, teasing, frightening or intentional disturbing of wildlife nesting, breeding or other activities.

(3) Possessing unlawfully taken wildlife or portions thereof.

(b) Hunting and trapping.

(1) Hunting shall be allowed in park areas where such activity is specifically mandated by Federal statutory law.

(2) Hunting may be allowed in park areas where such activity is specifically authorized as a discretionary activity under Federal statutory law if the superintendent determines that such activity is consistent with public safety and enjoyment, and sound resource management principles. Such hunting shall be allowed pursuant to special regulations.

(3) Trapping shall be allowed in park areas where such activity is specifically mandated by Federal statutory law.

(4) Where hunting or trapping or both are authorized, such activities shall be conducted in accordance with Federal law and the laws of the State within whose exterior boundaries a park area or a portion thereof is located. Nonconflicting State laws are adopted as a part of these regulations.

(c) Except in emergencies or in areas under the exclusive jurisdiction of the United States, the superintendent shall consult with appropriate State agencies before invoking the authority of 1.5 for the purpose of restricting hunting and trapping or closing park areas to the taking of wildlife where such activities are mandated or authorized by Federal statutory law.

(d) The superintendent may establish conditions and procedures for transporting lawfully taken wildlife through the park area. Violation of these conditions and procedures is prohibited.

(e) The Superintendent may designate all or portions of a park area as closed to the viewing of wildlife with an artificial light. Use of an artificial light for purposes of viewing wildlife in closed areas is prohibited.

(f) Authorized persons may check hunting and trapping licenses and permits; inspect weapons, traps and hunting and trapping gear for compliance with equipment restrictions; and inspect wildlife that has been taken for compliance with species, size and other taking restrictions.

(g) The regulations contained in this section apply, regardless of land ownership, on all lands and waters within a park area that are under the legislative jurisdiction of the United States.

AUTHORITY:

16 U.S.C. 1, 3, 9a, 462(k).

36 CFR 2.4 NATIONAL PARKS

2.4 Weapons, traps and nets.

(a) (1) Except as otherwise provided in this section and Parts 7 (special regulations) and 13 (Alaska regulations), the following are prohibited:

(i) Possessing a weapon, trap or net

(ii) Carrying a weapon, trap or net

(iii) Using a weapon, trap or net

(2) Weapons, traps or nets may be carried, possessed or used:

(i) At designated times and locations in park areas where:

(A) The taking of wildlife is authorized by law in accordance with 2.2 of this chapter;

(B) The taking of fish is authorized by law in accordance with 2.3 of this part.

(ii) When used for target practice at designated times and at facilities or locations designed and constructed specifically for this purpose and designated pursuant to special regulations.

(iii) Within a residential dwelling. For purposes of this subparagraph only, the term "residential dwelling" means a fixed housing structure which is either the principal residence of its occupants, or is occupied on a regular and recurring basis by its occupants as an alternate residence or vacation home.

(3) Traps, nets and unloaded weapons may be possessed within a temporary lodging or mechanical mode of conveyance when such implements are rendered temporarily inoperable or are packed, cased or stored in a manner that will prevent their ready use.

(b) Carrying or possessing a loaded weapon in a motor vehicle, vessel or other mode of transportation is prohibited, except that carrying or possessing a loaded weapon in a vessel is allowed when such vessel is not being propelled by machinery and is used as a shooting platform in accordance with Federal and State law.

(c) The use of a weapon, trap or net in a manner that endangers persons or property is prohibited.

(d) The superintendent may issue a permit to carry or possess a weapon, trap or net under the following circumstances:

(1) When necessary to support research activities conducted in accordance with 2.5.

(2) To carry firearms for persons in charge of pack trains or saddle horses for emergency use.

(3) For employees, agents or cooperating officials in the performance of their official duties.

(4) To provide access to otherwise inaccessible lands or waters contiguous to a park area when other means of access are otherwise impracticable or impossible.

Violation of the terms and conditions of a permit issued pursuant to this paragraph is prohibited and may result in the suspension or revocation of the permit.

(e) Authorized Federal, State and local law enforcement officers may carry firearms in the performance of their official duties.

(f) The carrying or possessing of a weapon, trap or net in violation of applicable Federal and State laws is prohibited.

(g) The regulations contained in this section apply, regardless of land ownership, on all lands and waters within a park area that are under the legislative jurisdiction of the United States.

AUTHORITY:

16 U.S.C. 1, 3, 9a, 462(k).

36 CFR 2.2

Commentary

Notice at the end of both of these regulations prohibiting weapons and firearms in national parks appear the words " AUTHORITY: 16 U.S.C. 1, 3, 9a, 462(k)." This tells us that the director of the National Park Service must be able to point to a federal code section enacted by Congress from which he gets his authority to promulgate regulations. In this instance he looks to 16 U.S.C. 1, 3, 9a and 462(k) for authority to deprive a citizen of the United States of the right to protect himself and his family with a firearm in a national park. One would assume that when depriving a citizen of such an important right (a right to defend himself and his family from deadly force - indeed, a right to life itself) Congress would have stated this very plainly and carefully. But when you look up these four code sections in the United States Code, the words "weapon" and "firearm" do not appear. Certainly the Director of National Parks will argue that to carry out his responsibilities it was necessary to deprive law-abiding citizens of their Second Amendment rights; that it wasn't enough to have hundreds of federal laws prohibiting us from assaulting or harming another person with a firearm. I don't know about you, but that argument doesn't hold water with this cowboy. I'm enclosing the full text of these four code sections in this commentary so you can see the "stretch" of authority yourself (but in a smaller font to save a little space - so use a magnifying glass if you can't read it).

16 USC 1   (2000) TITLE 16, CONSERVATION, CHAPTER 1, NATIONAL PARKS, MILITARY PARKS, MONUMENTS, AND SEASHORES, NATIONAL PARK SERVICE

1. Service created; director; other employees

There is created in the Department of the Interior a service to be called the National Park Service, which shall be under the charge of a director who shall be appointed by the President, by and with the advice and consent of the Senate. The Director shall have substantial experience and demonstrated competence in land management and natural or cultural resource conservation. The Director shall select two Deputy Directors. The first Deputy Director shall have responsibility for National Park Service operations, and the second Deputy Director shall have responsibility for other programs assigned to the National Park Service. There shall also be in said service such subordinate officers, clerks, and employees as may be appropriated for by Congress. The service thus established shall promote and regulate the use of the Federal areas known as national parks, monuments, and reservations hereinafter specified, except such as are under the jurisdiction of the Secretary of the Army, as provided by law, by such means and measures as conform to the fundamental purpose of the said parks, monuments, and reservations, which purpose is to conserve the scenery and the natural and historic objects and the wild life therein and to provide for the enjoyment of the same in such manner and by such means as will leave them unimpaired for the enjoyment of future generations.

16 USC 3   (2000), TITLE 16, CONSERVATION, CHAPTER 1, NATIONAL PARKS, MILITARY PARKS, MONUMENTS, AND SEASHORES, NATIONAL PARK SERVICE

3. Rules and regulations of national parks, reservations, and monuments; timber; leases

The Secretary of the Interior shall make and publish such rules and regulations as he may deem necessary or proper for the use and management of the parks, monuments, and reservations under the jurisdiction of the National Park Service, and any violation of any of the rules and regulations authorized by this Act shall be punished by a fine of not more than $ 500 or imprisonment for not exceeding six months, or both, and be adjudged to pay all costs of the proceedings. He may also, upon terms and conditions to be fixed by him, sell or dispose of timber in those cases where in his judgment the cutting of such timber is required in order to control the attacks of insects or diseases or otherwise conserve the scenery or the natural or historic objects in any such park, monument, or reservation. He may also provide in his discretion for the destruction of such animals and of such plant life as may be detrimental to the use of any of said parks, monuments, or reservations. No natural, curiosities, wonders, or objects of interest shall be leased, rented, or granted to anyone on such terms as to interfere with free access to them by the public: Provided, however, That the Secretary of the Interior may, under such rules and regulations and on such terms as he may prescribe, grant the privilege to graze livestock within any national park, monument, or reservation herein referred to when in his judgment such use is not detrimental to the primary purpose for which such park, monument, or reservation was created, except that this provision shall not apply to the Yellowstone National Park. And provided further, That the Secretary of the Interior may grant said privileges, leases, and permits and enter into contracts relating to the same with responsible persons, firms, or corporations without advertising and without securing competitive bids: And provided further, That no contract, lease, permit, or privilege granted shall be assigned or transferred by such grantees, permittees, or licensees without the approval of the Secretary of the Interior first obtained in writing.

16 USC 9a (2000), TITLE 16. CONSERVATION, CHAPTER 1. NATIONAL PARKS, MILITARY PARKS, MONUMENTS, AND SEASHORES, NATIONAL PARK SERVICE

9a. Government of parks, etc.; violation of regulations as misdemeanor

The Secretary of War [Secretary of the Army] is hereby authorized to prescribe and publish such regulations as he deems necessary for the proper government and protection of, and maintenance of good order in, national military parks, national parks, battlefield sites, national monuments, and miscellaneous memorials as are now or hereafter may be under the control of the War Department [Department of the Army]; and any person who knowingly and willfully violates any such regulation shall be deemed guilty of a misdemeanor and punishable by a fine of not more than $ 100 or by imprisonment for not more than three months, or by both such fine and imprisonment.

16 USC 462 (2000) TITLE 16. CONSERVATION, CHAPTER 1A. HISTORIC SITES, BUILDINGS, OBJECTS, AND ANTIQUITIES, GENERAL PROVISIONS

462. Administration by Secretary of the Interior; powers and duties enumerated

The Secretary of the Interior (hereinafter [in 16 USC 461--467] referred to as the Secretary), through the National Park Service, for the purpose of effectuating the policy expressed in section 1 hereof [16 USC 461], shall have the following powers and perform the following duties and functions:

. . .

(k) Perform any and all acts, and make such rules and regulations not inconsistent with this Act [16 USC 461--467] as may be necessary and proper to carry out the provisions thereof. Any person violating any of the rules and regulations authorized by this Act [16 USC 461--467] shall be punished by a fine of not more than $ 500 and be adjudged to pay all cost of the proceedings.

[So where do these two statutes give bureaucrats the authority to take away our right to protect ourselves and our families with a firearm? Huh? Huh? Dammit you federalies, stop treading on our rights! Pancho]

36 CFR 261.10 & 261.58 [Shooting and Hunting in National Forests]

"Plain Talk"

Unless there is a specific order prohibiting it (and the only two orders in Utah I could find are the ones for Davis and Washington Counties set forth below) it's okay to possess a firearm and hunt in Utah's national forests. But you can't shoot within 150 yards of buildings, camps or people. You also can't shoot across or on forest service roads or across bodies of water adjacent to roads or into caves (you don't want to plunk a spelunker) .

ACTUAL TEXT

261.10 Occupancy and use. NATIONAL FORESTS

The following are prohibited:

. . .

(d) Discharging a firearm or any other implement capable of taking human life, causing injury, or damaging property as follows:

(1) In or within 150 yards of a residence, building, campsite, developed recreation site or occupied area, or

(2) Across or on a Forest Development road or a body of water adjacent thereto, or in any manner or place whereby any person or property is exposed to injury or damage as a result in such discharge.

(3) into or within any cave.

. . .

261.58 Occupancy and use. NATIONAL PARKS

When provided by an order, the following are prohibited:

. . .

(m) Discharging a firearm, air rifle, or gas gun.

. . .

(v) Hunting or fishing.

FEDERAL REGULATIONS THAT OUTLAW SHOOTING ON RECREATIONAL PROPERTY IN UTAH

"Plain Talk"

The following two "regulations," prohibit the use of firearms in two areas of the State of Utah. The first relates to the poorly defined areas of forest service land east of Centerville in Davis County and the second to the "Red Cliffs Area" near St. George.

1. Davis County Closure

The Davis County closure has a penalty of up to 6 months in jail and a $5,000 fine. Copies of the maps are in Appendix G. The only way of determining exactly where the boundaries are depends upon a reading of the imprecise map contour lines. There are no signs telling people where the boundaries of the U.S. Forest Service properties are subject to this closure. Davis County shooting enthusiasts are in serious risk of huge fines and imprisonment without any reasonable notice of where they are not supposed to shoot. THIS IS A REAL PROBLEM HERE IN THE WEST WHERE AS MANY PEOPLE SHOOT AND HUNT AS PLAY GOLF!

2. Red Cliffs Closure

The "Red Cliffs closure" affects camping, fires, the use of motorized vehicles, rock climbing, the removal of wild plants and animals, and pets, but we have not included those sections because they do not relate directly to the subject matter of this book. Simply stated, this regulation outlaws shooting any weapon including modern guns, muzzle loaders and archery equipment, except during hunting season. Violators are guilty of a class A misdemeanor. Hunters and shooters can tolerate such closures if they have notice and signs on the boundaries inform them where they are not supposed to shoot.

ACTUAL TEXT

1. Davis County Closure - Vol. 63, No. 154, SHOOTING IN THE FOOTHILLS BETWEEN WARD AND FARMINGTON CANYON ROADS SPECIAL ORDER OF FOREST SUPERVISOR

United States Department of Agriculture

Forest Service

8230 Federal Building, 125 South State Street

Salt Lake City, Utah 84138

SHOOTING IN THE FOOTHILLS BETWEEN WARD AND
FARMINGTON CANYON ROADS SPECIAL ORDER OF FOREST
SUPERVISOR

WASATCH-CACHE NATIONAL FOREST

SALT LAKE RANGER DISTRICT

Pursuant to 36 CFR 261.50 (a) and (b), the following act is prohibited on all areas described below and as shown on the map. All lands affected are located on the Salt Lake Ranger District, Wasatch-Cache National Forest. This order is in effect until further notice.

1.   Discharging a firearm. [36 CFR 261.58 (m)]

Pursuant to 36 CFR 261.50 (e), the following acts, or persons, are exempt from this order:

1.   Persons with a permit or contract authorizing the otherwise prohibited act.

2.   Authorized Federal, state, or local officers, or members of an organized rescue or firefighting force in the performance of official duty, when authorized by the District Ranger.

3.   Any person discharging a firearm within the boundaries of an approved public/private shooting range.

4.   Any properly licensed person discharging a firearm in conjunction with legal hunting activities as provided by Utah State Code, wildlife rules or proclamations established by the Utah Wildlife board.

<u>Area Described</u>: All National Forest Lands along the Wasatch Front foothills located between Ward Canyon Road and Farmington Canyon Road below 5100 feet elevation (approximately the "high water" mark or "bench" for the Lake Bonneville Shoreline) as shown on the attached map.

/Bernie Weingardner/, dated 10/31/97

Forest Supervisor

Wasatch-Cache National Forest

Violation of this prohibition is punishable by fine of not more than $5,000 or imprisonment of not more than 6 months or both (16 U.S.C. 551; 18 U.S.C. 3559 and 3571 (b) (6)).

This order supercedes any previous orders/notices for the above described areas, and same said violation(s).

Order Number <u>04</u>   <u>19</u>   <u>90</u>

                 Region   Forest   Numeric Sequence

2. Red Cliffs Closure - Publication of Closure and Restriction Order for the Red Cliffs Desert Reserve 63 FR 42869 DATE: Tuesday, August 11, 1998

FEDERAL REGISTER,Vol. 63, No. 154, Notices, DEPARTMENT OF THE INTERIOR (DOI) , Bureau of Land Management (BLM), [UT-045-00-7122-00; 9560]

Publication of Closure and Restriction Order for the Red Cliffs Desert Reserve 63 FR 42869. DATE: Tuesday, August 11, 1998

The public land in the following described lands will be affected:

[This is great public notice if you happen to work for a title company!]

Salt Lake Meridian, T. 41 S., R. 13 W., Sec.(s) 17 thru 19; (all) Sec.(s) 20; 21; 22; 27; 28; (all) Sec. 29, N 1/2NE 1/4, N 1/2S 1/2N ½, N 1/2S 1/2SW 1/4NE 1/4, SE 1/4SE 1/4SW 1/4NE 1/4, S 1/2SE 1/4NE 1/4, NE 1/4NW 1/4, N 1/2SW 1/4SW 1/4NW 1/4, NE 1/4NE 1/4SE 1/4, N 1/2NW 1/4NE 1/4SE 1/4; Sec. 30, N 1/2N ½, embracing that portion of land north of the Virgin River, S 1/2NE 1/4 T. 41 S., R. 14 W., Sec. 13, SE 1/4NE 1/4, S 1/2S ½, NE 1/4SE 1/4; Sec.(s) 15 thru 22; (all) Sec. 23, W 1/2SW 1/4, embracing that portion of land west of I-15 corridor; Sec. 24; (all) Sec. 25, Lots 1 thru 10, SW 1/4NE 1/4, NE 1/4SW 1/4NW 1/4, E 1/2SE 1/4NW 1/4, NW 1/4SE 1/4NW 1/4, E 1/2NE 1/4SW 1/4, E 1/2W 1/2NE 1/4SW 1/4, SE 1/4SW 1/4, W 1/2SE 1/4; Sec. 26, Lot 4, embracing that portion of land west of I-15 corridor; Sec. 27, embracing that portion of land west of I-15 corridor; Sec.(s) 28 thru 31; (all) Sec. 32, embracing that portion of land north and west of I-15 corridor; [*42870] Sec. 33, embracing that portion of land north and west of I-15 corridor; Sec. 34, embracing that portion of land north and west of I-15 corridor; T. 41 S., R. 15 W., Sec.(s) 13 thru 36; (all) T. 41 S., R. 16 W., Sec. 4, S ½; Sec.(s) 5 thru 9; (all) Sec. 10, embracing that portion of land west of the SR-18 corridor, Lot 4; Sec.(s) 11 thru 13; (all) Sec. 14, N ½, NE 1/4SE 1/4; Sec. 15, embracing that portion of land west of the SR-18 corridor, E 1/2NE 1/4; Sec.(s) 16 thru 21; (all) Sec. 22, W ½, W 1/2E ½, embracing that portion of land west of the SR-18 corridor; Sec. 24, E ½, E 1/2W ½; Sec. 25, E ½, E 1/2W ½; Sec. 27, SW 1/4NE 1/4, NW 1/4NW 1/4, S 1/2NW 1/4, SW 1/4, W 1/2SE 1/4; Sec.(s) 28 thru 34; (all) Sec. 36; (all) T. 41 S., R. 17 W., Sec.(s) 1, 12, 13, 24; (all) T. 42 S., R. 14 W., Sec. 5, embracing that portion of land west of I-15 corridor; Sec. 6, embracing that portion of land west of I-15 corridor; T. 42 S., R. 15 W., Sec.(s) 1 thru 9; (all) Sec. 12; (all) Sec.(s) 16 thru 19; (all) Sec. 20, (all) T. 42 S., R. 16 W.,

Sec.(s) 1 thru 3; (all) Sec.(s) 11 thru 14; (all) Sec. 24, (all) EFFECTIVE DATE: August 11, 1998. This interim closure and restriction order will be superseded when the detailed recreation management plan for the Red Cliffs Desert Reserve is completed and approved by Washington County. FOR FURTHER INFORMATION CONTACT: Mark Harris, BLM Ranger, Dixie Resource Area, 345 E. Riverside Dr, St. George, UT 84790 telephone (435) 688-3371.

SUPPLEMENTARY INFORMATION: To implement decisions of the Washington County Habitat Conservation Plan which established the Red Cliffs Desert Reserve, and to protect valuable and fragile natural resources, and provide for public safety and enjoyment, and to provide consistency with regulations that have been passed by Washington County, the Utah School and Institutional Trust Land Administration, and the cities of St. George, Washington, Ivins, and Hurricane the following closures and restrictions are established for the public lands which are included in the areas described.

. . .

Weapon Use

No firearm or other weapon may be discharged except during regulated hunting within prescribed seasons. Propelling an arrow by a bow shall be considered a discharge of a weapon. Any device loaded with powder, other explosive, or any gun actuated by compressed air shall be considered a firearm.. **[This definition of "firearm" conflicts with the definition in the Gun Control Act of 1968 that excludes most black powder and muzzle loader rifles and pistols unless they were designed to use modern ammunition (18 U.S.C. 921(3)(16))].**

. . .

The above regulations do not apply to emergency vehicles or personnel, or vehicles owned by or persons employed by the United States, the State of Utah, Washington County, or any municipality in Washington County when such vehicles or personnel are used or acting in the performance of official duties, or for authorized users of rights of way, or for owners of private land to access their private land.

Authority: The authority for issuing a closure and restriction order is contained in CFR Title 43 Subpart 8364.1a. A copy of these restrictions will be available in the Dixie Resource Area Office, which manages these lands.

Violations are punishable as class A misdemeanors. Dated: July 31, 1998. James D. Crisp, Area Manager.

CHAPTER XIV:
CIVIL RIGHTS LAWSUITS TO ENFORCE
THE RIGHT TO BEAR ARMS

Pancho's Wisdom
Happiness is a warm barrel.

Anti-gun advocates like Sarah Brady would like the public to believe that gun owners have no enforceable civil rights. In a recent *Hearst Newspaper* article entitled "Guns in America, Part III," Sarah Brady is reported to have told interviewers:

> Asked about differences between her group and gun rights groups such as the National Rifle Association, Brady said, "Our objective is to cut down deaths and injury.
>
> "They [the NRA] are looking only to protect gun owners' quote -- and I stress that -- rights, because I DON'T BELIEVE GUN OWNERS HAVE RIGHTS . . ."

Contrary to Brady's claims, the several courts have handed down important decisions protecting the rights of gun owners. We have already discussed how the Supreme Court struck down part of the Brady law in the *Printz* case and how it found the Gun Free School Zone Act unconstitutional in the *Lopez* case (see discussion in Chapter XIII). In addition to these victories, three cases have recently held that gun owners can enforce their civil rights against state and local governments that try to infringe on their rights to own and possess guns, including concealed weapons.

One of the most dramatic cases was *Kellogg et. al. v. City of Gary et. al.*, 562 N.E.2d 685 (Indiana 1990). During the 1970s, the State of Indiana required a permit to possess a handgun. For years the City of Gary, Indiana had routinely given out permits (it appears residents had to obtain permits from the city in which they lived). Then on January 1, 1980, the police chief and mayor stopped handing out permits and from that time forward, Gary citizens could no longer buy a handgun.[94] Several citizens, including an attorney, joined to sue

---

[94] Any questions about the danger of requiring gun owners to have a federal or state permit to possess a firearm or a handgun? What are you going to do when the bureaucrats administering the permit program decide to stop issuing permits? Sue? Did you notice how long it took this case to

to enforce their rights under the federal Civil Rights Act. The Indiana Supreme Court held that Gary officials had violated the equal protection clause of the Fourteenth Amendment of the United States Constitution. The Court explained that Gary's police chief and mayor had deprived these citizens of rights that other Indiana citizens enjoyed, i.e., the right to obtain a permit to own a handgun. The justices observed that issuing the mayor's bodyguards permits while denying them to common citizens was unequal.[95] Furthermore, the Indiana Supreme Court held that there was a "liberty" and a "property" interest created by the right to bear arms guaranteed in the Indiana State Constitution (containing language similar to Utah's), which is in turn, protected by the Fourteenth Amendment of the United States Constitution. The Court stated:

> We . . .find that this RIGHT of Indiana citizens to BEAR ARMS for their own self-defense and for the defense of the state IS AN INTEREST IN BOTH LIBERTY AND PROPERTY which is PROTECTED BY THE FOURTEENTH AMENDMENT to the Federal Constitution . . . by its actions, the city denied the citizens access to the state's procedural process which guaranteed them a substantive right under the Indiana Constitution (emphasis added).

562 N.E.2d at 694. The holding that gun permits are a "property right" is very relevant and important to Utah concealed weapon permit holders. Indiana's handgun permit statute was a "shall issue" statute like Utah's concealed weapon law (see analysis in Chapter VIII). The Indiana court held that when government officials must issue a permit to qualified applicants, this creates a property interest which cannot be taken away without due process of law. *Id.* at 695, 696.

---

get to the Indiana Supreme Court [10 years]? What are you going to do if you need a gun in the meantime to defend yourself or your family from criminal attack?

[95] Does this remind you of an Ex President who has committed perjury, who is still being protected by secret service agents with machine guns, and who doesn't want citizens with clean criminal records to have semiautomatic "assault weapons"?

A jury awarded over $800,000 in damages against the city and over $500,000 in attorney fees. Although the Supreme Court of Indiana reduced these amounts, the case stands as a warning to states, counties and cities that gun owners and concealed weapon permit holders have civil rights that can be enforced under a federal statute.

In *Miller et. al. v. Collier et. al.*, 878 P.2d 141(Colo. App. 1994) two private investigators were having a terrible time trying to get state officials to issue them concealed weapon permits. It seemed to them that police officers, former police officers and government employees could get the permits,[96] but they (the plaintiffs) couldn't. They sued alleging they weren't being treated the same (denial of equal protection). Their complaint relied on the federal civil rights law, 42 U.S.C.1983 that states:

> Every person who, under color of any statute, ordinance, regulation, custom, or usage, of any State or Territory, subjects, or causes to be subjected, ANY CITIZEN of the United States or other person within the jurisdiction thereof to DEPRIVATION OF ANY RIGHTS, PRIVILEGES, OR IMMUNITIES SECURED BY THE CONSTITUTION AND LAWS, SHALL BE LIABLE to the party injured in an action at law, suit in equity, or other proper proceeding for redress (emphasis added). **[Stated simply, if a government official, acting under a state law or local ordinance, deprives a citizen of a right guaranteed by the U.S. Constitution or a federal law, the official can be sued for damages in a civil rights lawsuit]**.

The Court held that the intent of Section 1983 is to "create a civil remedy for persons who prove that one acting under the color of state law has illegally deprived them of rights guaranteed by the Federal Constitution or by Federal law." 878 P.2d at 146. The Court took special note of the fact that the Plaintiffs had alleged in their complaint:

> . . . that their applications were handled differently than those submitted by private investigators who are current or retired law enforcement officers and that defendants are, in effect, "attempting to protect the outside employment of current law enforcement officers and

---

[96] It's not what you know, it's who you know!?

retired law enforcement officers to conduct private business at the expense of the plaintiffs." Plaintiffs claim there is no rational reason for this disparate treatment and that defendants are thus acting arbitrarily and capriciously.

Id. at 146. The Court of Appeals of Colorado held that these allegations were sufficient to state a claim for relief under Section 1983 of the Civil Rights Act for violation of Plaintiffs' rights to equal protection under the law.

In *Ford v. Turner,* et. al., 531 A.2d 233 (D.C. App. 1987), the District of Columbia Court of Appeals applied Section 1983 of the Civil Rights Act to spank Washington, D. C. officials for confiscating and keeping unregistered firearms without notice and a hearing. The court held a law allowing confiscation of firearms without notice and a hearing, deprived the heirs of the deceased gun owner procedural due process. The court held in assessing damages the court or jury could look to "impairment of reputation . . ., personal humiliation, and mental anguish and suffering." 531 A.2d at 240.

Utah courts should follow these legal precedents to ensure that government officials do not deprive law-abiding Utahns of the right to bear arms to protect themselves, their families, their homes and businesses. State and local agencies infringing upon such rights should be held liable for large civil damage awards, including attorney fees.

CHAPTER XV CONCLUSION:

PANCHO'S MP-5

(Pancho's Pet Peeves +P)

Pancho's Wisdom

If you're too busy to teach yer kids to shoot and hunt, you're too damned busy.

Pancho cut his teeth in the Crossroads of the West shooting vintage Colts and lever guns. They're beautiful to look at, but slow. Recently, however, he achieved NIRVANA during a therapy session of 30-round bursts from a 9 mm MP-5 sub-machine gun. *"Muy bueno!!"* Full auto rocks!

Likewise, in every chapter until this one, we have limited Pancho to one or two "shots" (Pancho's Wisdom) at those low-downed Kel-Tec confiscators. One or two shots at a time is kinda like shootin' them ol' single actions with black powder cartridges - SLOW. For Pancho to get the full therapeutic effect of speakin' his peace, we needed to let him CUT LOOSE, like a sustained burst from a subgun, and air his grievances. So put your hands together to help me welcome Pancho! (while the Gun Nite Show band plays B-B-B-B-B-B-Bad, Bad to the Bone.) Rock-n-Roll, Who loves ya Baby? Come on you annoying PEEVES, stand up and take your verbal[97] hits from Pancho!

GOV. MIKE LEAVITT - Pancho heard it through the copvine that the Gov maintains an entourage of troopers totin' MP-5's or P-90's (the sheik new subguns w/ armor piercing bullets) as his personal bodyguards, but he won't let non-law-enforcement state employees with concealed weapon permits carry unloaded guns in the trunks of their cars while on duty. Federal law permits anyone to travel anywhere in the U.S., even Washington D.C., with an unloaded gun in his or her trunk. Governor Leavitt won't let his employees carry guns for personal protection, even when he sends them to the Four Corners area near Blanding where government officials have

---

97 Notice I said "verbal." I don't want the "peeves" to read this out of context and claim Pancho advocates shooting people that don't possess the "wisdom" he does.

been ambushed.   So what's good for the Gov ain't good for the goslings? Ain't that a tad bit elitist?

"SAFE TO LEARN, SAFE TO WORSHIP" - This ballot initiative (which incidently has failed twice already) is aimed solely at disarming Utah's concealed weapon permit holders in churches and schools.   Nothing about this ballot initiative makes schools or churches safer; it makes them more dangerous by disarming the innocent. Whoever dreamed up this title graduated from the BILL CLINTON FINISHING SCHOOL OF CATCHY, DISHONEST HEADLINERS TO DECEIVE THE IGNORANT MASSES. It leaves you with that soiled, unclean feelin' like when someone makes unwanted advances toward you while seductively whispering "REASONABLE GUN CONTROL."

Oh, and while we're talking eerie, University of Utah professor **BILL NASH**, vice-admiral of Utahns Against Gun Violence, just announced that from now on he/she will be known as "Barbara"! In the words of Crocodile Dundee, "CRIKEY HE'S A SHEILA!" Pancho always felt there is something KINKY about a college professor who doesn't trust adult U. of U. students to defend their TRADITIONAL families with a firearm in married-student housing. Barbara is nervous around college students with legal guns, but he/she apparently isn't afraid of COLD SURGICAL STAINLESS! Of course, the news media informed us that fellow U. of U. professors and students heralded Nash's closet exit as "courageous." (At the University, coming out of the closet is commendable, but wanting to defend your family with a gun is uncivilized.) If Nash's political agenda hadn't convinced you that he (oops! she) was confused, well, you now have confirmation.   Have you ever asked yourself why those who live DEVIANT LIFE STYLES work so hard to deprive those who have TRADITIONAL VALUES of the right to possess firearms? Could it be that they realize ultimately, we won't let their PERVERTED IDEALS dominate our TRADITIONAL FAMILY VALUES without a fight? And if there is going to be a fight, they don't want us to have guns. (Oh Pancho, BEHAVE!)

PHYLLIS SORENSEN, president of the Utah Education Association **(UEA)**, supports the ballot initiative mentioned above misleadingly entitled "Safe to Learn, Safe to Worship." Amazingly, after such an assault on Utah gun owners by the UEA, she wants Utah voters, over half of which are gun owners, to support pay raises for teachers. Pancho wants teachers to be fairly compensated , but he's certainly not going to support their cause, if their union attacks his.

Hey, Phyllis, us 40,000 concealed weapon permit holders went to a lot of effort to get our permits. Voting takes a lot less effort. Oh, and Phyllis, by the end of 2002, there will be 100,000 of us (ALL VOTERS)!!! YOU WANT YOUR TEACHERS TO GET RAISES? THEN STOP MESSIN' WITH OUR RIGHT TO DEFEND OURSELVES WHILE AT SCHOOL OR CHURCH! (Pancho, you play dirty!)

INTERNET AND COMPUTER SOFTWARE BILLIONAIRES contribute millions of dollars to lobbyists to disarm the economically less fortunate (meaning most of us). Forget the fact that they abide in absolute safety in fantastic fortresses manned by machine-gun-macho mercenaries, behind finger-fryin' parameter fences confining frothing, fanged Dobermans. Seems like their ivy-league lawyers have advised them the Second Amendment means . . . "the Right of the ~~People~~ Rich to Keep You Out! and Bear ~~Arms~~ Armies shall not be infringed."

The A.C.L.U. - It claims to defend our Bill of Rights, but when gun owners, including the author, have called to complain of infringement of Second Amendment rights, we never get a call back. So how does the A.C.L.U. count to ten? One, ...Three, Four . . . What's A.C.L.U. stand for? Anti-Church, Lewd and Unnatural!

OUR NATIONAL PARK DIRECTOR - says you can't take a loaded gun into a National Park to protect yourself from animal and human predators. The Chief Federal Promulgator (a lesbian lawyer from Nantucket) assures him this is permissible because the Second Amendment has two plausible meanings, (1) The right of the BEARS to gnaw off your ARMS shall not be infringed, or (2) the right of ARMED tent invaders to BEAR your wife and daughters to their lairs shall not be infringed.

NEWS EDITORS of The Salt Lake Tribune and Deseret News - These champions of the First Amendment never seem to miss a chance to demand tighter restrictions on gun-owners' Second Amendment rights. Fine, but would they agree to the same kinds of restrictions on their First Amendment rights? After all, the pen is mightier than the broad sword. What if, before they could publish an article in the newspaper, they had to submit to FBI background checks that could take as long as five days and ultimately could deprive them their right to publish? How about agreeing to register their pens, their word processors and their writing styles with the Federal Government as a **PRIOR RESTRAINT** to help reduce the risk of libelous attacks on individuals?   Come on fellows, what's wrong with a little "reasonable pen control" on your precious right to take cheap shots at hundreds of thousands of innocent Utah gun owners?

EMPLOYERS who impose "no-weapons policies" on their employees - Your boss has established a "no weapon policy" so he can convince your grieving family at your funeral that he did everything in his power to protect you from "violence in the workplace." "Gee, we just didn't expect someone with six illegal guns hell-bent on murdering dozens, to RISK LOSING HIS JOB by violating company policy! And it was totally unpredictable that from the time we called 911, that this temporarily insane individual (who, of course, doesn't deserve the death penalty because we oppose taking another human life) had reloaded four times and fortunately was out of ammunition when the cops arrived. Oh, and six of the people murdered were concealed weapon permit holders who obediently left their guns at home. Otherwise there could have been a dangerous cross-fire and innocent people might have been shot!"

PINKERTON SECURITY as well as other security companies - pin bright shiny badges on their UNARMED security guards so they can look like cops. The badges, of course, make great targets in the dark. No worry. Instead of guns, PINKERTON issues "armor piercing" walkie-talkies to its guards so they can take on AK commandos from North Hollywood. No wonder the Pinkertons could never catch Jesse James and the Younger Gang. It wasn't until Jesse and Frank met up with ARMED CITIZENS (not law enforcement) of Northfield, Minnesota that they met their Waterloo.

JUDGES - who can't read and understand the plain language of the Second and Fourteenth Amendments of the United States Constitution. They conclude that states have the right to pass gun control laws to "protect the children" (teenage gangbangers marking their drug turf with the blood of rival homees). If children are so important to them, why have their decisions led to the slaughter of over a million innocent children a year since *Roe v. Wade* in 1972*(*The American Holocaust*)*? Although "abortion" appears nowhere in the Bill of Rights, they "see" it while remaining blind to the phrase "right to bear arms."   Do they think such inconsistencies give educated Americans confidence in our judicial system? Don't they realize we know they are deciding these cases based upon their life- style choices and NOT based upon the plain language of the U.S. Constitution?

These judges won't permit overly-broad prior restraints in the context of the First and Fourth Amendments to the Constitution. For example, they would NEVER give police officers a warrant to search every house in a city block in which a fugitive was last seen. This would violate the rights of too many innocent persons. And they would NEVER say newspaper editors can't print articles unless a government censorship body approves the article in advance. This would be a PRIOR RESTRAINT on freedom of speech and the press. So WHY permit laws to be passed that prevent innocent people from buying guns and accessories to protect themselves, their families and their country? Fourteen-year-old crack dealers can score concealable handguns in less than a Clinton/Lewinsky minute, but under current laws a nineteen year old woman will have to wait TWO YEARS to buy a handgun from a gun dealer to protect herself from a stalker. Such a prior restraint could ultimately deprive her of her FUNDAMENTAL RIGHT TO LIFE! Come on you Judges! Don't let U.S. Supreme Court Justices Thomas and Scalia be the only judges on the bench to have the courage to take the heat of being labeled "CONSTITUTIONALISTS" (as if there were something the matter with that).

Pancho's Wisdom

Ain't it interesting that the same politicians who grab guns to "protect the children," (e.g. California Senators Barbara Boxer [D-Sodom] and Diane Feinstein [D-Gomorrah])claim women have a "right" to an abortion. Abortions kill 1.6 million unborn children a year!

My Fellow Red-Neck-Gun-Nuts WHO THINK IT'S ABOUT RACE OR ETHNIC ORIGIN - As you see in the previous peeve, Justice Thomas (a black) and Justice Scalia (of Italian decent) are making it popular again to read and follow to the language of the United States Constitution. As the "Melting Pot" of the world, the U.S. accepts freedom-loving people of all races and ethnic backgrounds. The obvious ethnic image of Pancho on the front and back covers of this book is a hint that it's NOT about race or ethnic origin; it's STILL about FREEDOM.

UNITED STATES MILITARY - for issuing "ball ammo" to our irreplaceable young soldiers. Police officers and self-defense instructors will tell you that "ball ammo" (full metal jackets) go right through an attacker without disconnecting his trigger finger. Military "brass" stick our precious young men and women up against waves of enemy soldiers whose brains have been freeze dried on clouds of opium and don't issue our troops the ammunition they need to immediately put the bad boys down.

ROSIE O'DONNELL - Has been slapped so many times for her hypocrisy that Pancho doesn't need to slap her again. (Who said Pancho wasn't a compassionate guy!) Let her bruises heal, and maybe she won't be so hard to look at.

TRAP and SKEET SHOOTERS WHO DON'T BELONG TO THE NRA - you be lettin' us handgunners carry all the load. Don't be thinkin' Brady, Schumer and Feinstein ain't set their sights on snaggin' yer scatterguns!

SUMMIT COUNTY PROSECUTORS prosecuted deer hunter Paul Wayment for the death of his little boy due to exposure. That means that every parent who has lost a child by letting him or her get locked in the trunk of a car, backing over the child, or letting the child fall into a swimming pool is guilty of negligent homicide. Let's face it, Paul Wayment was prosecuted because he was a deer hunter, a gun guy. I told you that gun owners were turning into one of the most persecuted segments of our society.

THOSE WHO BELIEVE that being LESS PREPARED to fight tyranny, foreign enemies and crime, is BETTER than being MORE PREPARED.

THOSE WHO TRUST the United Nations and Federal troops with the most technologically advanced light weapons, including machine guns, bazookas and hand grenades while us peon masses are relegated to outdated weapons such as bolt actions, lever actions, and guns with low-capacity magazines. "Will you protect us and make life safer?" "Sure, we'll TAKE CARE of you!" DUH!

MAYORS OF CITIES WHO HAVE SUED GUN MANUFACTURERS: They have created their own crime problems by disarming their innocent constituents with the strictest gun control laws in the country. No telling how many innocent people have died because they can't buy a gun to protect themselves in these urban hell holes. Rather than accept responsibility for their mistakes, they sue gun manufacturers as "scape goats." Members of minorities are often the unfortunate victims of urban gun control. They have no weapons to protect themselves so they call the police. When the cops show it seems they shoot the first minority person they encounter, all too often, the innocent victim.

LIBERAL DEMOCRATS who tempt minorities, welfare recipients, union members and the elderly to give up their ideals for a "mess of pottage." "If you vote for us we'll give you free cigarettes, higher union wages, increased amounts of welfare, and more social programs for the elderly. All you have to do is sleep with the Devil by voting for us so we can trash the traditional ideals that made America great."

THE FAMILIES AND "FRIENDS" of GANG BANGERS, who have been shot or killed, who refuse to cooperate with police investigators. Sheriff Pancho would simply instruct his officers to give such crimes the LOWEST priority. "You want to be in a gang, you know the risk. You get killed, oh well. We're sorry, but we just don't have time to investigate this incident." Pancho's solution for the gang problem is Utah's version of SURVIVOR. Put all the "G's" on Fremont Island with Mac 11's. The last homee standing gets a million dollars of seized cocaine and a one-way ticket to Colombia. The machine gun stays.

ANOREXIC FASHION MODELS - Do we have to believe that anorexic women are beautiful just because some gay, crackhead photographer who rocks out on techno-music while sniffing lines on a mirror, thinks so? What's this got to do with guns? Nothing, but it's my book and I'm taking shots at whoever and whatever bugs me! For example, some of Mike Dillon's[98] reloadin' cover girls look like they've been run through a case trimmer. Before his next photo shoot, he should buy 'em a couple o' Whoppers with cheese and watch 'em for an hour or two to make sure they don't dump their powder prematurely. Yep, Pancho's a loose cannon — wanted by the Federalies for $5,000 U.S.

---

98 To avoid misunderstanding, NONE of what appears in the first sentence of this "peeve" i.e. "gay, crackhead . . .sniffing" applies to Mike Dillon. He's a great man, with a superior product to which Pancho can personally attest. However, Pancho is concerned that if any of our daughters see the Blue Press laying around the house, they could get the impression that the A,B, C's of attracting men who shoot, are Anorexia, Bulimia and Calcium deficiency.

Mitch: "Give a Revolutionary Pistolero a couple of bursts and he wears out the barrel! How'd that feel, Pancho?"

Pancho: "Ahhhh! It soothes the soul to send a ton o' lead down range!"

Mitch: "But, you still seem a little irritable."

Pancho: "I'm afraid I forgot someone!"

Mitch: "You couldn't have. You're the Last Man Standing! Besides, Just save it for the next edition."

Pancho: "We'll run out of subtitles!"

Mitch: "I know, we'll call it 'Pancho's Warning!'"

Pancho: "Bueno!"

Mitch: "Do you have anything POSITIVE to say about anyone?"

Pancho: "Now that you mention it. . ."

SO NO ONE THINKS PANCHO IS A "NEGATIVE" SORT OF PISTOLERO:

BRAVO! to the good-hearted, hard-working union people in Tennessee, Arkansas and West Virginia who put FREEDOM FIRST and their POCKETBOOKS SECOND by voting for George W. Bush. As you know, these three states have traditionally voted Democratic. This is because Democrats "buy" union votes by promising union "perks." 270 electoral votes were needed to win the presidential election. Bush had 271, Gore had 267. Tennessee (Gore's home state) had 11 electoral votes, Arkansas (Clinton's "White Water" splashing ground) had 6 and West Virginia 5. Had Gore taken any of these states, he would have won the election. Clinton has publically acknowledged that Gore's stance on gun control is probably what beat him in these states. The good ol' boys (and girls) on the Mason-Dixon Line taught us all a lesson to remember - FREEDOM'S MORE VALUABLE THAN DIAMONDS!

PANCHO'S PARTING SHOTS

If urban liberals want gun control let them have it. Invite them to build 12-foot-barbed-wire fences around their cities and call themselves the Independent Nation of Hell. Let them institute the devilish doctrines they list to embrace, atheism, pornography, adultery, sexual perversions, generations of welfare, drug addiction, abortion, and lack of criminal accountability (such as doing away with the death penalty). Watch the criminals migrate in. The innocent will migrate out, to America the way it was meant to be, to the rural sanctuaries of the Heartland, the Rocky Mountains and Dixie, the Land of the Free and the Home of the Brave and a nation UNDER GOD!

Adios, my Brave, Free and Armed Amigos!

Pancho

CHAPTER XVI:
PRO-SELF-DEFENSE ORGANIZATIONS

Pancho's Wisdom

Crimes against women will stop when CRIMINALS KNOW that ANNIE KNOWS where to get her gun.

Many readers have asked what they can do to help stop the expungement. Following is a list of organizations that have benefitted gun owners. Apologies to any worthwhile organization we unintentionally omitted. We'll catch you in the next edition.

The Utah Gun Owners Legal Defense Fund (U-GOLD) is a non-profit corporation created to educate Utahns about their right to bear arms and to enforce this right in the Utah courts. U-Gold c/o Gary Travis, 8773 South 450 East, Sandy, Utah 84070, www.u-gold.org

Concealed Weapon Permit Holders Association, Inc. (CWPA) represents the interests of Utah's nearly forty thousand concealed weapon permit holders (CWPs). One of several benefits CWPA offers its members is a PRE-PAID LEGAL PLAN. For a membership fee of less than $100 per year per member, CWPA provides an attorney to represent members charged with a felony after a defensive shooting. The pre-paid legal plan has no deductible, but some restrictions apply. For a complete description of plan benefits call Curt Oda at 1 (801)898-6875. www.cwpa.net

Additional pro-self-defense organizations include:

National Rifle Association (NRA)
11250 Waples Mill Road
Fairfax, VA 22030

Utah Shooting Sports Council (USSC)
P.O. Box 1975
Layton, UT 84041-6975
www.utahshootingsports.org

Utah Gun Owner's Alliance (UGOA)
PO Box 1185
Sandy, UT 84091-1185

Gun Owners of Utah (GOUtah)
P.O. Box 1185
Sandy, UT 84091-1185
(801) 566-1625 for voice mail and fax
www.utgoa.org

Utah Self Defense Instructor's Network (US-DIN)
PO Box 71677
Salt Lake City, UT 84171

Women Against Gun Control (WAGC)
PO Box 95357
South Jordan, UT 84095
Pancho asked we put his in:
The Pink Pistols (a gay/lesbian pro-gun group!)
www.pinkpistols.com
Telephone (617) 678-5762

Each organization has a slightly different approach to fighting infringement. The values of one or more of these organizations may be compatible with yours. We encourage you to get involved in some way to help preserve our Right to Bear Arms.

Mitch: Wait a minute, Pancho, what's with your endorsing the Pink Pistols? With all the gay and lesbian "put downs" I though you strongly condemned such a life style.

Pancho: I do. The proliferation (big word for a bandito) of homosexuality has been connected to the destruction of several great societies including Ancient Greece, Ancient Rome, not to mention Sodom and Gomorrah. I'm not exactly sure why, certainly the practice undermines the family unit. And it's my First Amendment right to point this out.

Mitch: Then why do you mention the "Pink Pistols", a gay pro-gun group, in a positive light?

Pancho: In a free society, everyone has the right to express his or her opinions, but NO ONE has the right to resort to violence to silence another person's free speech. I applaud this group for publically announcing that its members are armed and will "never again" tolerate "hate crimes." By encouraging armed self defense, the Pink Pistols will do much more to protect gays and lesbians from violence than some politically correct legislator passing "Hate Crimes Legislation." I believe homosexuality is immoral, but I champion the right of gays and lesbians to defend themselves.

Mitch: How's that?

Pancho: As far as I know, no one has organized the "Pink Pistols" locally. When they do organize, I am volunteering your services as a certified CWP instructor to certify the first six members for free!

Mitch: Why me?

Pancho: Because BCI doesn't authorize imaginary revolutionary pistoleros to certify anyone for a CWP.

Mitch: Okay, I'll do it. They can get a hold of me using the contact info in the front of the book. But after all we have written, these people are likely to tell both of us to take this free offer and shove it!

Pancho: That's their right to free speech. But if they do, they may miss the chance to break down barriers between two groups that have common goals.

Pancho's Wisdom

Hate Crimes will stop only when Haters comprehend that the Victims of Hate (Minorities including Gays and Lesbians) are armed.

Mitch: I never thought I'd be having a Socratic dialogue with an imaginary revolutionary pistolero!

Pancho: Don't feel like you're alone; schizos and multiples do it ♫. . .all the time.

Mitch: Why you Son of a Beretta!

CHAPTER XVII:
ABOUT THE AUTHOR

Pancho's Wisdom

Pancho defines "plinking" as "recycling aluminum the MAN'S WAY!" (To enhance natural decomposition ALL bulk garbage should be properly aerated [preferably with .45 inch diameter holes] before being taken to the landfill.)

James D. "Mitch" Vilos is a graduate of Utah State University and the J. Reuben Clark Law School at Brigham Young University. He has practiced law since 1978 and is a member of the Utah Bar Association and Alabama Bar (currently inactive status). Mr. Vilos' practice focuses on primarily two areas of law, personal injury law and firearms law. He has obtained numerous six and seven figure verdicts and settlements on behalf of injured people and is a Member of the Million Dollar Advocates Forum. He has authored articles relating to personal injury litigation and insurance law in legal publications such as the Utah State Bar Journal and Utah Trial Lawyers Journal.

Mitch has extensive expertise in firearms law. He has his Federal Firearms License (FFL), is a member of the National Rifle Association, the American Self-defense Institute, and Single Action Shooting Society (Badge No. 10,586, Alias "Pancho Vilos"). He is the author of *Utah Gun Law: Good, Bad and Ugly* and the *Utah Spotlighting and Night Hunting Manual*. He has written an article entitled, "Not Guilty But Bankrupt, Civil Liability for Negligent Self Defense," published in the American Self-Defense Institute's ASDI Oracle, 1997, Issue 2. He is a Utah State authorized concealed weapon instructor. Mitch is also a graduate of the Ogden Metro Swat Basic Training Course (affectionately known as "Hell Week") and Davis County Sheriff's Citizen's Academy.

Mr. Vilos has lectured to many groups about negligence law, medical malpractice, insurance law, representing people with traumatic brain injuries, constitutional law and gun law.

APPENDIX A:

Parental Consent Form for Minor to Possess Handgun

PRIOR WRITTEN CONSENT FOR JUVENILE TO POSSESS
HANDGUN AND/OR HANDGUN AMMUNITION.

I _____, hereby certify I am the parent
and/or guardian of _____, a juvenile whose date
of birth is _____.

I certify that I am not prohibited by Federal, State or local law from
possessing a firearm. I hereby give my prior written consent for the
juvenile above-named to temporarily possess a handgun and/or handgun
ammunition for the following temporary use:

    □A.   In the course of employment, or

    □B.   In the course of ranching or farming at the residence of
said juvenile, or

    □C.   On property used for ranching or farming where the
juvenile has permission of the property owner or lessee
to possess a handgun, or

    □D.   Target practice, or

    □E.   Hunting, or

    □F.   To take a course of instruction on the safe and lawful
use of a handgun.

I have explained to said juvenile that the handgun must be unloaded
and kept in a locked container to and from the activity described above and
that this consent is temporary and only extends to, from and during the
activity described above.

I have instructed said juvenile to keep this written consent in
possession at all times while possessing said handgun.

Inasmuch as Federal law requires compliance with local law, in the
event that said juvenile is less than 14 years of age, he/she has been
instructed that he/she may not possess said handgun under any
circumstances unless accompanied by a responsible adult.

DATED this _____ day of _____, 200_.

_____
             Parent and/or Guardian

Note: This consent is for temporary use only. The juvenile should be instructed that once the activity described
on the previous page ceases, the juvenile must return the handgun to the owner and that while traveling to and from
the activity, the handgun must be unloaded and carried in a locked container.

CAUTION: There are several Utah state laws that impose additional restrictions on minors possessing
firearms. Appendix F of this book shows how all of the state and federal laws interrelate. DO NOT allow
a minor to possess a firearm or hunt without reviewing the law.

APPENDIX B:

Order form for additional copies of
Utah Gun Law II: Pancho's Wisdom

Order extra copies of the *Utah Gun Law II: Pancho's Wisdom* for family, friends and legislators.

Just fill out this form and mail it to:

Attorney "Mitch" Vilos

PO Box 1148

Centerville, UT 84014

❏ Please send me copies of *Utah Gun Law II: Pancho's Wisdom*

_____ Copies x $18.76 each $_____

_____ Copies x $3.60

(shipping & handling) $_____

_____ Copies x $1.24

(sales tax) $_____

Total $_____

(Make check or money order payable to James D. Vilos. $20.00 penalty for all returned checks. Author may hold books until personal checks clear. For immediate delivery send cashier's check or money order).

Total for one book = $23.60, two books = $47.20, etc. **Bulk order rates available!** Call (801) 295-3340 for details. Dealers call for dealer prices.

Where we should send your books.

Name:_____

Address:_____

_____

_____

Phone # (   )_____

APPENDIX C:

Order form for the
Utah Spotlighting and Night Hunting Manual

Order extra copies of the *Utah Spotlighting and Night Hunting Manual* for family and friends.

Just fill out this form and mail it to:

Attorney "Mitch" Vilos

PO Box 1148

Centerville, UT 84014

❏   Please send me copies of the

     Utah Spotlighting and Night Hunting Manual

_____ Copies x $14.95 each $_____

_____ Copies x $2.95

       (shipping & handling) $_____

_____ Copies x $.95

       (sales tax) $_____

           Total $_____

(Make check or money order payable to James D. Vilos. $20.00 penalty for all returned checks. Author may hold books until personal checks clear. For immediate delivery send cashier's check or money order).

Total for one book = $18.85, two books = $37.70, etc. **Bulk order rates available!** Call (801) 533-0222 for details. Dealers call for dealer prices.

Where we should send your books.

Name:_____

Phone # (**)**_____

Address:

          _____

e-mail _____

APPENDIX D:

Request to be Notified of Future Changes in
Utah Gun Law

Nearly every year the Utah Legislature, the Bureau of Criminal Identification (BCI), and the Division of Wildlife Resources (DWR) make changes to Utah gun law. As a shooter, hunter or perhaps a concealed weapon permit holder, you **NEED TO KNOW** what these changes are. If you would like to be informed of changes in the law, please fill out and mail us this form. We will place your name and address on our mailing list and will inform you if we have published a supplement or a subsequent edition of the book. We will send you an **ORDER FORM** for a supplement or a new edition **AT THAT TIME**. You may **THEN DECIDE** if you would like to order a supplement or updated edition. Prices of supplements will vary depending on the number of changes in Utah gun law during any given year.

I would like to be placed on your mailing list to be informed of a newly published supplement or newer edition of the book. I understand **this is NOT an order** for a supplement to your book and that **I will NOT be charged** for giving my name and address to you at this time. I also understand that after you publish a supplement or new edition, you will send me an order form and I can order at that time. I understand that the prices of the supplements, new editions and shipping and handling will vary from year to year depending upon the number of changes in Utah Gun Law. My name and address are:

Name:_____

Address:_____

_____

Email:_____

Mail to: Attorney "Mitch" Vilos

PO Box 1148

Centerville, UT 84014

APPENDIX E:
List of Attorneys General

Attorney General of Alabama
State House
11 South Union Street
Montgomery, AL 36130
334-242-7300

Attorney General of Alaska
State Capital
Post Office Box 110300
Juneau, AK 99811-0300
907-465-3600

Attorney General of Am. Samoa
Post Office Box 7
Pago Pago, AS 96799
684-633-4163

Attorney General of Arizona
1275 West Washington Street
Phoenix, AZ 85007
602-542-4266

Attorney General of Arkansas
200 Tower Building
323 Center Street
Little Rock, AR 72201-2610
501-682-2007

Attorney General of California
1300I Street
Suite 125
Sacramento, CA 95814
916-324-5437

Attorney General of Colorado
Department of Law
1525 Sherman Street
Denver, CO 80203
303-866-3052

Attorney General of Hawaii
425 Queen Street
Honolulu, HI 96813
808-586-1282

Attorney General of Idaho
P.O. Box 83720
Boise, ID 83720-0010
208-334-2400

Attorney General of Illinois
State of Illinois Center
100 West Randolph Street
12th Floor
Chicago, IL 60601
312-814-2503

Attorney General of Indiana
219 State House
Indianapolis, IN 46204
317-232-6201

Attorney General of Iowa
Hoover State Office Building
Des Moines, IA 50319
515-281-3053

Attorney General of Kansas
Judicial Building
301 West Tenth Street
Topeka, KS 66612-1597
913-296-2215

Attorney General of Kentucky
State Capitol
Room 116
Frankfort, KY 40601
502-564-7600

Attorney General of Mississippi
Department of Justice
Post Office Box 220
Jackson, MS 39205-0220
601-359-3692

Attorney General of Missouri
Supreme Court Building
207 West High Street
Jefferson City, MO 65101
573-751-3321

Attorney General of Montana
Justice Building
215 North Sanders
Helena, MT 59620-1401
406-444-2026

Acting Attorney General
Administration Building
Saipan, MP 96950
670-332-4311

Attorney General of Nebraska
State Capitol
Post Office Box 98920
Lincoln, NE 68509-8920
402-471-2682

Attorney General of Nevada
Capital Complex
Carson City, NV 89710
775-684-1100

Attorney General of N Hampshire
33 Capitol Street
Concord, NH 03301-06397
603-271-3658

Attorney General of Connecticut
P.O. Box 120
Hartford, CT 06141-0120
203-566-2026

Attorney General of Louisiana
Department of Justice
Post Office Box 94095
Baton Rouge, LA 70804-4095
504-342-7013

Attorney General of New Jersey
Richard J. Hughes Justice Cmplx
25 Market Street, CN 080
Trenton, NJ 08625
609-984-9579

Attorney General of Delaware
Carvel State Office Building
820 North French Street
6th Floor
Wilmington, DE 19801
302-577-3838

Attorney General of Maine
6 State House Station
Augusta, ME 04333-0006
207-626-8800

Attorney General of New Mexico
Post Office Drawer 1508
Santa Fe, NM 87504-1508
505-827-6000

Corporation Counsel of D.C.
441 4th Street NW
Washington, DC 20001
202-727-6248

Attorney General of Maryland
200 Saint Paul Place
Baltimore, MD 21202-2202
410-576-6300

Attorney General of New York
120 Broadway
New York, NY 10271
212-416-8519

Attorney General of Florida
The Capitol
PL 01
Tallahassee, FL 32399-1050
904-487-1963

Attorney General of Mass
One Ashbury Place
Boston, MA 02108-1698
617-727-2200

Attorney General of N.C.
Department of Justice
Post Office Box 629
Raleigh, NC 27602-0629
919-733-3377

Attorney General of Georgia
40 Capitol Square, S.W.
Atlanta, GA 30334-1300
404-656-4585

Attorney General of Michigan
Post Office Box 30212
525 West Ottowa Street
Lansing, MI 48909-0212
517-373-1110

Attorney General of North Dakota
State Capitol
600 East Boulevard Avenue
Bismark, ND 58505-0040
701-328-3640

Attorney General of Guam
Judicial Center Building
120 West O'Brien Drive
Agana, GU 96910
871-475-3324

Attorney General of Minnesota
State Capitol
Suite 102
St. Paul, MN 55155
612-296-6196

Attorney General of Ohio
State Office Tower
30 East Broad Street
Columbus, OH 43266-0410
614-466-3376

Attorney General of Oklahoma
State Capitol
2300 N. Lincoln Blvd, Rm 112
Oklahoma City, OK 73105
405-521-3921

Attorney General of S. Dakota
500 East Capitol
Pierre, SD 57501-5070
605-773-3215

Attorney General of Virginia
900 E. Main Street
Richmond, VA 23219
804-786-2071

Attorney General of Oregon
Justice Building
1162 Court Street NE
Salem, OR 97310
503-378-6002

Attorney General of Tennessee
John Sevier Building
500 Charlotte Ave.
Nashville, TN 37243-0486
615-741-3491

Attorney General of Washington
Post Office Box 40100
905 Plum Street, Building 3
Olympia, WA 98504-0100
360-753-6200

Attorney General of Pennsylvania
Strawberry Square
16th Floor
Harrisburg, PA 17120
717-787-3391

Attorney General of Texas
Capitol Station
Post Office Box 12548
Austin, TX 78711-2548
512-463-2191

Attorney General of West Va
State Capitol
Charleston, WV 25305
304-558-2021

Attorney General of Puerto Rico
Post Office Box 192192
San Juan, PR 00902-0192
809-721-7700

Attorney General of Utah
236 State Capitol
Salt Lake City, Utah 84114
801-538-1326

Attorney General of Wisconsin
State Capitol, Suite 114 East
P.O. Box 7857
Madison, WI 53707-7857
608-266-1221

Attorney General of Rhode Island
150 S. Main Street
Providence, RI 02903
401-274-4400

Attorney General of Vermont
109 State Street
Montpelier, VT 05609-1001
802-828-3171

Attorney General of Wyoming
State Capitol Building
Cheyenne, WY 82002
307-777-7841

Attorney General of South Carolina
1000 Assembly Street
Post Office Box 11549
Columbia, SC 29201
803-734-3970

Attorney General of the Virgin Island
Department of Justice
G.E.R.S. Complex, 48B-50C
Kronprinsdens Gade
St. Thomas, VI 00802
809-774-5666

APPENDIX F:
Youngsters, Guns and Ammo

Age	≥ 21[1]	$\geq 18 < 21$[2]	$\geq 16 < 18$	$\geq 14 < 16$	$\geq 12 < 14$	< 12
Concealed Weapon Permit	Yes, if Good Character	No	No	No	No	No
Buy Handgun	Yes	No/Yes[3]	No[4]	No	No	No
Possess[5] Handgun	Yes	Yes	For limited purposes w/ Parents written permission on person[6]	For limited purposes w/ Parents written permission on person[7]	For limited purposes w/ Parents written permission on person and accomp'd by responsible adult[8]	For limited purposes w/ Parents written permission on person and accomp'd by responsible adult[9]
Buy Handgun Ammo	Yes	No/Yes[10]	No	No	No	No
Possess Handgun Ammo	Yes	Yes	For limited purposes w/ Parents written permission on person[11]	For limited purposes w/ Parents written permission on person	For limited purposes w/ Parents written permission on person	For limited purposes w/ Parents written permission on person
Buy Rifle Shotgun	Yes	Yes	Not from dealer, but from anyone else if accomp'd by parent[12]	Not from dealer, but from anyone else if accomp'd by parent	Not from dealer, but from anyone else if accomp'd by parent	Not from dealer, but from anyone else if accomp'd by parent

Age	≥ 21[13]	≥ 18 < 21[14]	≥ 16 < 18	≥ 14 < 16	≥ 12 < 14	< 12
Possess Rifle Shotgun	Yes	Yes	Yes, but must be permitted OR accomp'd by parent[15]	Yes, but must be permitted OR accomp'd by parent[16]	Yes, but must be accomp'd by responsible adult[17]	Yes, but must be accomp'd by responsible adult[18]
Buy Rifle Shotgun Ammo	Yes	Yes	Not from a gun dealer,[19] but from anyone else	Not from a gun dealer, but from anyone else	Not from a gun dealer, but from anyone else	Not from a gun dealer, but from anyone else
Possess Rifle Shotgun Ammo	Yes	Yes	Yes	Yes	Yes	Yes
Hunt Big Game	Yes	Yes	Yes	Yes, accomp by parent, or adult 21 and OK w/ Parent[20]	No/Yes for 13 yr old who turns 14 yr of hunt[21]	No
Hunt Small Game	Yes	Yes	Yes	Yes, must be accomp'd by adult[22]	Yes, must be accomp'd by parent[23]	No[24]
Possess Other Dangerous Weapon	Yes	Yes	Yes, but must be permitted OR accomp'd by parent[25]	Yes, but must be permitted OR accomp'd by parent	Yes, must be accomp'd by responsible adult[26]	Yes, must be accomp'd by responsible adult
Possess Machine Gun	Yes, under certain conditions[27]	No	No[28]	No	No	No

1. Just in case you've forgotten your math symbols, this means, "greater than or equal to 21" years of age, or put another way, 21 years old or older.

2. One more translation just in case your have a mental block for math symbols. This means, "greater than or equal to 18, but less than 21" years of age, i.e., 18, 19, and 20 years of age.

3. A person at least 18, but younger than 21 cannot buy a handgun from a gun dealer, 18 U.S.C. 922(b)(1). However, 18, 19 and 20 year old people can buy a handgun from a person who is not a gun dealer, 18 U.S.C. 922(x)(1) (see Chapter XIII of this book). DO NOT BE TEMPTED TO ACT AS A "MIDDLEMAN" TO BUY GUNS FROM GUN DEALERS FOR PEOPLE UNDER 21! IT'S A FELONY! U.C.A. 76-10-527 (4) "A person is guilty of a felony of the third degree who purchases a handgun with the intent to: (a) resell or otherwise provide a handgun to any person who is ineligible to purchase or receive from a dealer a handgun; or (b) transport a handgun out of this state to be resold to an ineligible person." This law splits hairs. As long as the non-dealer does not have the INTENT AT THE TIME HE OR SHE PURCHASES THE GUN, to transfer it to a person under 21, it can legally be sold to a person 18 or older, but younger than 21. It's legal for grandpa, who bought his pistol 5 years ago, intending to keep it, to give or sell it, to his granddaughter who is 18; but he cannot buy it from a dealer with the intent to transfer it to his granddaughter.

4. Federal law, 18 U.S.C. § 922(x)(1), forbids anyone to sell a handgun to a person under 18 years of age. State law, U.C.A. 76-10-509.9 states, "(1) A person may not sell any firearm to a minor under 18 years of age unless the minor is accompanied by a parent or guardian. (2) Any person who violates this section is guilty of a third degree felony." Unfortunately, Utah state law suggests that a person could sell a handgun to a minor under 18 years of age if the minor was accompanied by a parent or guardian. Of course, this is illegal under federal law. Therefore, state law could mislead a person into violating federal law.

5. These handgun rules assume the person is not hunting. If a minor is hunting, he will usually need to be accompanied by someone older and with a closer relationship than if he is merely shooting, but not hunting. For example, a 13 year old who is not hunting needs only to be accompanied by a responsible adult, i.e., someone older than U.C.A. 76-10-509(2), (found in Chapter VII of this book). However, if the 13 year old is hunting, he must be

accompanied either by a parent or guardian, or someone 21 or older, approved by his parent or guardian, U.C.A. 23-20-20(2), (discussed in Chapter IX).

6. Federal law requires a minor to keep a parent's written permission with him or her while possessing a handgun. 18 U.S.C. 922(x)(2),(3). Read more about this in Chapter XIII. The state law is U.C.A. 76-10-509, which says:

"(1) A minor under 18 years of age may not possess a dangerous weapon unless he:

(a) has the permission of his parent or guardian to have the weapon; or

(b) is accompanied by a parent or guardian while he has the weapon in his possession."

Notice that there is an "or" between (a) and (b) above. This means if a child is under 18 years of age and has the permission of his parent or guardian, he need not be accompanied by the parent or guardian (unless he is under 14 years of age or hunting, see applicable rules below). Therefore, if kids 14-17 years of age have written permission from their parents to possess a handgun, they do not need to be accompanied by a parent or guardian.

7. Same rule applies to kids 14 and older, but less than 16; see footnote 6 above.

8. U.C.A. 76-10-509(2) "Any minor under 14 years of age in possession of a dangerous weapon shall be accompanied by a responsible adult." (Read more about this in Chapter VII).

9. U.C.A. 76-10-509(2) "Any minor under 14 years of age in possession of a dangerous weapon shall be accompanied by a responsible adult." (Chapter VII).

10. A person at least 18, but younger than 21 cannot buy handgun ammunition from a gun dealer, 18 U.S.C. 922(b)(1), but can buy handgun ammunition from a person who is not a gun dealer, 18 U.S.C. 922(x)(1) (Chapter XIII). But see "middleman" precautions in footnote 3 above.

11. 18 U.S.C. 922(x)(2), (3), discussed in Chapter XIII.

12. A person younger than 18 cannot buy a any weapon from a gun dealer, 18 U.S.C. 922(b)(1), but there is no federal prohibition for a minor to buy a rifle or shotgun from someone who is not a gun dealer. This is left to state

law and Utah has enacted U.C.A. 76-10-509.9 that states: "(1) A person may not sell any firearm to a minor under 18 years of age unless the minor is accompanied by a parent or guardian. (2) Any person who violates this section is guilty of a third degree felony." See Chapters VII and XIII.

13. Just in case you've forgotten your math symbols, this means, "greater than or equal to 21" years of age, or put another way, 21 years old or older.

14. One more translation just in case your have a mental block for math symbols. This means, "greater than or equal to 18, but less than 21" years of age, i.e., 18, 19, and 20 years of age.

15. U.C.A. 76-10-509(1), Chapter VII in this book.

16. U.C.A. 76-10-509(1), Chapter VII in this book.

17. U.C.A. 76-10-509(2) "Any minor under 14 years of age in possession of a dangerous weapon shall be accompanied by a responsible adult." (At first blush, this looks like it's less restrictive than for kids 14 - 17 years old; but the older kids don't need to be accompanied if they have their parents permission).

18. U.C.A. 76-10-509(2), ditto (for you Rush Limbaugh fans).

19. 18 U.S.C. 922(b)(1), the text of which is in Chapter XIII. Because federal law prohibits the sale of any ammunition to a person under 18 years of age, a person buying ammunition with the intent of "acting as a middle man" could be held criminally liable for "aiding and abedding" a gun dealer to violate federal law by selling rifle or shotgun ammunition to someone under 18. If, however, a person possesses rifle or shotgun ammunition and later decides to sell to a minor, this is probably legal.

20. U.C.A. 23-20-20(3) "A person of at least 14 years of age and under 16 years of age must be accompanied by his parent or legal guardian, or other responsible person of the age of 21 years or older and approved by his parent or guardian, while hunting big game with any weapon."

21. Children under 14 years of age may not hunt big game in Utah except 13 year olds may hunt big game if they turn 14 during the year of the hunt. R657-5-4, Chapter IX.

22. U.C.A. 23-20-20(4) "A person of at least 14 years of age and under 16 years of age must be accompanied by a person of the age of 21 years or older while hunting wildlife, other than big game, with any weapon."

23. U.C.A. 23-20-20(2) "A person under the age of 14 years must be accompanied by his parent or legal guardian, or other responsible person of the age of 21 years or older and approved by his parent or guardian, while hunting with any weapon." R657-22-18, we talk about this in Chapter IX.

24. Children under 12 may not hunt "protected wildlife," U.C.A. 23-20-20(5), suggesting they may hunt "unprotected wildlife" like jack rabbits, if accompanied by responsible adult, at least 21 years of age and who is approved by the child's parent, U.C.A. 23-20-20(2).

25. U.C.A. 76-10-509(1), see discussion in Chapter VII.

26. U.C.A. 76-10-509(2), Chapter VII.

27. One way to qualify is to obtain a Federal Firearms License (FFL). A person must be 21 or older to apply for an FFL, 18 U.S.C. 923(d)(1). There are other ways to legally own and possess a machine gun but they are beyond the scope of this book. Check with the BATF. If a person possesses a machine gun illegally, the penalty is imprisonment up to 10 years, 18 U.S.C. 922(o), 18 U.S.C. 924(2). See Chapter XIII.

28. U.C.A 76-10-509.4(4) makes it a third degree felony for minors to possess a machine gun or a sawed-off shotgun or rifle. It is also a felony for an adult to let a minor have access to any of these weapons U.C.A. 76-10-509.5. See discussion in Chapter VII.

APPENDIX G:
Maps of National Forest Lands in Davis County Closed to Shooting

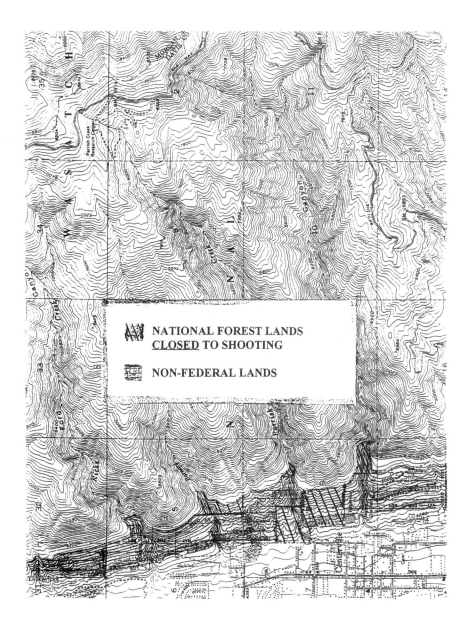

NATIONAL FOREST LANDS
CLOSED TO SHOOTING

NON-FEDERAL LANDS

<----- FARMINGTON CANYON ROAD

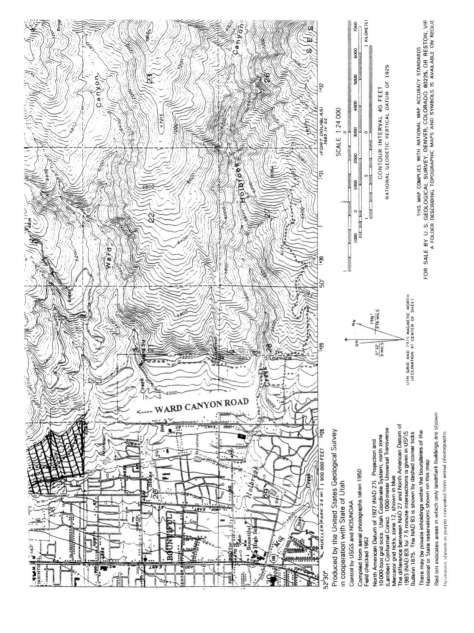

WARD CANYON ROAD

Produced by the United States Geological Survey
in cooperation with State of Utah

Control by USGS and NOS/NOAA

Compiled from aerial photographs taken 1950
Field checked 1952

North American Datum of 1927 (NAD 27) Projection and
10 000-foot grid ticks: Utah Coordinate System, north zone
(Lambert Conformal Conic). 1000-meter Universal Transverse
Mercator grid ticks, zone 12, shown in blue
The difference between NAD 27 and North American Datum of
1983 (NAD 83) for 7.5 minute intersections is given in USGS
Bulletin 1875. The NAD 83 is shown by dashed corner ticks

There may be private inholdings within the boundaries of the
National or State reservations shown on this map

Red tint indicates areas in which only landmark buildings are shown

Revisions shown in purple compiled from aerial photographs

SCALE 1:24 000

CONTOUR INTERVAL 40 FEET
NATIONAL GEODETIC VERTICAL DATUM OF 1929

THIS MAP COMPLIES WITH NATIONAL MAP ACCURACY STANDARDS
FOR SALE BY U. S. GEOLOGICAL SURVEY, DENVER, COLORADO 80225, OR RESTON, VIR
A FOLDER DESCRIBING TOPOGRAPHIC MAPS AND SYMBOLS IS AVAILABLE ON REQUE

UTM GRID AND 1975 MAGNETIC NORTH
DECLINATION AT CENTER OF SHEET

APPENDIX H:

QUICK DRAW GUN LAW

Pancho's motto is to "Shoot Fast and Often!"[99] Fast shooters need quick access to Utah's gun laws. The following two tables provide "simplified" rules for possessing guns in different places. Notice that Table I applies to people WITHOUT a concealed weapons permit and Table II applies to people WITH a concealed weapon permit. Consult relevant statutes (primarily found in Chapters VII, VIII and XIII) for detailed discussion.

TABLE I

POSSESSING A FIREARM

WITHOUT A CONCEALED WEAPON PERMIT

Place of possession	Is Firearm permitted WITHOUT CWP?	Relevant statutes(Bold indicates Federal statutes)
Home	Yes - loaded (76-10-511)	U.C.A. 76-10-500 and 501 (Chapter VII)
Place of business	Yes	U.C.A. 76-10-500 and 501 (Chapter VII)
Curtilage (place immediately around your house)	Yes - Utah code doesn't specifically address this in weapons laws but 511 says "at (as opposed to in) place of residence" which probably could be interpreted to mean immediately around.	500, 501, 511 (unless otherwise stated these sections are in Title 76, Chapter 10 -Weapons, which are discussed in depth in Chapter VII of this book)
Temporary Residence, camp	Yes - okay loaded (76-10-511) definition of loaded (502)	501, 511 (Chapter VII)

---

99. Words of wisdom imparted to me by my good friend and shooting mentor Gary Travis.

Place of possession	Is Firearm permitted WITHOUT a CWP?	Relevant statutes (Bold indicates Federal statutes)
Private motor vehicles	Yes, but not loaded (505) and not concealed (504). Not considered concealed if it is "securely encased" which means unloaded and completely enclosed in container, even though not locked, or in a gun rack. However, gun cannot be placed in glove box or console. (501)	501, 504, 505 (Chapter VII)
Open Carry	Yes, but if loaded cannot carry on public street. Caution: carrying openly could get you arrested for disturbance of the peace or threatening with a deadly weapon if your intentions are misinterpreted by someone.	505 (Chapter VII)
Concealed Carry	No	504 (Chapter VII)
Public places	Yes, but if loaded cannot carry on public street.	505 (Chapter VII)

Place of possession	Is Firearm permitted WITHOUT a CWP?	Relevant statutes (Bold indicates Federal statutes)
State Government offices	Yes (see 502, 505), but you cannot take gun into secured area of jail, mental institution, or courthouse.	502, 505, 523.5 and 529 (Chapter VII)
Federal facilities (including post office)	No, if posted or you know it's illegal (now you know)	**18 USC 930 (Chapter XIII)**
Natl Park or monument	Yes, buy only if locked away to prevent ready use, or if permitted for hunting under state law	**36 CFR 2.4 (Chapter XIII)**
Natl Forest	Yes, unless subject to federal closure order	**36 CFR 261.10 & 261.58** (Ch. XIII) e.g. Appendix G
State Park	Yes, in camp or tent, but watch out for regulation prohibiting firearms in state parks (this reg is probably unenforceable if you are using gun to protect a temporary dwelling)	500, 501 and 511, (Chapter VII) but see R651-612-1 (Chapter IX)
Schools	No	505.5 (Ch. VII); 53A-3-502 (Ch. VIII)

Place of possession	Is Firearm permitted WITHOUT a CWP?	Relevant statutes (Bold indicates Federal statutes)
Churches, another person's private residence	Yes, unless notified orally or in writing that firearms are prohibited	530 (Ch. VII)
Interstate Transit (airplanes, buses and trains)	No guns allowed in passenger compartment. Weapons must be declared and locked in case in luggage compartment.	1504, **18 U.S.C. § 922(e)** Chapters VII and XIII
Local Buses (UTA) and TRAX	No, and it's a felony if you do!	1504, Chapter VII
Secured Areas (with metal detecrots) in Courts, Airports, Jails, Olympic venues	No	523.5 and 529,(Ch. VII) U.C.A. 53-5-704 (Ch. VIII)
Interstate Transportation	Call attorneys general - okay to transport through states and cities where firearms prohibited if not loaded and not readily accessible	**18 U.S.C. § 926A** **(Chapter XIII)**

TABLE II

POSSESSING A FIREARM

WITH CONCEALED WEAPON PERMIT

Place of Possession	Is Firearm permitted WITH CWP?	Relevant statutes (Bold indicates Federal statutes)
Home	Yes - loaded (76-10-511)	U.C.A. 76-10-500 and 501 (Ch. VII)
Place of business	Yes, permit is valid throughout the state without restriction	U.C.A. 76-10-500 and 501, (Ch. VII) U.C.A. 53-5-704 (see summary at end of Ch. VIII)
Temporary Residence, camp	Yes - okay loaded (76-10-511) definition of loaded (502)	500, 501 (Ch. VII)
Private motor vehicles	Yes, even loaded and concealed	505, 523 (Ch. VII)
Open Carry	Yes, even loaded. Caution: carrying openly could get you arrested for disturbing the peace or threatening with a deadly weapon if your intentions are misinterpreted	505, 523 (Ch. VII)
Concealed Carry	Yes	U.C.A. 53-5-704 (Ch. VIII)
Public places	Yes	U.C.A. 53-5-704 (Ch. VIII)

Place of Possession	Is Firearm permitted WITH CWP?	Relevant statutes (Bold indicates Federal statutes)
State government offices	Yes, but not in secured areas of jail, mental institution, or courthouse	523.5 and 529 (Ch. VII)
Federal facilities (including post office)	No, if posted or you know it's illegal (you know now)	**18 USC 930.** **(Chapter XIII)**
Natl Park or monument	Yes, but only if locked away to prevent ready use, or if permitted for hunting under state law	**36 CFR 2.4** **(Chapter XIII)**
Natl Forest	Yes, unless subject to federal closure order	**36 CFR 261.10 & 261.58** (Ch. XIII) e.g. Appendix G
State Park	In camp or tent, but watch out for regulation prohibiting firearms in state parks (probably unenforceable)	500, 501 and 511, (Ch. VII) but see R651-612-1 (Ch. IX)
Schools	Yes	505.5; 53A-3-502 (Ch. VII)
Churches, another person's private residence	Yes, unless notified orally or in writing that firearms are prohibited	530 (Ch. VII)

Place of Possession	Is Firearm permitted WITH CWP?	Relevant statutes (Bold indicates Federal statutes)
Interstate Transit (airplanes, buses and trains)	Not in passenger compartment, but okay w/ luggage if declared to bus company and locked in case in suitcase in luggage compartment	1504, **18 U.S.C. § 922(e)** Chapters VII and XIII
Local Buses (UTA) and TRAX	Yes	1504 (Ch. VII)
Secured Areas (with metal detectors) in Courts, Airports, Jails, Olympic venues.	No	523.5 and 529,(Ch. VII) U.C.A. 53-5-704 (Ch. VIII)
Interstate Transportation	Yes, if just passing through and firearm is unloaded and not readily accessible - Call attorneys general of different states (Appendix E)	**18 U.S.C. § 926A** **(Chapter XIII)**
Curtilage (place immediately around your house)	Utah code doesn't specifically address this in weapons laws but 511 says "at (as opposed to in) place of residence" which probably could be interpreted to mean immediately around	500, 501, 511 (unless otherwise stated these sections are in Title 76, Chapter 10 -Weapons and discussed in detail in Chapter VII)